THE EMERGING EURO-MEDITERRANEAN SYSTEM

MANCHESTER
UNIVERSITY PRESS

EUROPE
IN
CHANGE

SERIES EDITOR EMIL KIRCHNER

already published

Committee governance in the European Union
THOMAS CHRISTIANSEN AND EMIL KIRCHNER (EDS)

Theory and reform in the European Union
DIMITRIS N. CHRYSSOCHOOU, MICHAEL J. TSINISIZELIS, KOSTAS IFANTIS, STELIOS STAVRIDIS

Greece in a changing Europe
Between European integration and Balkan disintegration?
KEVIN FEATHERSTONE AND KOSTAS IFANTIS (EDS)

The new Germany and migration in Europe
BARBARA MARSHALL

Turkey's relations with a changing Europe
MELTEM MÜFTÜLER-BAC

Righting wrongs in Eastern Europe
ISTVAN POGANY

Two tiers or two speeds?
The European security order and the enlargement of the European Union and Nato
JAMES SPERLING (ED.)

Recasting the European order
Security architectures and economic cooperation
JAMES SPERLING and EMIL KIRCHNER

Dimitris K. Xenakis & Dimitris N. Chryssochoou

THE EMERGING EURO-MEDITERRANEAN SYSTEM

MANCHESTER UNIVERSITY PRESS
Manchester and New York

distributed exclusively in the USA by Palgrave

Published by Manchester University Press
Oxford Road, Manchester M13 9NR, UK
and Room 400, 175 Fifth Avenue, New York, NY 10010, USA
http.//www.manchesteruniversitypress.co.uk

Distributed exclusively in the USA by
Palgrave, 175 Fifth Avenue, New York,
NY 10010, USA

Distributed exclusively in Canada by
UBC Press, University of British Columbia, 2029 West Mall,
Vancouver, BC, Canada V6T 1Z2

British Library Cataloguing-in-Publication Data
A catalogue record for this book is available from the British Library

Library of Congress Cataloging-in-Publication Data applied for

ISBN 0 7190 6013 3 *hardback*

First published 2001

07 06 05 04 03 02 01 10 9 8 7 6 5 4 3 2 1

Typeset in Minion with Lithos
by Northern Phototypesetting Co Ltd, Bolton
Printed in Great Britain
by Bookcraft (Bath) Ltd, Midsomer Norton

To our fathers,
Kimon D. Xenakis and Nikitas D. Chryssochoou

Some have pointed to a modern 'clash of civilisations' as inevitable. We who live at the crossroads disagree – indeed, we are living proof that different cultures and different faiths can co-exist in peace.

His All Holiness Bartholomew I,
Archbishop of Constantinople – New Rome and Ecumenical Patriarch,
University of Exeter, 13 July 2000.

Contents

	Series editor's foreword	*page* ix
	List of abbreviations	xi
	Introduction	1
Part I	**Transformation and complexity**	7
1	Transformative orders	9
2	On Mediterranean complexity	25
Part II	**Policy and process**	55
3	European policies towards the Mediterranean	57
4	The Barcelona Process: structure and evolution	74
Part III	**Theorising sea-change**	95
5	Conceptualising Euro-Mediterranean governance	97
6	The emerging Euro-Mediterranean system	116
	Select bibliography	127
	Index	152

Series editor's foreword

The events of 1989 unleashed a number of significant changes in European development, bringing in their wake consequences such as the dismantling of the iron curtain, the transformation of communist regimes, German reunification, dissolution of the Warsaw Pact and the Soviet Union, an end to the Cold War syndrome, and the arrival of a host of new states. The consequences of these changes affect nation states, the European Union, and European security and stability. Whilst Europe as a whole has moved from enmity towards friendship and from conflict to cooperation in economic, political and military fields, the internal stability and cohesion of many states has been adversely affected. The result has been civil wars, fragmentation, migration, and economic and social hardship. Parallel to these developments are attempts by the EU for a larger and more integrated entity.

How Europe is responding to these changes and developments and their consequences is the focus of this book series, appropriately entitled, *Europe in Change*. Books in this series take both a historical and interdisciplinary perspective in order to compare the post-1989 situation with earlier periods in European history and benefit from the theoretical insights of different disciplines in analysing both events and developments.

The aspect of *change* is a central concern to the book *The emerging Euro-Mediterranean system*. As the authors argue, fundamental changes in the structure and operation of institutionalised shared rule among distinct culturally defined and socially organised polities pose new challenges to the interminable search for a viable political order based on stable authority patterns of governance not only within but, increasingly, between states and peoples. These ascending challenges necessitate the integration of domestic and international politics and, by extension, the conditions for developing a more profound understanding of the relationship between *continuity and change*, unity and fragmentation, sovereignty and interdependence, autonomy and control.

For peaceful change to occur in the Mediterranean region, which has been traditionally marked by volatility and often protracted conflicts, the authors attribute a central role to the 1995 established Euro-Mediterranean partnership (EMP). They are, however, cautious in their interpretation, arguing that effective order building.can not be realised under the present (weak) institutional configuration of the EMP. In their view, at the moment the EMP represents a balance of separate national preferences, rather than a common Euro-Mediterranean interest per se. For the authors, the EMP is propelled by a certain 'economism' whose financial rather than trade implications are favourable to the non-EU partners. In return for the above the EU has linked issues of economic liberalisation to a set of political principles. Looking to the future, the authors argue that the search for a new legitimacy in Euro-Mediterranean relations depends on the partners' capacity to resist the forces of polarisation and segmentation, as well as on the credibility of their commitment to rediscovering a sense of process (and purpose) based on humanism, pluriformity and social justice.

The book engages effectively conceptual tools, such as transformation, regime theory, and governance, in the assessment of the empirical development in the Mediterranean and provides a very interesting analysis of the EPM and its likely future development. By addressing key influences on, and developments of, the EPM process, and by employing international relation theories and European integration approaches in the analysis, the Xenakis and Chryssochoou book provides a timely and interesting analysis of developments in the Mediterranean region, and of the role the enlarged EU will play in it.

Emil J. Kirchner
General Series Editor

ABBREVIATIONS

ACP	African, Caribbean and Pacific
BWC	Biological Weapons Convention
CAP	Common Agricultural Policy
CBMs	confidence-building measures
CFSP	Common Foreign and Security Policy
CJTF	Combined Joint Task Force
CSBMs	confidence and security-building measures
CSCE	Conference on Security and Co-operation in Europe
CSCM	Conference on Security and Co-operation in the Mediterranean
CTBT	Comprehensive Test Ban Treaty
CWC	Chemical Weapons Convention
ECU	European currency unit
EEA	European Economic Area
EFTA	European Free Trade Area
EIB	European Investment Bank
EMP	Euro-Mediterranean partnership
EP	European Parliament
ESDI	European Security and Defence Identity
GCC	Gulf Co-operation Council
GDP	Gross Domestic Product
GMP	Global Mediterranean Policy
HFA	Helsinki Final Act
IMF	International Monetary Fund
MEFTA	Mediterranean Free Trade Area
MENA	Middle East–North Africa
MPCs	Mediterranean Partner Countries
NATO	North Atlantic Treaty Organisation
NGOs	non-governmental organisations
NPT	Non-Proliferation Treaty
OSCE	Organisation on Security and Co-operation in Europe
PBMs	partnership-building measures
RMP	Renovated Mediterranean Policy
WEU	Western European Union
WTO	World Trade Organisation

Introduction

At a time when power is becoming more widely dispersed and low politics areas acquire greater salience for both students and practitioners, the Mediterranean finds itself in limbo, between order and change, affirmation and transformation. Against a background of unprecedented global transformations that constantly redefine the conditions on which international life is organised, while reactivating basic questions of order and governance, this book represents an attempt at assessing developments in Euro-Mediterranean governance since the signing of the Barcelona Declaration in November 1995. Its principal aim is to investigate the extent to which the Euro-Mediterranean partnership, only a handful of years since its inception, has been able to ascribe new meaning to the concept of regional order-building through peaceful means. This is no easy task, given that 'the Mediterranean' denotes a volatile region *par excellence*, long characterised by autochthonous and often protracted conflicts.

Indeed, over the last few years, Mediterranean politics has come alive, rising as it were from the lethargy imposed on it by some fifty 'cold years' based on inelastic 'images of polarity' as well as a fixed conception of order held together by the ideological glue of two diametrically opposed worldviews. Interestingly, underlying the conduct (or praxis) of international politics throughout the largely unimaginative years of Cold War diplomacy was the preservation of the status quo in a divided Europe and of a relatively stable international system, at least as compared to the dynamism, unpredictability, uncertainty – but also the excitement – of the post-1989 era. Today, the critical question is whether the Euro-Mediterranean process can sustain its newly instituted 'partnership' for any significant length of time without first having to transform itself into a system of patterned behaviour based on norms of good governance and the principles of mutualism and reciprocity: namely, without generating a notion of the rules of the game capable of steering and, in time, structuring international behaviour.

The Mediterranean – for many, Europe's birthplace – has been described as a dense network of diversities and dividing lines between different political and socio-economic (sub)systems, cultures and regimes, as well as languages, forms of expression and religious denominations. Historically, the region has occupied a prominent role in the attainment of European peace and security, not least due to its crucial geopolitical and geostrategic position, representing both the crossroads and the natural bridge between Europe, Asia and Africa. Being a space where several civilisations have influenced and enriched each other, as well as a crossroads for multiple cultural, human and economic exchanges, the Mediterranean combines a wide range of diverse and often conflicting interests. Although some might claim that its peoples have exhibited a distinctively Mediterranean sense of belonging, albeit at different levels of intensity and to varying extents, they have not (as yet) laid down the foundations of a communal journey. Notwithstanding the Braudelian rhetoric of a historical and cultural destiny nourished by shared myths and ideals, the Mediterranean remains simultaneously a place of peaceful human activity as well as a zone of real or potential tensions and rifts.

Much like Europe itself, the Mediterranean remains a composite of diverse civilisations, each sharing some portions of a distinctive culture based on a body of rich histories, traditions, philosophies and values. To borrow a phrase, it is 'a patchwork of images, composed partly of myths, partly of realities'. Today, the extent to which old images are replaced by new in the Mediterranean cultural tapestry is an open question, answers to which depend in part on the differing religious and secular understandings of the region's sense of unity and identity, diversity and differentiation. Mythical constructs aside, in the light of current constellations of order and change the Mediterranean is characterised by a new pluricausal and multilogical dynamism pushing towards a new mapping of its component collectivities. Elements of both convergence and divergence in its coastal parts are reformulated through a dialectical union of old stereotypes, novel ways of life, modified perceptions of belonging and an ascending pluralism in the emerging patterns of human governance and interaction.

Changes in patterns of thinking and acting are in the air, finding expression either in the form of new social movements that cut across established boundaries or in the formulation of a politics of institutionalised rule. Still, though, the effects of its changing social, political and economic scenery are frequently concealed, sometimes by the forces of conservatism, sometimes by adherents of a much-idealised and allegedly glorified past. What is certain, however, is that these are exciting times for revisiting and reconceptualising the region's social structures, cultural distinctiveness, economic orientation and, crucially, political future. As noted above, there is no doubt that encouraging the development of new possibilities and opportunities in the Mediterranean has been the launching of the Barcelona Process.

Although current discourses reach different conclusions as to the existence of an identifiable Mediterranean 'entity' or 'unity', the one thing that seems to be constant is that the bonds of unity and diversity between its coastal parts will continue to form part of an open-ended debate. Throughout history, the Mediterranean has been a laboratory for the cross-fertilisation of diverse cultures, amounting to a synthesis of heterogeneous religious and ethnic groups along the lines of a 'heterarchical space'. And given the levels of unequal economic development, the plurality of political regimes, divergent perceptions of security and, crucially, uneven demographic growth, one can easily identify the difficulties facing any attempt to come to grips with Mediterranean complexity. For the purposes of this study, however, 'the Mediterranean' is taken to denote a heterarchical regional space, where geography, history and politics intermesh with culture and religion with enormous complexity, resulting in a composite system of partial regimes, each reflecting a particular sense of being and belonging.

To students of international relations, the challenging question posed by the emerging governance structures of the new Euro-Mediterranean process is whether the regional partnership, rising as it were from the legacy of state-controlled and largely unco-ordinated European policies towards the Mediterranean (pursued either on an individual basis through separate foreign policy agendas or collectively through the institutional machinery of the then European Community), will prove capable of giving birth to an international regime with a life of its own based on clearly defined rules as well as mutually reinforcing principles, norms and decision-making procedures. The stability and development of the Mediterranean is not a new theme in the history of European diplomacy. It is one, however, that is characterised by considerable variation and, more often than not, poor results. The extent to which the Mediterranean can really be seen as a *region* further complicates the discussion about the appropriate scope and level of a common European policy towards the Mediterranean. Partly as a result of the EC's Mediterranean enlargements in the early and mid-1980s, and partly due to the changing geopolitical and geostrategic conditions post-1989, Mediterranean affairs have come to occupy a significant amount of the European Union's external relations.

The signing of the Barcelona Declaration has undoubtedly sparked new interest in the governance of the Euro-Mediterranean space, particularly in terms of studying its envisaged transformation from a dispersed system of bilateral arrangements (composed mainly of trade agreements and financial protocols) to the eventual framing of institutionalised patterns of shared rule based on the development of common understandings and the achievement of mutually rewarding interactions. Notwithstanding the rhetoric of high-ranking diplomats and politicians, and despite the different levels of enthusiasm with which the partner states have welcomed its declared principles and objectives, one could legitimately claim that the Barcelona Conference inaugurated a new era in Euro-Mediterranean relations. Clearly, crucial questions remain to be addressed as to whether the whole exercise will be crowned with success; what can the EU deliver in terms of furthering liberalisation and the building of democratic structures in the partner countries; which norms are likely to emerge in regional security building (especially in the sensitive area of conflict management); will a more equitable regime of economic exchange be established between the poor and the rich of the region; and – to keep this almost naturally expanding list relatively short – what might be the prospects of a new politics of institutional accommodation, given the existing levels of complexity, heterogeneity, fragmentation and difference that, for centuries now, have shaped the physiognomy of this 'unique body of water'?

Related areas of concern to students of the new Euro-Mediterranean landscape include the relationship between order and change, autonomy and interdependence, pluralism and control. Added to these are questions of political democracy and good governance, civil society and human rights, multiculturalism and inter-faith communication among distinct culturally defined, socially structured and politically organised states and societies; a good part of which, it needs to be emphasised, are presently characterised by political instability, weak or almost non-existent civic organisations, disjunction between the wishes of the ruling elites and their respective publics, and, in general, what might be called 'horizontal divisions' that cut across the spectrum of domestic cleavages.

At a more specific level, for the EU to achieve the intended outcomes and improvements, and its expressed ambition to present itself as a single polity with its own voice in international affairs, the identification of a commonality of interests, aspirations and, crucially, a shared vision towards the Mediterranean will be necessary. For their part, southern Mediterranean and Middle Eastern countries would also have to employ strategies capable of mobilising their energies towards the achievement of a more balanced network of relations in their dealings with their European partners based on the forces of mutualism, reciprocity and, where possible, reconciliation. In this context, a new 'hermenautics of civilisational dialogue' through reciprocal exchanges and a philosophy of mutual understanding is deemed necessary to alleviate culturally and historically rooted prejudices and misperceptions, which have often in the past offered a convenient apology for keeping regional co-operation out of reach. For, ultimately, it is this 'capacity for dialogue' that remains crucial for revitalising a cross-fertilisation between heterogeneous units, opening a whole new range of possibilities for the realisation of the conditions of peace, stability and prosperity in the region. Such a capacity, however, in an era of greater complexity, flexibility and differentiation, requires the acknowledgement of cultural pluralism and symbiotic association for a meaningful regional process of emerge and consolidate itself. The search for a new legitimacy in Euro-Mediterranean relations rests on the partners' capacity to resist the forces of polarisation and segmentation, and rediscover a sense of process (and purpose too) based on humanism, pluriformity and social justice.

At an institutional level, there also appear to be more questions than answers regarding the necessary means for systematising Euro-Mediterranean relations, transforming political principles into concrete political achievements, structuring the interaction of the various 'baskets' involved (including the issue of conditionality and the means towards its operationalisation), the levels of flexibility to be allowed within the governance arrangements of the partnership and the preferred strategies for the implementation of agreed commitments (including the question of compliance). Of importance here are the EU's strategic choices for the promotion of norms of good governance, given the tensions arising from different conceptions of the 'good polity'. It is equally crucial to assess whether there are any insurmountable cultural barriers to furthering the prospects of the Euro-Mediterranean partnership, keeping in mind the recent re-embrace of radical Islamism and Arab nationalism. Above all, the question is whether the co-operative ethos embedded within the Barcelona Declaration can go beyond the level of contractual inter-state obligations to move closer to a genuine partnership between interdependent polities within a transformative order. It is only in that sense that the evolving regional process will act as a prelude to new and far-reaching beginnings.

Finally, a few words are in order about the organisation of the book. It is divided into three parts, each reflecting a particular concern with the structure and dynamics of order-building in the Euro-Mediterranean space. Part I accounts for the realities of the post-1989 international order and assesses the nature of Mediterranean complexity. Part II focuses on European policies towards the Mediterranean before and after the launching of the Barcelona Process and the extent to which the latter represents a break with the pre-1995 state of affairs. Finally, Part III justifies the centrality of theory to the development of a more profound understanding of complex social and political phenomena, and conceptualises the emerging Euro-Mediterranean system through the intersection of regime theory and international governance.

PART I

Transformation and complexity

1

Transformative orders

International system change

The end of the Cold War unleashed widespread speculation on what international politics would bring: instability or global co-operation; sovereign equality or great-power domination; world-wide democratisation or old-fashioned despotism; a 'new world order' or a return to hyper-nationalism? As international and regional orders find themselves in transition, so do most international institutions and organisations formed during the Cold War. In attempting to capture the new dialectic of international system change in the early 1990s, Barber has asserted that the world is 'falling precipitately apart and coming reluctantly together at the very same moment'.[1] The recent sea-change in international politics has ignited new thinking about 'a new world order',[2] 'the end of history',[3] 'blood and nationalistic belongings',[4] 'the clash of civilisations',[5] 'grey areas',[6] 'coming chaos',[7] 'between chaos and order'[8] and 'world disorders'.[9] Despite these prophecies, however, some of which arguably have occasioned the gloomiest of prognostications, there are still reasons for being optimistic when looking at the future of international relations.

Post-1989 transformations have led to a state of unpredictable change and, as often admitted, 'disorder', with increased perceptions of instability stemming from the collapse of the 'deterrence regime' that ascribed a sense of balanced hierarchy to the international system. The new era was marked also by a dramatic shift in Soviet strategic perceptions, an attempt by Western powers to exploit the strategic/military advantage following the Soviet retrenchment, and the absence of a major international war to act as a catalyst for change. The UN has emerged as a major actor in world politics, and after the Gulf Crisis has become the cornerstone of a 'new world order' through a massive military operation.[10] Also, human rights norms have become organising principles of the new order, 'just as anti-communism was for the Cold War'.[11] Although these events opened the way for a Kantian-inspired 'perpetual peace',[12] the task of civilising international politics was to be taken up by 'Grotian' agents.[13]

Assertions about the end of the Cold War inevitably imply a Eurocentric bias; but if one considers geopolitics from an Asian perspective, then the narrative line is far more ambiguous. Many of the tensions associated with the Cold War have persisted: Korea remains divided, while China continues to adhere to a Marxist/Maoist ideology and has an uneasy relationship with its neighbours that poses a potential geopolitical challenge. Moreover, 'the coming anarchy', in the words of Kaplan, reflects the multi-dimensional meltdown experienced by many African states.[14] As for the Western world, the era of bipolarity has been replaced by one of relative stability, where co-operation tends to shape relations among leading countries on most issues. This trend was epitomised by Western responses to the Gulf Crisis in 1990–91, where a strategic consensus among Western powers laid the foundations for effective collective action.

The perceived stability characterising the Cold War system was also reflected in the dominant theories of international relations, which emphasised elements of continuity.[15] But the complexity of the new era clearly highlights the need for a novel approach, capable of taking dynamic change seriously.[16] In some interpretations, 'complexity' is merely used to describe what is complicated and not well understood. Stein explains:

> Complexity is almost a theological concept; many people talk about it, but nobody knows what 'it' really is. For example, organizations and systems are often called complex, not because they are seen as dynamic and adaptive, but because they defy easy notions as to how they are organized or function.[17]

The momentous political upheaval after 1989 has sparked renewed interest in the study of international politics as scholars turn to the past for insights and categories of analysis with which to get to grips with a present that is in a state of flux. These premisses are summarised well by King, Keohane and Verba, who argue that scholars would learn a lot if they could re-run history with everything constant, save for an 'investigator-controlled explanatory variable'.[18] This view posits that the best way to understand the world is through linear models, a logic that falls within the macroscopic approach of this book.

During bipolarity, military threats to security dominated all others in the eyes of most international security specialists. The end of the Cold War era, which arguably changed 'all the answers and all the questions',[19] has brought with it numerous suggestions that resources once devoted to coping with military threats can now be used to deal with 'soft' security issues. Since 1989, the changing nature of conflicts – i.e. from international to internal conflicts – has altered established perceptions of sovereignty and the principle of non-intervention in the domestic affairs of states. At a time when more than thirty wars are reported on daily,[20] present-day world turbulence demonstrates the difficulties arising from the debris of the Cold War. New challenges are easy to identify in the case of Balkan insecurities, reflecting the lack of effective conflict management by the international community. In the Yugoslav and Chechnya cases, lack of agreement on the interpretation of international law, dilemmas within democracies on the use of force, the return to national reflexes rather than collective solidarity, and the real or perceived inappropriateness of international institutions have seriously undermined the operational capacity of the international community.[21]

A natural inclination of any potential synthesiser in the discipline of international relations is to focus on alarming trends that may have tragic consequences for peace and stability, if not shatter the existing order by sowing the seeds of chaos. Defining and recognising conditions of stability during the bipolar era was relatively easy and analytically less demanding. The by-products of globalisation – international organised crime, terrorism, refugee problems, demographics, and environmental issues, together with massive changes in the global economy, technological advances in transport and communications, and diminished governmental control – have radically changed our classical perceptions of security and the context in which international pathologies endure. Security, in this sense, tends to take on an abstract quality intertwined with the complexities of socio-political interaction. But, if too broadly defined, 'security' begins to lose its meaning as a concept, making it almost impossible to set priorities for collective action. While theoretical agreement on the meaning of 'security' post-1989 is still problematic,[22] the term can no longer be gauged in strictly military terms. New security considerations must be based on a pluridimensional approach to cope with the new agenda which, according to Dewit, focuses on 'the reach of impact, the complexity of the causal process, the range and capabilities of actors involved, and the acknowledgement that threat and response are no longer within the sole or even primary purview of the military'.[23] As geopolitics plays such a crucial role in the global system, a new dialectic is added, linking together the various domains of security.

Neorealists have suggested that the removal of the 'bipolar overlay' meant an increasingly intense struggle for power between competing states within an anarchical system, 'with the possibility of a war always in the background'.[24] The 1991 Gulf War further complicated things, for it turned on the talk of a 'new world order' in much more conflictual terms. Although the threat of nuclear confrontation has been reduced, the new era is likely to be more complex and unstable rather than less. For example, in the Balkans and the Trans-Caucasus, bitter and long-standing ethnic divisions that simmered for years under a tight bipolar lid have boiled over.[25] Many regimes that were pawns in the superpower confrontation have been set adrift by their former benefactors and are struggling for survival. Yet, the prophecies advanced by realists have not been fulfilled. Rather, there are still signs of optimism that the new century can sustain a world order within which international disputes are resolved through reason and, in any case, by means other than force. A clear trend has thus emerged to replace unilateral relations and power-politics behaviour with a multilateral institutionalised context. Hence, post-1989 world politics should not be viewed as a historically frozen realm of power-hungry states, but rather as a dynamic process of interaction among individuals, groups, states and international institutions.

We have recently witnessed the emergence of a form of regional multilateralism that binds together regions around the world into the global system. As a result, regional actors are increasingly recognising that their futures are intermeshed and are taking steps to co-ordinate their course of action. Today, the multilateral management of international problems occupies a central position in political, socio-economic, environmental and security issues. The fast-paced integration of the world economy, new pressures towards internationalised (economic) governance and novel forms of transnational action, by adding to the challenges confronting the new global agenda, have also increased the currency of institutionalised multilateralism. In the economic sphere, the existence of organisations such as the International Monetary Fund (IMF), the World Trade Organisation (WTO) and the World Bank, and an ever-expanding array of transnational networks suggests that the shift toward market liberalisation is intimately linked with new forms of multilateral regulation, management and political lobbying. In general terms, institutionalised multilateralism can be taken to denote a particular – Western – way of bringing together international actors to support global governance, incorporating principles of non-discrimination and diffused reciprocity.[26]

As early as 1977, Keohane and Nye warned us of the inadequacy of Realism as an analytic framework for a world in transition to a condition of complex interdependence.[27] As the realist paradigm failed to predict and explain the ending of the Cold War,[28] some scholars have embarked on an intellectual journey to reconsider 'the power of power politics'.[29] An alternative view to realism holds that globalisation, rather than some hostile constellation of external forces, represents a real threat to popular well-being. This view, by undermining the significance of geopolitical imperatives, does not take the end of the Cold War as a decisive threshold, but rather looks to the emergence of transnational social forces as agents of historical change. Cox argues that in the era of globalisation the state becomes a transmission belt from the global to the national economy: 'where heretofore it had acted as the bulwark defending domestic welfare from external disturbances … [now] different forms of state facilitate this tightening of the global/local relationship for countries occupying different positions in the global system'.[30] As Held rightly notes, economic, political and cultural interdependencies undermine the sovereignty of states in all aspects of their security:

> *the operation of states in an evermore complex international system both limits their autonomy and infringes increasingly upon their sovereignty.* Any conception of sovereignty that interprets it as an illimitable form of public power is undermined. Sovereignty itself has to be conceived today as already divided among a number of agencies – national, regional and international – and limited by the very nature of this plurality.[31]

The sovereign state currently lies at the intersection of a vast array of international regimes and organisations assigned the task of managing whole areas of trans-national activity and collective policy problems. The growth of new forms of organising politics reflects the growing diffusion of foreign and domestic policy, and the corresponding desire by most states for international governance and regulation.

As Nierop asserts, 'virtually all nation-states have gradually become enmeshed in and functionally part of a larger pattern of global transformations and global flows',[32] calling into question the authority of the territorial state in an ever-borderless world-market. Indeed, a simple touch on the keyboard by a powerful money dealer may hold individuals and states to ransom.[33] Neoliberal ideas may still form the ideological cement that keeps this transformed globe together,[34] but we are also reminded of the fragility of the international financial system.[35] Ironically, inequality is growing, at a time when the triumph of liberal politics and economics was expected to inaugurate a new era of freedom and opportunity. After 1989, Gray argues, 'the world … has passed through a brief period of euphoria about a New World Order, the end of history, an emerging universal democratic peace, and suchlike juvenilia'.[36] In fact, the current state of affairs is still influenced by the legacy of realism. In Hassner's words, if the description of the Cold War system was one of 'neither peace nor war', that of the post-Cold War period is one of 'both peace and war'.[37] The new international system is not the result of a 'real war', where victors impose their own rules of the game. Rather, it emerges through negotiation and agreement, and the final outcome will depend not on abstract and impersonal forces of history but on collective institutional action.

That the emerging multipolarity will differ markedly from that of the previous era is a point well made in the relevant literature,[38] and so is the view that the new order is being shaped by regional dynamics that had operated all along under the surface of superpower politics.[39] But while globalisation has altered the patterns of geopolitics and geogovernance, 'our conceptual frameworks and menu of policy prescriptions are indelibly infused with a Cold War political logic'.[40] In this context, 'power' will be more evenly spread as regional economic blocs expand their geopolitical influence.

The role of international institutions becomes crucial here, for it is through them that states know what to expect from each other. Indeed, mutual expectations and reciprocal behaviour represent the very fabric of a viable international order. When referring to 'international order', we imply that the international society of states and institutions is 'governed' in the loose sense of the term. Yet, one should bear in mind that the pattern of rule that governs relations among states is one that conforms to the idea of 'governance without government'.[41] As change transforms international politics, the prospects for global governance become a transcendent issue. Regime theory explains that this idea refers to the role that governance systems, in contrast to organisations or material entities, play in solving collective-action problems under conditions of complex interdependence.[42] International regimes are central in maintaining a reliable system of international security, thus offering the assurance of joint decisions or the avoidance of common dilemmas.[43] Two basic images of global governance emerge here: the first projects a world of rules and laws respected by all; the second reflects a global process, whereby the lawless lead the world to a state of chaos and injustice.

The European order transformed

Post-1989 Europe has been 'transformed' and 'redefined'.[44] It is no longer under the threat of mutual nuclear destruction, no longer in fear that every crisis might escalate into a wider East–West conflict. Germany has been reunited for more than a decade now, and Russia is a new polity with a new foreign policy agenda.[45] As Gray rightly points out, however, we are not yet on the threshold of a golden age of assured peace:

> The 1990s are an inter-war, as well as a post-war period, because bad times assuredly will return. That, at least, is what history should be allowed to teach as. Just possibly, the future of world politics might witness a radical improvement over the past, but Europeans cannot prudently order their security affairs upon such a slender hope.[46]

The redefinition of the European order is still incomplete. As Mayall and Miall assert, 'the phase of deconstruction has probably not yet ended'.[47] Europe is now shaped by a multitude of often competing forces: integration and disintegration; internationalisation and re-nationalisation; balance of power and struggle for power. The collapse of Communism has given way to the disintegration of multinational states, a painful process of transition to liberal democracy (or polyarchy) and market economy, and the resurgence of the suicidal effects of (ethnic) nationalism. The explosion of political liberty in central and eastern Europe has inflicted upon this transformative European order signs of regional turbulence. Although no immediate military threat exists, new risks and challenges have emerged. They include:

- historically based mistrust and friction among ethnic groups;
- aggressive nationalism;
- proliferation of biological and mass-destruction weapons;
- social disruption in light of radical economic reforms;
- illegal migration;
- drug-trafficking; and
- ecological threats.

An indication of the many uncertainties embedded within the new European security system is also the relative increase in the defence spending of so-called 'rival states'.[48] Moreover, given the fact that 'Islamic fundamentalism' is also directed against moderate regimes in North Africa and the Middle East, should the besieged Turkish, Egyptian and Algerian Governments succumb to radical Islamic movements, then Europe's southern flank would be in fragile hands. All the above are major challenges confronting the internal and external security of the new Europe.[49]

More than twenty years ago, Hassner tried to assess the possibilities for Europe beyond the Cold War and concluded that security integration would be imperative in the absence of superpower hegemony. He explained: 'Some multilateral framework, some collective arrangement committing stronger states to the protection and restraint of smaller ones, must be an essential part of any European system.'[50] But the new European security order, he warned, must evolve in living history, from the security requirements of the new political order, rather than by conscious and manipulative design; only failure awaits 'a rational, intellectual or mechanical and deliberate construction as opposed to a natural, organic or historical product with all its confusions and hazards'.[51] This point is equally valid today. As Heisbourg points out,

> we must beware of spending too much time quarrelling about European security architectures, for however important they may be for the long term, the qualities which we will need in the next few months or years will be those of the navigator, not the architect: adaptability and mobility combined with a sense of direction.[52]

All European security organisations have responded to the new challenges, engaging themselves in a great deal of rethinking.[53] This is especially true of the North Atlantic Treaty Organisation (NATO) and the Western European Union (WEU), but even more so of the then Conference and now Organisation on Security and Co-operation in Europe (OSCE), for it transformed itself from a periodic platform for East–West dialogue into an international organisation proper with operational capabilities of its own.[54]

The early 1990s was a period of idealism in which the newly independent states appealed to the UN and the OSCE with every minor complaint, much as they had turned to the Central Committee of the Communist Party in earlier days. The second stage was a period of 'romantic maximalism', during which the leaders of the post-Soviet states believed that international organisations possessed unlimited resources which would be used to address all their major problems. The third stage was one of cynicism towards international organisations, most sharply felt in Russia. The view that international organisations lack either the interest or the capacity to become involved in Eurasia led to the conclusion that membership of these organisations is of little value.[55] Herein lies the institutional paradox of the first post-Cold War decade: while there exist several overlapping security institutions with competing responsibilities, the post-1989 systemic reality has been instrumental in sustaining the actors' faith in co-operative frameworks and in advancing rule-governing state behaviour.[56]

The end of the Cold War found western Europe highly institutionalised. As Keohane and Nye put it: 'state behaviour was to a considerable extent governed by rules. This system therefore only distantly resembled the textbook portrayal of sovereign states pursuing self-help policies under conditions of anarchy.'[57] Yet, if such relations seem to be an example of peacefulness at the international level, this is due not to the absence of conflicts but rather to the existence of various forms of non-violent and even integrative conflict management.[58] Western Europe is well accustomed to the politics of reciprocal co-operation, and, recently, a state of political co-determination has emerged among the component polities of the European Union (EU),[59] while growing economic integration has increased the intensity and levels of interdependence among them. EU initiatives towards central and eastern Europe can be seen as part of a wider evolution towards pan-European integration. As the EU has become the centre of gravity for its periphery, one might expect that its leadership potential would face up to its growing international responsibilities. Yet, painful structural adjustments lie ahead for Europe to compete in a globalised economy, while urgent reforms must precede the accession of the applicant countries to the EU.[60]

Today, there is no lack of European security institutions. But the question is over *who decides* on European security arrangements. Out of a massive literature, three issues figure prominently: the transformation and eastward enlargement of NATO and the EU; the transatlantic partnership and the role of the US in European security; and the future shape and role of the OSCE.[61] The Atlantic Alliance remains at the centre of European security, for it has succeeded in building political consensus, managing threats, defending its members, organising multinational military operations and keeping the US involved in Europe. In June 1996, NATO adopted a European Security and Defence Identity (ESDI) and set up the Combined Joint Task Force (CJTF). In May 1997, NATO and Russia agreed to establish a Joint Permanent Council, and two months later NATO agreed to admit three new members.[62]

Although NATO can protect its members through the force of arms, security involves much more than military might. It has crucial social, political and economic dimensions. The other European security organisations alongside NATO work to ensure that comprehensive security has a firm foundation through the strengthening of democratic institutions within the new members. The dilemma is that, while former Communist Europe is drawn into the European security framework, security can never really be achieved without a change in the political cultures of the newly admitted states. In Klebes's words: 'the problem is to ensure that Western Europe reunites with Eastern Europe in terms of its democratic values and other institutions that promote a pervasive and formidable foundation for continental and transatlantic security'.[63] The defining properties of a 'security community' are co-operation and confidence, and the central and eastern European states cannot be part of such a community unless they establish co-operative practices of conflict resolution. But as the Franco-German experience has clearly illustrated, not all such conflicts have to be resolved before these states are fully integrated into the envisaged European security community.[64]

The Mediterranean between order and disorder

One of the effects of the 1989 *annus mirabilis* was to shift the focus from the East–West towards the North–South divide. At the same time, the Western world witnessed the beginning of a period of – relative – geopolitical moderation conducive to co-operative ventures. Another clear trend was the increasing interconnectedness between geopolitical and cultural zones: these are now open to the emergence of new power centres. Concomitantly, the Mediterranean space has not only witnessed a sense of renewed scholarly excitement, but has become the focus of policy makers, especially since the mid-1990s with the launching of the Barcelona Process. No other part of the globe exemplifies better the post-1989 trends towards fragmentation and the revival of 'ancient feuds' than the Mediterranean, with security issues becoming increasingly indivisible. Notwithstanding the successive Yugoslav and Gulf Crises, the renaissance of a wider interest in the Mediterranean is based on the growing importance the region enjoys in the strategic calculus of the new European order. While EU members along the northern rim are increasingly prosperous as they find themselves locked in a dual process of economic and political union, most countries located at the southern rim seem to be moving in the opposite direction. Such a widening gap causes dramatic structural instability in Europe's international system, while projecting images of instability to the rest of the world.

From a macro-historical perspective, and due to its geopolitical and geostrategic position, the Mediterranean has always played a decisive role in the attainment of European peace and security, representing simultaneously the crossroads and the natural bridge between three continents: Europe, Asia and Africa. Being a space where several civilisations and religions have influenced and enriched each other, as well as a crossroads for multiple cultural, human and economic exchanges, the Mediterranean combines a wide range of diverse and often conflicting interests which, taken together, prevent its peoples from laying down the foundations of a communal journey. Despite the Braudelian rhetoric of a historical and cultural destiny nourished by commonly shared myths and ideals, the region remains at the same time a place of human activity, as well as a zone of political, economic, social and religious tension.

Located in the midst of the 'global village', the Mediterranean has been prone to the disruptive effects of protracted local disputes. With its complex structures and diverse systems, it has served as the battlefield of numerous wars in the history of humankind. In recent years the wider Mediterranean has witnessed the breakout and prosecution of diverse armed conflicts (both within and between nations) and the appearance of shaky socio-political dynamics. The Gulf War in the early 1990s has also served as a reminder of the region's potential to fall victim to similar disputes over regional hegemony. Moreover, the recent revival of Islamic activism is perceived as a threat to vital Western interests. In particular, the existence of large Islamic communities in Europe has increasingly led to hostile reactions, as these communities are frequently portrayed as a threat to Europe's socio-cultural cohesion. This has exacerbated an already evident alertness associated with complex socio-economic, demographic and political challenges (low politics), as well as with traditional military security anxieties (high politics). Some of these phenomena are linked to the systemic complexity of the Mediterranean region itself, where the existence of diverse types of conflict signals the appearance of others. Today, an unfortunate consequence of these trends is that the region approximates a hotbed of tensions, often resulting in brutal confrontations. Being an area of potential disorder, it is interesting to note that, especially after the Cold War and Gulf Conflicts, no real security threats exist in south–south relations. But the region being also a mosaic of cultures and civilisations, theorising the Euro-Mediterranean condition requires a thorough examination of competing normative orders and structures of meaning, rather than a resort to the demagogic myths that have long surrounded the Arabs' arduous journey to modernity and beyond. These problems are further compounded by transatlantic competition over this 'unique body of water'[65] and by the existing levels of European disharmony that effectively pervade the whole range of Euro-Mediterranean relations.

Although strategic orientation and co-ordinated action of all the actors involved are vital for the stability of the Euro-Mediterranean order, it was not until the mid-1970s that signs of an enhanced European interest in the Mediterranean became manifest, namely with the launching of the Euro–Arab dialogue. The same occurred in the early and mid-1980s with the accession of Greece, Spain and Portugal to the European Community (EC), and then again after the 1990–91 Gulf War. Although the Community retained only a marginal role in the Mediterranean during the Cold War, it had developed conventional relations with the littoral countries as early as 1962 (and even earlier with former French colonies) and had also participated in some major political processes in the region – e.g., the Middle East Peace Process and the Cyprus question.

The then dominant security perception of oil supplies, the preservation of the territorial status quo, the socio-cultural and historical heritage, and the management of new regional challenges were all dealt with by the Community via an economic prism, aimed at diffusing endogenous socio-economic pressures.[66] Yet, the 'Mediterranean question' – how to encompass ways of keeping the area peaceful and stable – was never really absent from the Community's foreign policy agenda. For one thing, European economic vulnerability to the Middle East crisis, revealed by the oil embargo in 1973, pushed the Community to install a dialogue with the Arab League from 1974 onwards, following the Yom Kippur War.[67] Despite the setting up of regular working groups and joint committees, the Euro–Arab dialogue eventually faded away, not least due to internal divisions within the Arab community. Frozen for most of the 1970s and 1980s as a result of superpower rivalry, the Euro–Arab dialogue received a new push in 1989, before being completely abandoned after the 1990 Iraqi invasion of Kuwait. The failure of the Euro–Arab initiative is attributed to the lack of agreement between the parties regarding agenda-setting issues. While the

Community gave priority to the economic dimension of security (energy supplies), the Arabs pushed for the inclusion of the Palestinian problem into the agenda.[68] In short, the European approach towards the Mediterranean was patterned on the following triptych: trade concessions; financial co-operation; and project aid. But these actions proved insufficient to sustain regional economic progress. The same can be said of all pre-1989 efforts by the Community to promote political dialogue and horizontal policy co-ordination in the region. Crucially, such efforts lacked a formal and comprehensive dialogue component due to their predominant bilateralism.

The early 1990s signalled the beginning of an entirely new era. Prima facie, the post-Cold War environment offered new opportunities for peace and prosperity in the Mediterranean, but in reality it increased the prospects for future instability, since the superpowers were no longer in a position to dampen conflicts. Mediterranean countries lost the geographic advantage they used to have because of their proximity to the EU at a time when eastern Europe was not allowed to have open exchanges with the West. As Hoekman points out, the relatively low wages and significant stocks of human capital put central and eastern European states in competition with Mediterranean states that had to implement more far-reaching liberalisation, privatisation and deregulation.[69] As EU foreign policy architects were directing their attention towards eastern Europe, southern EU members had to resume responsibility to deal with the growing scale of conflicts and disputes in parts of the Mediterranean.

Such a renewed interest in Euro-Mediterranean politics focused on solving collective-action problems, satisfying region-wide stability conditions, managing complex interdependence, and striking a balance between order and change. As a result, a number of comprehensive and partial multilateral initiatives emerged, most notably the 'global' Conference on Security and Co-operation in the Mediterranean (CSCM) – patterned along the lines of the CSCE model – and the rather more limited exercises of the 'Five plus Five' initiative, in the western Mediterranean, and the Mediterranean Forum, extending further east. Such projects, however, did not gain much success, not least due to their limited membership. The Yugoslav Crisis (and the CSCE's incapacity to resolve it) was a serious handicap for launching the CSCM. Munuera and Wrede regard the latter as an international forum capable of coping with a broad range of pressing issues,[70] a view that reflects a renewed interest in a CSCM-like project following the signing of the Barcelona Declaration in November 1995. Henceforth, Euro-Mediterranean politics were to acquire a multilateral framework. At the same time, creating a commonality of interests on economic as well as political and socio-cultural issues became the major challenge to the Barcelona project. The aim of the Barcelona Declaration is to commit its members to a set of basic principles of international co-operation and peaceful relations for a meaningful partnership to emerge within a pluralist regional order. They include: democratisation, liberalisation and pluralism; the rule of law; respect for human rights and minorities; and good-neighbourly relations. The crucial question here is not only whether the evolving Euro-Mediterranean partnership (EMP) will deal effectively with the dramatic level of systemic regional complexity (and sub-systemic diversity), but whether it will resolve any policy contradictions that may arise as the Barcelona project proceeds.[71]

As institutionalists of all kinds would argue, goal attainment is affected by the institutional context within which international actors operate. Olsen and Peters assert: 'Institutions contain some sort of governmental DNA and tend to transmit that genetic code to the individuals who take up roles within them.'[72] But one should not also forget that the success of order building is predicated on the extent to which it can accommodate change without violence. This requires new and constructive action by international institutions. In this context, the normative question that this study poses is whether institutions really matter in complex, fragile and fragmented orders. Neoliberal institutionalists offer what seems a plausible answer, arguing that the construction of international institutions stabilises domestic structures and facilitates co-operation.[73] In fact, these are all the more crucial since, according to Adler, 'in the future, the foreign policy architects of the European security-community [and, let us immediately add, the Euro-Mediterranean space] still must compete with and fight against strongly reified power-political practices and conflicting identities'.[74]

Although opinions differ on the extent to which institutions reformulate preferences and interests,[75] one could safely argue that 'in a world politics constrained by state power and divergent interests, and unlikely to experience effective hierarchical governance, international institutions operating on the basis of reciprocity will be components of any lasting peace'.[76] Although claiming too much for the effectiveness of institutionalised governance in the Euro-Mediterranean space might in the end prove to be a 'false promise',[77] it would be wrong to dismiss institutions as epiphenomena to the distribution of power: institutions do reshape states' definitions of interests and patterns of interaction.[78] In a nutshell, institutionalised governance matters and so does its design. This is the premise upon which this book is based.

Notes

1 See B. Barber, 'Jihad Versus McWorld', *The Atlantic Monthly*, March (1992), 53–63.
2 G. Bush, Address to the United Nations, 11 September 1990.
3 F. Fukuyama, *The End of History and the Last Man* (New York, Free Press, 1992).
4 M. Ignatieff, *Blood and Belonging: Journeys into the New Nationalism* (Toronto, Viking, 1993).
5 S. P. Huntington, 'The Clash of Civilizations?', *Foreign Affairs*, 72: 3 (1993) 22–49.
6 M. Manwaring (ed.), *Gray Area Phenomena: Confronting the New World Disorder* (Boulder, CO, Westview Press, 1993).
7 K. J. Holsti, 'The Coming Chaos? Armed Conflict in the World's Periphery', in T. V. Paul and J. A. Hall (eds), *International Order and the Future of World Politics* (Cambridge, Cambridge University Press, 1999), pp. 283–310.
8 See J. Chace, 'Between Chaos and Order', *World Policy Journal*, 16: 3 (1997).

9 S. Hoffman, *World Disorders: Troubled Peace in the Post-Cold War Era* (Oxford, Rowman & Littlefield, 1998).

10 In the new era, the UN started to intervene in the internal affairs of states in cases of domestic conflict, human rights violations and disregard of basic humanitarian principles. In this ascending normative order, where individual rights overwhelm the rights of states, the plight of the affected people became a new legitimising tool for collective action.

11 D. Rieff, 'Imperialism or Barbarism', *Prospect*, 43: July (1999), 36.

12 In the pursuit of perpetual peace, Kant proposed a world federation of states, through which the majority of states could unite to punish any one state that committed aggression.

13 S. M. Tarzi, 'The Role of Norms and Regimes in World Affairs: A Grotian Perspective', *International Relations*, 14: 3 (1998), 71–84.

14 R. D. Kaplan, 'The Coming Anarchy', *The Atlantic Monthly*, February (1994), 44–76.

15 The continuity observed was as much a product of the perceptions of scholars in the discipline of International Relations of what was considered important as it was a product of an 'objective' view of 'reality'.

16 See J. L. Gaddis, 'International Relations Theory and the End of the Cold War', *International Security*, 17: 3 (1992–93) 5–58; Cf. J. N. Rosenau, *Turbulence in World Politics* (Princeton, NJ, Princeton University Press, 1990).

17 D. L. Stein (ed.), *Lectures in the Sciences of Complexity* (Redwood City, CA, Addison-Wesley, 1989), p. xiii.

18 G. King, R. O. Keohane and S. Verba, *Designing Social Inquiry: Scientific Inference in Qualitative Research* (Princeton, NJ, Princeton University Press, 1994), p. 82.

19 C. W. Kegley, Jr, 'The Neoidealist Moment in International Studies? Realist Myths and the New International Studies', *International Studies Quarterly*, 37 (1993), 141.

20 M. Booth, 'Global Warring', *The Independent Magazine*, 30 January 1999.

21 Thus the probability of new hostilities in the Balkans after the Kosovo Crisis is great, for the region remains internally unsettled. See N. Gnesotto, 'Lessons of Yugoslavia', *Chaillot Papers*, 14, WEU Institute for Security Studies, 1994; and S. Clément, 'Conflict Prevention in the Balkans: Case Studies of Kosovo and the FYR of Macedonia', *Chaillot Papers*, 30, WEU Institute for Security Studies, Paris, 1997.

22 See B. Buzan, O. Waever and J. De Wilde, *Security: A New Framework for Analysis* (London, Lynne Rienner, 1998); and K. Krause and M. Williams, *Critical Security Studies: Concepts and Cases* (London, University College Press, 1997).

23 D. B. Dewitt, 'Introduction: The New Global Order and the Challenges of International Security', in D. B. Dewitt, D. Haglund and J. Kirton (eds), *Building a New Global Order: Emerging Trends in International Security* (Oxford, Oxford University Press, 1993), p. 1.

24 J. J. Mearsheimer, 'The False Promise of International Institutions', *International Security*, 19: 3 (1994–95), 5–49. See also K. Waltz, 'The Emerging Structure of International Politics', *International Security*, 18: 2 (1993), 44–79.

25 J. J. Mearsheimer, 'Why We Will Soon Miss the Cold War', *The Atlantic Monthly*, 266: 2 (1990) 35–50.

26 The possibility for multilateral management of regional and international problems transcends traditional intellectual, disciplinary and area studies divides. For instance, the world economy, human rights, the environment, population, security issues, non-proliferation and cultural affairs, all constitute possible issues for further investigation. See further in R. O. Cox (ed.), *The New Realism: Perspectives on Multilateralism and World Order* (Tokyo, United Nations University Press, 1997).

27 R. O. Keohane and J. S. Nye, Jr, *Power and Interdependence: World Politics in Transition* (Boston, MA, Little, Brown, 1977), especially pp. 23–37.

28 F. V. Kratochwill, 'The Embarrassment of Changes: Neo-Realism as the Science of *Realpolitik*', *Review of International Studies*, 19 (1993) 63–80; R. N. Lebow, 'The Long Peace, the End of the Cold War, and the Failure of Realism', in R. N. Lebow and

T. Risse-Kappen (eds), *International Relations Theory and the End of the Cold War* (New York, Columbia University Press, 1995), pp. 23–56.

29 J. A. Vasquez, *The Power of Power Politics: From Classical Realism to Neotraditionalism* (Cambridge, Cambridge University Press, 1998).

30 R. O. Cox, 'Global Restructuring: Making Sense of the Changing International Political Economy', in R. Stubbs and G. R. D. Underhill (eds), *Political Economy and the Changing Global Order* (London, Macmillan, 1994), p. 49. Cf. J. N. Rosenau, *Along the Domestic–Foreign Frontier: Exploring Governance in a Turbulent World* (Cambridge, Cambridge University Press, 1997).

31 D. Held, 'Democracy, the Nation-State and the Global System', in D. Held (ed.), *Political Theory Today* (Cambridge: Polity Press, 1991), p. 222.

32 T. Nierop, *Systems and Regions in Global Politics: An Empirical study of Diplomacy, International Organisation and Trade 1950–1991* (John Wiley, Chichester, 1994), p. 171.

33 For a more analytical view, see D. Held, A. McGrew, D. Goldblatt and J. Perraton, *Global Transformations* (Cambridge, Polity Press, 1999), especially pp. 32–86.

34 See F. Fukuyama, E. Hobsbawm, T. Garton Ash, R. Cooper, E. Luttwak and P. Hassner, 'The Global Order in the 21st Century: A Round Table', *Prospect*, August/September (1999), 50–8.

35 See S. Strange, *Casino Capitalism* (Manchester and New York, Manchester University Press, 1997). Cf. R. O. Cox, '"Take Six Eggs": Theory, Finance and the Real Economy in the Work of Susan Strange', in R. O. Cox, *Approaches to World Order* (Cambridge, Cambridge University Press, 1996), pp. 174–90.

36 C. Gray, 'The Geopolitics of European Defence in 2020', in M. Duffy, T. Farrell and G. Sloan (eds), *European Defence in 2020* (Exeter, University of Exeter, 1998), p. 23.

37 P. Hassner, 'An Overview of the problem', in N. Gnesotto (ed.), *War and Peace: European Conflict Prevention, Chaillot Papers*, 11, WEU Institute for Security Studies, Paris, 1993.

38 As Tucker has observed, whereas the multipolarity of the 1970s and 1980s took on meaning within the broader context of a persisting bipolarity, this is not the case with the multipolarity of the 1990s. See R. W. Tucker, '1989 and All That', *Foreign Affairs*, 69: 4 (1990), 96–7. See also C. W. Keagley and G. Reymond, *A Multipolar Peace? Great-Power Politics in the Twenty-First Century* (New York, St. Martin's Press, 1994). A somehow different view is offered by K. Waltz, 'The Emerging Structure of International Politics', *International Security*, 18: 2 (1993), 44–79.

39 The Middle East Peace Process, for example, was fuelled by regional pressures and not by the intervention of any superpower. Regional interests also drive the Russian project of reconstructing a sphere of influence in its near abroad of the Commonwealth of Independent States. See P. J. Katzenstein, 'Regionalism in Comparative Perspective', *ARENA Working Papers*, 1, 1996.

40 K. D. Bush and E. F. Keyman, 'Identity-Based Conflict: Rethinking Security in a Post-Cold War World', *Global Governance*, 3: 3 (1997), 311.

41 J. N. Rosenau, 'Governance, Order and Change in World Politics', in J. N. Rosenau and E. Czempiel (eds), *Governance Without Government: Order and Change in World Politics* (Cambridge, Cambridge University Press, 1992), pp. 1–29.

42 O. R. Young, *International Governance: Protecting the Environment in a Stateless Society* (Ithaca, NY, Cornell University Press, 1994), p. 16.

43 A. Stein, 'Co-ordination and Collaboration: Regimes in an Anarchic World', in S. Krasner (ed.), *International Regimes* (Ithaca, NY, Cornell University Press, 1983), pp. 124–5.

44 See respectively, W. Wallace, *The Transformation of Western Europe* (London, Pinter, 1990) and H. Miall (ed.), *Redefining Europe: New Patterns of Conflict and Cooperation* (London, Pinter, 1994).

45 M. Mandelbaum (ed.), *The New Russian Foreign Policy* (Washington, DC, Brookings Institute, 1998).

46 Gray, 'The Geopolitics of European Defence in 2020', p. 23.

47 J. Mayall and H. Miall, 'Conclusion: Towards a Redefinition of European Order', in Miall (ed.), *Redefining Europe*, p. 262.

48 R. F. Lehman II, 'Global and Part-Regional Trends in Arms Control and Confidence Building: Implications for the Mediterranean Region, North Africa and the Middle East', in F. Tanner (ed.), *Arms Control, Confidence-Building and Security Cooperation in the Mediterranean, North Africa and the Middle East* (Malta, MEDAC, 1994).

49 See further in A. Politi, 'European Security: The New Transnational Risks', *Chaillot Papers*, 29, WEU Institute for Security Studies, Paris, 1997.

50 P. Hassner, 'Change and Security in Europe: In Search of a System', *Adelphi Papers*, 49, Part II, International Institute for Strategic Studies, London, 1968, p. 21.

51 *Ibid.*, p. 4.

52 F. Heisbourg, 'Challenges to European Security and How to Meet them', Speech to the European Movement's Conference 'European Foreign and Security Policies', 7 June 1991, p. 6.

53 See W. Park and G. Wyn Rees (ed.), *Rethinking Security in Post-Cold War Europe* (London, Longman, 1998); O. Waever, 'Insecurity, Security, and Asecurity in the West European Non-War Community', in Adler E. and M. Barnett (ed.), *Security Communities* (Cambridge, Cambridge University Press, 1998), pp. 69–118; and D. Mahncke, 'Parameters of European Security', *Chaillot Papers*, 10, WEU Institute for Security Studies, Paris, 1993.

54 On the *raison d'être* of European security institutions, see J. Sperling and E. Kirchner (eds), *Recasting the European Order* (Manchester and New York, Manchester University Press, 1997).

55 A. Kortunov, 'Regional and International Institutions in Conflict Prevention and Peacekeeping', in G. W. Lapidus and S. Tsalik (eds), *Preventing Deadly Conflict: Strategies and Institutions* (New York, Carnegie Corporation of New York, 1994).

56 See I. Peters (ed.), *New Security Challenges: The Adaptation of International Institutions* (New York, St. Martin's Press, 1996), pp. 11–18.

57 R. O. Keohane and J. S. Nye, 'Introduction: The End of the Cold War in Europe', in R. O. Keohane, J. J. Nye and S. Hoffman, (eds), *After the Cold War: International Institutions and State Strategies in Europe, 1989–1991* (Harvard, Harvard CT, University Press, 1993), p. 2.

58 V. Rittberger (ed.), *International Regimes in East–West Politics* (London, Pinter, 1990), p. 256.

59 See D. N. Chryssochoou, *Democracy in the European Union* (London and New York, I. B. Tauris, 1998); and *Theorizing European Integration* (London, Sage, 2001).

60 See H. Grabbe and K. Hughes, *Eastward Enlargement of the European Union* (London, Royal Institute of International Affairs, 1997).

61 A. D. Rotfeld, 'Europe: In Search of Cooperative Security', in SIPRI Yearbook 1997, *Armaments, Disarmament and International Security* (Oxford, Oxford University Press, 1997).

62 Although the accession of Poland, Hungary and the Czech Republic to NATO will not affect these tasks or for that matter fundamentally change the Alliance's ability to successfully conduct them, that would not be the case if the post-Soviet states were to be included. See K. Schake, 'Europe After NATO Expansion: The Unfinished Security Agenda', *Policy Papers*, 38, University of California Institute on Global Conflict and Cooperation, 1998.

63 See H. Klebes, 'The Quest for Democratic Security', *Peaceworks*, 26 (1998).

64 I. Gambles, 'Conclusion: Prospects for the Expansion of the European Security-Community', in I. Gambles (ed.), *A Lasting Peace in Central Europe?*, *Chaillot Papers*, 20, WEU Institute for Security Studies, Paris, 1995.

65 The term is borrowed by T. Couloumbis and T. Veremis, 'Introduction: The Mediterranean in Perspective', in S. Stavridis *et al.* (eds), *The Foreign Policies of the European Union's Mediterranean States and Applicant Countries in the 1990s* (London, Macmillan, 1999), p. 1.

66 E. Regelsberger and W. Wessels, 'European Concepts for the Mediterranean', in G. Luciani (ed.), *The Mediterranean Region: Economic Interdependence and the Future of Society* (London, Croom Helm, 1984), p. 246.

67 D. Allen, 'The Euro–Arab Dialogue', *Journal of Common Market Studies*, 16 (1977–78), 324.

68 E. Regelsberger, 'The Euro–Arab Dialogue: Procedurally Innovative, Substantially Weak', in G. Edwards and E. Regelsberger (eds), *Europe's Global Links. The European Community and Inter-Regional Cooperation* (London, Pinter, 1990), pp. 57–65. See also A. Bin, 'Mediterranean Diplomacy: Evolution and Prospects', *Jean Monnet Working Papers in Comparative and International Politics*, 5, University of Catania, 1997.

69 B. Hoekman, 'The World Trade Organization, the European Union, and the Arab World: Trade Policy Priorities and Pitfalls', *Working Papers in International Economics*, Private Sector Development Division, World Bank, September 1995.

70 G. Munuera and H. Wrede, 'Prospects for Security and Cooperation in the Mediterranean After the PLO–Israel Agreement: A CSCM Revisited?', *Helsinki Monitor*, 2 (1994), 48–59.

71 The envisaged democratising and liberalising effects of the Barcelona project are rendered more difficult by the social tensions spawned by unpopular market reforms in view of the MEFTA objective.

72 J. P. Olsen and B. G. Peters, 'Learning from Experience', *ARENA Reprints*, 96/5, 1996, p. 28.

73 R. O. Keohane, 'Institutional Theory and the Realist Challenge After the Cold War', in D. Baldwin (ed.), *Neorealism and Neoliberalism: The Contemporary Debate* (New York, Columbia University Press, 1993), pp. 269–300.

74 E. Adler, 'Seeds of Peaceful Change: The OSCE's Security Community-Building Model', Adler and Barnett (eds), *Security Communities* (Cambridge, Cambridge University Press, 1998), p. 149. Central to the discussion about the development of 'security community' is the work of K. W. Deutsch on peaceful problem solving through the intensification of avenues of communication among nations (non-state international exchanges). A 'security community' is a framework of social interactions within which war would eventually become, in the relevant region, both unthinkable and impractical. Deutsch's notion of 'security community' could take the form of being either 'pluralistic' (where no formal/legal merger has occurred among the constituent units) or 'amalgamated' (where the component parts have been formally incorporated into a higher authority). See K. W. Deutsch *et al.*, *Political Community and the North Atlantic Area* (Princeton, NJ, Princeton University Press, 1957).

75 B. Rothstein, 'Political Institutions: An Overview', in R. E. Goodin and H. D. Klingemann (eds), *A New Handbook of Political Science* (Oxford, Oxford University Press, 1996).

76 R. O. Keohane and L. L. Martin, 'The Promise of Institutionalist Theory', *International Security*, 20: 1 (1995) 50.

77 J. J. Mearsheimer, 'The False Promise of International Institutions', *International Security*, 19: 3 (1994–95), 7.

78 R. R. Krebs, 'Perverse Institutionalism: NATO and the Greco-Turkish Conflict', *International Organization*, 53: 2 (1999), 368–9.

2

On Mediterranean complexity

Mapping the Mediterranean

It is fair to suggest that no consensus definition of 'the Mediterranean' has been recorded so far among its students. The latter are instead confronted with contradictory observations, often resulting in vague descriptions that the region constitutes a system of interactive states and societies whose mapping remains nebulous. Although 'different definitions and different criteria often produce different regions',[1] the definitional problem associated with the Mediterranean is that those who raise the same type of question fail to agree on a similar geographically bounded unit of analysis.

In geographical terms, the Mediterranean encompasses North Africa (the Maghreb), the south-western part of Asia (the Mashreq) and southern Europe. Its waters link up the Black Sea by the Turkish straits and the Red Sea by the Suez Canal, while the Gibraltar passage offers access to the Atlantic. Particular types of climate and a complex geology determine its coastal landscape, 'resulting in aggressive contrasts – sea, mountain, desert'.[2] Its coastline defines an enclosed body of water, a sort of 'liquid continent'. Simple geography means that there is a link between Europe and the Mediterranean; the former being contiguous with the Middle East at its Asian end, while it is only 16 kilometres away from its African end. Yet, the Mediterranean Sea appears to form a dividing line, an imaginary equator, between the European north and the Arab south.

Mapping the Mediterranean requires a more vigorous concept, taking into account that 'mental maps' and 'imagined spaces' are those that ultimately define communities and political regions.[3] Today, maps of the region from the pre-1945 era may look archaic and imperialistic; yet the way in which mental maps of the Mediterranean are drawn and have become accepted offers a powerful policy tool for controlling territories in the wider region. These maps develop into policies, capturing the minds of students of Mediterranean politics.

If there is a region in the international system where a clear mental divide exists between its north and south, one can hardly select a better example than the Mediterranean. But broad concepts, such as 'the West' or 'the Orient', that continue to divide the region cover no well-delineated territories. Their appeal is in the associations they conjure up, mixing geographical space with economic and social interaction, as well as with political and cultural identity to draw an imaginary, but still identifiable, divide.[4] A more studied analysis, though, reveals that the Mediterranean provides an efficient line of contact. After all, in the 'disorderly universe' of politics, it is perceptions that generate reality. The ability to manage such perceptions is thus of critical importance.

There is hardly another topic in international security discourse that has caused such a clear-cut split among scholars of different disciplines and members of the policy community: Christian Europe and the Islamic world. Both have found themselves locked in an almost interminable dynamic tension. To start with, one has to go back to the era of the ancient Greek civilisation and the days of the Roman *imperium.* This period witnessed an explosion of the Arab population, leaving a remarkable and lasting impact on a region that extended from Egypt to the 'Fertile Crescent'. Those living in this area were given a new religion, Islam, and a new language, Arabic. Of which, however, neither was capable of creating a melting pot through assimilationist techniques of enforced homogeneity, despite the fact that some commonly shared features did offer a bridge to overcoming diversity.

Undoubtedly, Western civilisation owes much to the Mediterranean.[5] Much like Christianity, Islam originates out of Hebrew monotheism and branches of Judaism, with common roots back to Patriarch Abraham.[6] But whereas the Hellenic–Judaic tradition, as Couloumbis and Veremis observe, captured the imagination of the Europeans with relatively little resistance, Islam failed to make any significant inroads in the West.[7] The influence of European thinking on the Arab–Muslim world dates back to the nineteenth century, while the Muslim civilisation marked its impact on European–Christian culture for several centuries. Not only did European culture have no particular influence on Muslims for over 1,000 years, but itself had benefited from the early Islamic 'enlightenment'.[8] Regardless of the socio-cultural and economic entanglements rooted in Mediterranean history, the modern European image of Islam sets its culture outside Europe; also, due to the burdened colonial past of the Europeans, the image of external 'otherness' to Europe is mirrored in the Muslim societies of the Mediterranean.[9]

Coming back to geographical considerations, defining the exact limits of Europe, Asia and Africa is no easy task. For example, Iceland tends to be perceived as being more 'European' than are the North African countries, although it is located further away from the centre of Europe and is far less influenced by Classical Greek and Roman cultures.[10] Unlike most northern Europeans, who generally regard North Africa as an incongruent and 'backward region' of no great strategic interest, Italy, Spain, France, Portugal and Greece hold a different view. Likewise, for many North Africans, the dividing line between Europe and Africa lies in the Sahara and not the Mediterranean, as is usually the case with Western perceptions.[11] Tempting as it may be to characterise the Mediterranean as 'a kind of horizontal dividing line' between the European north and 'an arc of crisis' located in the south, its division into Europe and 'other' fails to capture the dialectic between these two distinct yet intertwined geographical spaces. A theoretical framework of north–south conflict underestimates the realities of both north–north and south–south frictions and the sympathies that not only prevent the outbreak of autochthonous conflicts but underlie (western) European efforts to develop a set of harmonious and balanced, albeit non-symmetrical, relations across the Mediterranean.[12]

Does the Mediterranean extend from the Atlantic Ocean to the Suez passage, or is it better to consider its sub-regional settings separately? What, if anything, do the western Sahara, the Levant, the Aegean and the Balkans share that might suggest a meaningful 'Mediterranean approach'? Calleya argues that the Mediterranean encompasses at least two 'international regions': the geographical space which borders its north-western sector (EU) and the south-eastern sector (the Middle East). It also encompasses three sub-regional groupings: southern Europe (Portugal, Spain, France, Italy, Greece, Turkey, Cyprus and Malta); the Mashreq (Jordan, Israel, Lebanon, Jordan, Egypt and the Palestinian Authority); and the Maghreb (Morocco, Algeria and Tunisia).[13] Yet, there are many variations in these geographical divisions, presenting analysts with the problem of regional identities. From the perspective of international regionalism, Mediterranean sub-regional constellations need a complex re-conceptualisation of wider regional dynamics.

Important as it may be to focus on specific sub-regional constellations, it is still analytically useful to think about the Mediterranean as a single system (a totality). Some of the many security considerations around the basin derive from similar trends, such as unresolved questions of political legitimacy, slow growth to resurgent nationalism, religious radicalism, the search for regional dominance, arms supplies and strategic balances. Another Mediterranean paradox arises when considering that it is security, rather than societal, economic or cultural considerations, that legitimise a holistic approach to the study of Euro-Mediterranean politics.[14] But true as it may be that security problems in the area can best be handled at the regional level, the question is how to achieve coherent patterns of interaction among Mediterranean states, as well as between them and the rest of the world, so as to enhance regional stability.[15]

The Mediterranean has been described as a dense network of diversities and dividing lines between different political and socio-economic (sub)systems, cultures and regimes, as well as languages, forms of expression and religious denominations.[16] Historically, from Phoenicia to Greece, eminent settlements have emerged, each eager to defend the trade routes upon which its livelihood depended. The Mediterranean has facilitated colonisation, for several of its dominant civilisations were *thalassocracies* favourable to the free circulation of goods and ideas. The Romans were the first to conquer the entire Mediterranean seaboard, projecting the image of *Mare Nostrum*. History records that this activity was not limited to Mediterranean power-actors since other, non-littoral, ones have also established their presence in the area. In order to arrive at a penetrating understanding of the Mediterranean, one has to recognise that the region has always been a crossing point for conflict and co-operation, unity and diversity.

Current discourses assert that the Mediterranean exists as an 'entity' or 'unity'. This view chimes well with Braudel's, in that the Mediterranean formed a large-scale unity, whose history could only be understood by looking at the factors that tied its coastal parts together; a region that changed only over very long periods of time.[17] But, as Aliboni asserts, the special bonds of Mediterranean solidarity will continue to form part of an open-ended debate.[18] In this context, Lister makes the point that the question of a Mediterranean 'ideal' of unity is rarely explicitly spelt out; rather, 'it is usually a vague expression of goodwill and shared history'.[19] But such an ideal, she concludes,

> involves more than a dialogue among states but less than complete integration. It aspires to a condition of peace, harmony, cooperation and mutually beneficial exchange throughout the region. It bases its hope for the future on the close and productive relations of the past, often the ancient past.[20]

Throughout history, the Mediterranean has been as much a laboratory for the cross-fertilisation of diverse cultures as it has been a place of open and protracted conflicts. Being a heterogeneous synthesis of various religious and ethnic groups – along the lines of a 'heterarchy' – as well as of unequal economic development, a plurality of political regimes, divergent perceptions of security (threats), and uneven demographic growth, Mediterranean complexity occupies a prominent position between order and disorder. It emerges as an 'essentially contested project' for which a comprehensive framework of analysis is yet to become discernible. Accordingly, one could legitimately refer to the Mediterranean as a regional space where geography, history and politics intermesh with culture and religion with enormous complexity, resulting in a composite system of partial regimes, each reflecting a particular sense of being and belonging.

Threat (mis)perceptions

Many issues that are currently involved in both extra- and intra-regional fragmentation date back to the early stages of colonialism,[21] first practised by the South to the North and, later, *vice versa*. The Egyptian, Phoenician, Greek and Persian civilisations, and later the Roman Empire, have all found their way to the Mediterranean and sought to use it as a means of extending their power-base. The split between the Byzantine empire in the East and the Catholic/Germanic kingdoms in the West, the rise of Islamic and Arabic rule in the Middle East, North Africa and Spain, the impact of extra-territorial forces such as the crusaders, and the rise of regional powers like Moorish Spain, Venice and Genoa, have all contributed to the fragmentation of the region. Their impact has often turned the Mediterranean into a potentially explosive area, wherein the divisions among its peoples intermixed with their historical ties and related destiny. As a result, the Mediterranean has always run the risk of becoming a site of endemic conflicts.

From a macro-historical perspective, the fragmentation of this regional complex constitutes the major obstacle to substantive co-operation. Contemporary analysts point to both real and potential conflicts that originate in or impact on the region. In revisiting their respective causes, Balta distinguishes between conflicts that originate in the distant past and conflicts that emerged in the second half of the twentieth century.[22] Potential conflicts are divided into three categories: those inherited from colonialism (mainly territorial); those stemming from deeply divided societies (e.g. the Lebanon); and those originating in minority issues (e.g. Basques, Corsicans, Kurds, etc). Conflicts inherited from the past are closely associated with the three monotheistic denominations affecting Mediterranean societies. These inheritances exemplify the denominational fractures among Christianity, Judaism and Islam, and the schisms between the Catholic and Eastern Orthodox camps, as well as between the Sunnis and Shiites. Such conflicts are the Arab–Israeli dispute, the Greco-Turkish rivalry and the Cyprus question. The latter, for over a quarter of a century now, continues to frustrate all attempts at inter-communal reconciliation and, eventually, reunification. The Arab–Israeli issue has also featured prominently on the international agenda, due to its political and historical complexity, the depth of its emotional intensity and the recent revival of hope for a negotiated peace.

Following Spenser's analysis, the prevailing view during the Cold War era was that the Mediterranean represented 'a region of importance because of its proximity, potential instability and hence exploitation by the erstwhile Soviet Union, but of less importance as an "out of area" region in NATO terms'.[23] The Cold War had led to a reductive assessment of Mediterranean security issues, focusing on ways of countering the threat of the Soviet presence on Euro-American lines of communication, oil and trade routes. From the late 1980s, however, the emphasis shifted from global assessments of security issues to regional ones. In this context, Lesser has argued that in the new strategic environment, problems and interests have shifted towards the south.[24] The aftermath of the Cold War gave the impression, albeit briefly, that certain protracted conflicts might be resolved. But the easing of the East–West tension was not followed by a similar trend in Mediterranean politics. Rather, the removal of the bipolar 'safety net', and with it the view that wanted the Mediterranean to serve as a sub-theatre of superpower antagonism, introduced an idiosyncratic fragility at both regional and subregional levels.

Important security issues appear to be products of the new world (dis)order. The Gulf Crisis of 1990–91 was the first major international conflict to be recorded in the post-Cold War era of *pax Americana*, questioning the capabilities of European institutions, the impact of independent national diplomacies and the future of multinational crisis management. The Gulf Crisis interrupted Europe's new-found complacency about its own security, as it clearly showed that, without the US, Europe lacks the military capability to confront or deter its enemies in its southern flank.[25] Iraq's invasion of Kuwait also highlighted the fragility of Arab unity. Not only did it disprove the myth that Arabs do not attack their brethren, but it exposed the poorer countries' resentment towards the opulent life-style of the oil-rich conservative monarchies, as well as the shallowness of security arrangements in the Arab world.[26] At the same time, the initial euphoria of a universal collective security system hardly outlived the aftermath of the Gulf War, as the disintegration of Yugoslavia destroyed the illusion of what US President Bush called a 'new world order'.[27] Gnesotto concurs: '[Global] collective security is thus still an arbitrary system which is real and effective for certain areas of crisis but illusory and impossible for others. In Europe [and, let us immediately add, the Mediterranean] … it may be seen as nothing more than an inaccessible myth or a vague objective for the future.'[28]

Although the aftermath of the Gulf War sparked an interest in issues of conflict resolution in the Mediterranean,[29] soon after the termination of the civil war in Lebanon, there was a return to traditional power relations; the most striking examples being the stagnated Cyprus problem and the erratic Middle East Peace Process. Although the only bilateral conflict which threatens to erupt periodically is that between Greece and Turkey, a constant and potentially destabilising source of tension is the proliferation of all types of armament in the region, including ballistic missiles, chemical weapons and nuclear programmes for military purposes. To give but a rough estimate, annual military expenditures in the Middle East and the eastern Mediterranean only are approximately $50 billion, armed forces' personnel are about 3 million men, and there are 24,000 main battle tanks and 3,500 combat aircraft.[30] Hence, the arms escalation in the region is ever-present, not to mention the danger of using chemical and bacteriological weapons.[31]

As Jervis rightly points out, in international relations it is the threat itself as much as the perceptions of threat that guide policy makers.[32] Today, most analysts agree that the Mediterranean does not present Europe with a major military threat,[33] as the growing arms races in the region and, more generally, its militarisation are intended mainly for use on a south-south scale. But even the interstate Mediterranean tensions have rarely in the past led to war, save for the Arab–Israeli conflict. However crucial were the 1979 Camp David Accords, Arab–Israeli tensions persist, though the potential for another large-scale confrontation is greatly reduced. Successive defeats, coupled with internal frictions and factionalisation, have damaged Arab unity. Also, as Spencer asserts, their economic dependence on Europe sets the southern Mediterranean states more in competition than in conflict with one another, while external threats are not real enough to warrant greater organisational structures than already exist in the region.[34]

As a Mediterranean-inspired military threat to Europe appears unlikely, EU states are much more concerned about losing control over their energy supplies and growing illegal migration. Similarly, they are preoccupied with increased instability in parts of North Africa and the weakness of democratic institutions. Although issue-specific disputes are not to be ruled out, the main security risk is linked to the new challenges posed by radical movements and the growing economic asymmetries between the north and the south. Nor do southern Mediterranean countries perceive any direct military threat from Europe itself (perhaps with the exception of Libya),[35] for they tend to associate 'security' with predominantly domestic problems. Yet, the international management of domestic crises exacerbates anti-Western feelings: 'Even talking about it may have a destabilising effect.'[36] The same can be said of recent Western attempts to play an active role in Mediterranean security. This perception stems from a chain of events that has fuelled a deep sense of strategic insecurity in the Arab world. The Gulf War, the international isolation imposed on Iraq and Libya and, above all, the overwhelming US preoccupation with Israeli security have convinced Arab governments and publics that the Western world would not hesitate to strike out against them should its interests require so. At the same time, some North African states view the development of a European Security and Defence Identity and joint military exercises in the Mediterranean with suspicion.[37] As Chater notes, 'Europe … wants to cut off access from the south, building watchtowers to keep it under surveillance'.[38] Although paradoxical, the majority of North African regimes are sceptical of an alleged European unwillingness to play a decisive role in the Mediterranean, which they perceive also as a main cause for regional arms races.[39] Similarly, these regimes are suspicious of NATO's involvement in the region,[40] despite NATO's initiative for a 'Mediterranean Dialogue'.[41] For their part, finally, EU states have experienced some difficulty in dealing with Mediterranean security issues, in contrast to their ability to deal with similar problems in other transformative regions, such as central and eastern Europe. As Mortimer warns, 'the EU has to anticipate possible hostility in the Mediterranean without provoking it' (in a way similar to that in which it is handling Russia).[42]

Islamophobia and modernity

Mediterranean security issues are characterised by misunderstandings and distorted perceptions and images of (political) Islam, as well as of the threat of terrorism used by extremist nationalist movements. Other issues stem from the appropriation of Islam for political ends and the tensions arising from questions regarding universal values and norms of human rights. In large measure, these misunderstandings emanate as much from mutual ignorance as they do from intended confusion. One should also guard against the simplification, often suggested in the media, that 'Islamic fundamentalism' is a violent and merciless movement orchestrated by Iran with the help of other radical regimes.[43] As Essid points out, 'there is still a need to define and redefine terms which, rather than contributing to the dialogue we desire, reduce it to a series of parallel monologues and, at several levels, reinforce misunderstandings'.[44] It is thus of great importance that meaningful debate about Islam should dispel the clouds of deliberate myth-making and revengeful rhetoric that are so detrimental to a mutually rewarding dialogue.

During the Gulf War, the West was seriously concerned with the possibility of a militant Islamist backlash against intervention. The risk of terrorist attacks against the West was raised by Hussein's call for a 'holy war', soon after his invasion of Kuwait. His appeal rested on a three-pronged strategy,[45] unveiling several fault lines between and within Mediterranean societies. From an international relations perspective, this signalled a re-arrangement of world order, reducing the East–West confrontation to a minimum, while re-emphasising, in however complex terms, the Orient–Occident and North–South gaps. These events offered useful ammunition to those arguing that the dominant conflict post-1989 is one between Occidental and Oriental values, or between an Occidental economic/technological 'post-historical' world and an Oriental 'historical' world.[46]

Rather effortlessly, Huntington depicted multiple (sub-)regional 'clashes' as a result of the irrefutable existence of different cultures (civilisations), projecting a historical Mediterranean fragmentation, rather than unity.[47] His *The Clash of Civilizations* raised the question of the cultural dimension of security, in that the 'clash' occurs along the lines of a religion-based militancy against Western liberal values. But his analysis missed the underlying causes of Islamic resurgence, as it is obsessed with the cultural symbols or the retrieval of collective historical memories. A related criticism is that, by rewriting Muslim history, he failed to encourage intelligent dialogue between the two opposing cultures. As Sachedina asserts, such scholarship effectively corrupts the common moral and political language of the two cultures, fosters confrontation and prolongs historical stereotypes.[48] Arguing that the notion of 'Islam v. the West' will not represent the arena of the next ideological struggle, Fuller and Lesser suggest that a comprehensive reform is imperative in order to break away from authoritarianism, that political Islam threatens the established order in Muslim countries far more than does the West, and that confrontation can best be prevented by integrating Islam into the global process.[49]

Nevertheless, concern over an Islamic 'threat' to the West increased after the Gulf War, by the emergence of a new enemy stereotype after the demise of Communism, preparing a climate for a 'new cultural war'.[50] Rising anxiety in international relations is, according to Blunden, contagious.[51] Or, as Buzan puts it: 'the international system tends naturally to generate insecurity and suspicion, and once a pattern of hostility has been established each will tend to see the other as the enemy and to assume the worst about him'.[52] In fact, as Ayubi pointed out, 'even before the Gulf crisis, a theory started to take shape that it was not Communism that constituted the major threat for the West, but rather Islamic fundamentalism'.[53] All too often, Western foreign-policy makers have exploited a general public ignorance about 'Orientalism' to advance self-serving objectives. Since 'Islam is both a religion and a polity',[54] several extremist groups have used it for radical purposes. The traditional Western view of 'Orientalists' is that of Arabs/Muslims who 'show lack of coordination and harmony in organisation and function, nor have they revealed an ability for cooperation. Any collective action for mutual benefit or common profit is alien to them.'[55] Crucial to the creation of such stereotypes has been the role played by the Western media in equating Islam with 'fundamentalist Islam' and, hence, with a direct threat to the liberal–democratic West. Said makes the point well:

> the negative images of Islam are very much more prevalent than any others and such images correspond, not to what Islam 'is' ... but to what prominent sectors of a particular society take it to be: Those sectors have the power and the will to propagate that particular image of Islam, and this image therefore becomes more prevalent, more present, than all others.[56]

In this context, Said continues, 'there is a consensus on Islam as a kind of scapegoat for everything we do not happen to like about the world's new political, social, and economic patterns'.[57] Likewise, Espozito has suggested that the selective presentation of facts and biased analysis has contributed to a negative perception of Islamic religion on the part of mainstream Western society, reducing Islam and Islamic revivalism to stereotypes of 'Islam v. the West', 'Islam v. modernity', 'Muslim rage', extremism, fanaticism, and the like.[58] Similarly, Roberson argues that 'the Islamic threat is essentially a counterfeit issue imbued with stereotypical misperceptions and a casual commitment to analysis ... in some cases, a conscious exercise in image creation for tactical political purposes'.[59]

There has been a long-standing conflict between Islam and Western Christianity, each being perceived by the other as 'suspect'. Since the Crusades, the Western world has exported its civilisation through its imperial and colonial policies, often echoing the logic of *divide et impera* to secure its vital economic and trade interests. All other civilisations were measured by Western standards on the basis of the anthropocentric and individualistic worldviews reflected in the Greco-Roman and Christian traditions. These pre-liberal images were strongly influenced by the pre-eminent role attached to a value-driven distinction between the individual and the collective. It was part of the legacy of the Enlightenment that certain notions of 'civility' became linked to a more normative political language. Such a legacy has largely survived the present era, with the West attempting to monopolise global discourse on the democratic functions of government and human rights. But, much like those in the West, Muslims believe that their faith has a divine purpose, motivating them to set the world straight. They believe themselves to be the chosen people following the righteous path to 'judgement day'.

As much as a religion and a polity, Islam is also a culture with a different perception of the relationship between church and state. In an insightful analysis on Islam, Lapidus offers the following points:

> The Islamists believe that Islam provides a total system of beliefs and a model for a holy society and government. They see Islam as a comprehensive alternative to capitalism, communism, democracy, and other western ideological systems, and to the existing regimes in Muslim countries. They oppose the political elite, narrowly based military and family cliques, landlord coteries, oil-based economic elite in cahoots with local political leaders and western capitalists, and a decadent western culture steeped in sexual license and materialism. They believe that corrupt regimes and foreign influences breed injustice in their societies, undermine the natural order of the relations of men and women, and thus subvert the family and promote immorality. They have both a political and a religious solution to the problems of their societies: overthrow corrupted governments, expel foreign influences, and educate and elevate their own people through religious commitment.[60]

Despite the fact that the roots of this discourse can be traced to the revival of Classical Greek ideas and to the Renaissance, it was the coming of modernity that clearly exposed the differences between the cultures of the West and the East.[61] Most Arab societies were introduced to the logic of modernisation under the heavy pressure of colonial Europe. Modernisation was more successful in dismantling the traditional structures than in setting up their modern replacements.[62] The process of adaptation to modernity is still going on for Islamic countries. Although Gellner has argued that Islamic culture is endowed with a number of features that are congruent with requirements of modernity or modernisation,[63] many Muslim leaders still fight for a line 'back to the roots'. Arab governing elites are particularly eclectic in picking out those 'values of modernisation' that best fit their aims for maintaining power and control, like modern weapons, surveillance technology and consumer goods. Such processes of 'selective sorting out' and 'selective adaptation' do not allow the Western system of values and its culture of modernisation to be accepted by these societies. Instead, modernisation is often reduced to a symbol of moral decay, with Western influence, as something that increases the technological, military, economic and scientific superiority and/or hegemony of the capitalist world, having to be controlled.

In Western polities, a separation of state and religion – secularism – was necessary to safeguard the modernisation project and its assorted drive towards industrialisation, urbanisation, bureaucratisation, the expansion of technology, growth in communications, etc.; but Islam is still against any such separation.[64] Huntington observes that 'fundamentalist Islam' requires its political rulers to be practising Muslims: '*shari'a* [Islamic law] should be the basic law, and *ulema* [theologians and jurists] should have "a decisive vote in articulating, or at least reviewing and ratifying, all governmental policy"'.[65] From this view, modernity may only be reached within the framework of indigenous values and not through their assimilation to Western culture. As Aliboni asserts, modernisation through imitation of the West is but a trap leading to subordination.[66] In this context, Huntington notes, 'to the extent that governmental legitimacy and policy flow from religious doctrines and religious expertise, Islamic concepts of politics differ from and contradict the premises of democratic politics'.[67] This view accords with Diamond, Linz and Lipset's earlier analysis according to which 'the Islamic countries of the Middle East and Northern Africa … appear to have little prospect of transition even to semi-democracy'.[68] But it comes in direct opposition to Pool's claims that 'the view that Islam is utterly incompatible with democracy, whatever form the latter takes, is to view Islam from a limited and simplistic perspective. Contemporary Islam can be democratic, undemocratic and anti-democratic and the political orientations of Muslim and Islamic movements have exhibited similar variations.'[69] Although Curdy argues that democracy and Islam 'are contradictory only if democracy is defined by certain Western standards',[70] Pool is right to suggest that 'presidents and kings remain in charge of a state-controlled process of democratisation as part of strategies of … regime survival'.[71]

The revival of Islam *per se*, of political Islamism and of Islamic radicalism, is the product of these antitheses. Fragmented and struggling with modernity, Islam now faces a variety of challenges, including potentially violent movements. Lapidus explains:

> to cope with these movements we cannot merely deplore, hate, or fear them. We must understand what they are trying to say and the conditions that give rise to them. While the strengths and dangers of these movements can easily be overestimated, and frequently are, their seriousness and unsettling long-term potential cannot be ignored.[72]

The threat of radicalism currently manifested in the southern Mediterranean rim lies in the fact that many of its essential aspects represent a reaction to years of intolerable political and socio-economic conditions. In this sense, such a threat is not merely a symptom of deep-rooted differences between the West and Islam, but is a means of responding to post-colonial pressures towards liberalisation, which is perceived as threatening the 'inner cohesion' of the Islamic tradition. Here, religion is used to cover other deficits like economic, social and political: an alleged inferiority in self-perception, a dissatisfaction in terms of social development and a non-acceptance of the organisational/technocratic problem-solving capacity of 'the other'.

To conclude: it is worth recalling King Hasan's speech at the opening session of the Euro-Islam Conference in Stockholm in June 1995, in which it was said that 'authentic Islam represents no threat and means no harm to Europe. In it one finds nothing that would justify hostility against it or the accusation that all Muslims are extremists and closed to dialogue.'[73] It follows that that the creation and maintenance of a climate of meaningful and open dialogue in the Mediterranean is no easy task, especially given the tendency of both sides to fuel prejudices. But as long as misperceptions persist and differences are not tolerated, the relationship between Islam and Europe will remain tense, offering an apology for keeping sustainable co-operation without reach. Thus, a new 'hermeneutics of civilizational dialogue'[74] emanates as a *praesumptio juris et de jure*: a dialectic of cultural self-realisation through a reciprocal exchange based on a philosophy of mutual understanding that does away with any subjectivist view that wants the 'West' to act as a universal civilising force based on an almost metaphysical obligation to humanity.

The new security agenda

The tension in Euro-Mediterranean relations can be ascribed only in part to politico-military factors or the resurgence of radical Islam. The multidimensional character of Mediterranean security necessitates a comprehensive approach to security, taking into account socio-economic and cultural factors, and thus moving away from simplistic or convenient diagnoses that overemphasise the military aspects of security.[75] Lesser makes the point well: 'In the post-Cold War world, military power counts for less and diplomatic initiative and economic dynamism count more heavily.'[76] This is true, in that the most intricate Mediterranean problems are shaped by political upheavals, stemming mainly from a variety of socio-economic pressures. Bin concurs: 'many of the security-related concerns that have come to the fore in the region post-Cold War are non-military issues that may interact with more traditional security risks'.[77]

The new era has reactivated concern over the impact on Mediterranean politics and society of the north–south divide, itself part of the global debt problem.[78] Such a divide is determined by unequal economic development, a plurality of political regimes, divergent perceptions of security threats and changing patterns of demography. As Ireland put it: 'From Turkey to Morocco, the risks of social destabilisation build, as intense demographic pressures overwhelm evaporating economic opportunities.'[79] Also, the countries on the northern Mediterranean shore have an industrial output four times higher than that of their southern counterparts and have achieved self-sufficiency in agriculture, while southern countries, despite attempts at agricultural reform and nationwide modernisation, are constrained by the lack of equipment and by demographic pressures resulting in insufficient productivity and a structural deficit of food.[80]

Euro-Mediterranean affairs are also affected by Europe's dependence on oil and gas supplies. The Mediterranean represents for many industrial European countries the most important transport route (shipping and pipelines), through which the bulk of their raw materials travel from the Gulf and the Black Sea. For a long time, it was believed that the Cold War implied a threat to the security of raw material supplies, and this was accompanied by a feeling that the Soviet Union's policy towards the Arab world aimed to expose the West to the danger of having its oil supplies from the Middle East cut off.[81] Post-1989, the main danger lies in Europe's dependence on the Middle East as the main reservoir of crude oil, with 66 per cent of world reserves and deliveries accounting for approximately 50 per cent of total consumption. Toukan explains: 'The danger of its interruption could lead to external intervention.'[82] A trend towards co-operation has been recently observed between the Western oil companies of the importing countries and the national oil companies of the major producing ones. Such co-operation may lead to what Luciani calls 'vertical reintegration' in the oil industry through cross-investment and the stabilisation of global oil trade.[83] As for natural gas dependence, in the mid-1990s Algeria and Libya alone supplied 19.4 per cent of European gas demand, with a further 6 per cent supplied by the new Algeria–Spain gas pipeline via Morocco which was to be completed in June 1996, bringing the total up to one quarter of Europe's natural gas import needs.[84] The apparent lack of investment necessary for the creation of reliable transport infrastructures makes co-operation on the gas sector imperative, although developments in this sector are no longer to be considered as occurring mainly at the regional level, but rather at the global level. However, one should not ignore Brauch's telling remark that the future energy dependence of Europe will change fundamentally by the year 2050, as the fossil reserves in Algeria and Libya will then be depleted.[85] He also makes the point that the Europeans will have to reduce their carbon dioxide emissions under the framework convention on climate change and, hence, shift towards renewable energy systems – e.g. solar energy.

Turning to issues of complex economic disparity, Joffé emphasises the importance of the north–south ontology of the Mediterranean, linked to the rich–poor gap in the basin.[86] One can hardly select a better example within which a clear dividing line exists between a rich(er) north and a poor(er) south. Following Benyaklef's analysis, with the exception of Israel, all other non-European countries of the region suffer, *inter alia*, from low income, insufficient growth of GDP compared to their ever-increasing demographic growth, high inflation and unemployment, widespread illiteracy and inadequate health services.[87] A further indication of complex economic inequality in the region is the fact that 'the total GDP of EU Mediterranean states in the North is eleven times greater than that of its southern littoral counterparts'.[88] In addition to the above come Vasconcelos's remarks that North African countries are heavily dependent on Europe for their external trade (around 50–60 per cent), that there is hardly any evidence to suggest that a process of economic integration has been set in train among them and that trade between neighbouring countries represents no more than 3 per cent of the total.[89]

From the early 1960s to the mid-1980s, the southern Mediterranean outperformed all other regions of the world except East Asia, not only in income growth per capita, but in the equality of income distribution. Improvements in social conditions have been dramatic: life expectancy significantly increased (on average by 13 years), infant mortality rates were cut in half, primary-school enrolments became virtually universal and literacy among adults rose steadily. Southern Mediterranean governments were also effective in reducing poverty. For any given per capita income, poverty was lower in the Middle East and North African countries than elsewhere in the world and the distribution of wealth was more egalitarian than in many countries in East Asia and Latin America. These achievements were the result of rapid growth in the 1970s and early 1980s and the introduction of generous transfers to large sections of the population.[90] Since 1973, commercial relations between Europe and the Arab world have been determined by the variable of energy.[91] After the increase in oil prices in the early 1970s, the Middle Eastern and North African economies were greatly dependent on the export of oil and natural gas.[92] However, at the beginning of the 1980s, the slowdown of the earlier boom brought about a contraction of the Arab markets. Many Arab countries became heavily indebted and were forced to undergo sharp economic adjustments. Moreover, with the decline of oil prices during the latter part of the 1980s most of the Arab economies came to a grinding halt. The worsening of socio-economic conditions in the Mediterranean as compared to other, less developed, regions become evident by the 1990s. A report published by the World Bank in October 1995 explicitly stated that, since the mid-1980s, the southern Mediterranean countries have suffered the largest decline of real per capita income of all the other developing regions in the world (approximately 2 per cent annually), and a 0.2 per cent annual decline in the levels of productivity.[93]

As a response to these trends, the developing countries of the region accused the Europeans (and the wider West) of setting up and supporting a global economic system that works against their interests. From a historical perspective, such criticisms date back to colonial occupation and its powerful effects on the economic development of the Mediterranean south. As Joffé explains, the effects are particularly noticeable in the Maghreb, where the integration of that region into the French colonial sphere led to a situation whereby economic structures increasingly served the metropolitan market.[94] On the whole, economic co-operation in the Mediterranean is limited as much by the fragmentation of the southern economies (especially since protracted conflicts constitute a major hindrance to south–south economic relations) as by the absence of a coherent framework to manage north–south relations in a mutually advantageous manner.

Another undisputed feature of the Mediterranean is demography. The countries of North Africa, namely Mauritania, Morocco, Algeria, Tunisia, Egypt and Libya, have at present a population of 120 million, but over the next twenty-five years it is estimated that this population will cross the threshold of 200 million. By contrast, the population of northern Mediterranean countries, which in 1950 accounted for two-thirds of the total Mediterranean population, will fall to one-third by 2025, whereas on the southern shore of the basin, the growth rate is increasing rapidly. But the crux of the problem lies in the age-differences between the populations of the two Mediterranean shores. If there are no major demographic changes, the European countries will experience an increased ageing of their populations in the next thirty or so years, while in the southern rim the section of the population under 15 years of age will continue to rise steadily.[95] Among the major consequences of these fast-growing demographic trends will be a colossal demand for employment. This problem is further compounded by the fact that labour supply in southern Mediterranean countries is lagging far behind the expected increase in the labour force seeking work. Just to absorb the young people entering the labour market, these countries would have to create more than 2.5 million jobs annually, which is to say three times the present rate of job creation. Today, out of 250 million Arabs, 130 million are under 20. They will be entering the labour market over the next twenty or so years. In fact, never before in the history of the Mediterranean have there been as many youngsters on its southern shores, due to a robust demographic transition.[96] Should this market fail to absorb them, it is easy to imagine the frustration that this will generate, not to mention the accompanying levels of social protest and migratory pressures.[97] Until the conditions for the development of North African economies are properly in place, the only option available to a large section of their population will be to migrate to the more prosperous European countries, thus posing an additional challenge to regional stability.

Needed as cheap labour following the Second World War, Arab–Muslim migrants in western Europe have become a security issue.[98] Today, one easily identifies considerable migratory flows form ethnic communities that resist integration and/or assimilation to respective European host cultures, as some 6 million immigrants from the Maghreb alone reside in EU states, most notably France, Italy, Spain and Greece. In a period of heightening demographic fragility, immigration will continue to be seen as a major threat, leading to socially pathogenous phenomena such as intolerance, racism and xenophobia among a section of the host population. Yet, at a time when Europe is increasingly preoccupied with the perceived socio-economic and political consequences of foreign residents, one should not forget the valuable contribution of immigrants to Germany's post-war 'economic miracle',[99] regarded at the time more as a resource than a threat. Today, however, the capacity of the European labour market to absorb growing migratory flows appears to be far more limited. Contributing to the above has been the ever-growing flows of refugees and immigrants from eastern Europe and the Balkans post-1989, not to mention the additional currents of immigrants from other troubled parts of the globe.

Determining an appropriate policy response to the movement of immigrants and asylum seekers across national borders is one of the key challenges confronting both individual European governments and the EU collectively. Notwithstanding the EU's almost purely intergovernmental character, the incorporation into the formal treaty framework of a Justice and Home Affairs pillar with the signing of the Treaty on European Union in February 1992, and subsequent treaty amendments culminating in the signing of the Treaty of Amsterdam in October 1997 were, in large measure, a clear reflection of these mounting concerns.[100] In general, recent trends have resulted in restrictive legislation on immigrants and refugees which, as Aliboni says, comes in sharp contrast to the rationalist, democratic nature of modern European societies.[101] Collinson has also illustrated the profound influence of the migration question on the political and security agenda of the Mediterranean. Indeed, her book *Shore to Shore* demonstrates how EU policy toward the Maghreb has been increasingly defined by anxiety about the potential for rising immigration levels.[102] But even if Europe institutes new barriers to control the inflow of immigrants, a number of critical questions will remain, particularly with regard to the implementation of such measures and the way in and extent to which they will prove capable of discouraging potential immigrants from reaching Europe without reinforcing fragmentation. Arguably, in the existing patterns of north–south interaction, people (mainly through the media) clearly see the extent to which their living conditions differ from those of their northern neighbours. But the media also bring stereotypical and negative images of the southern Mediterranean, fuelling hostility and mistrust among the European peoples toward the Arab world. This xenophobic and, more accurately, Islamophobic trend serves to solidify the cultural divide across the Mediterranean. In Boutros-Ghali's words: 'Proximity in this case can only exacerbate differences.'

Disparities in wealth within the Mediterranean are undermining the social pillars of support that have traditionally sustained secular national orders and generate a creeping cultural radicalism towards rejection of 'the other'.[103] But such disparities have also allowed for other problems to come to the fore. In particular, due to their weak responses to the new challenges, the Arab regimes use 'regional nationalism' as a means of perpetuating the status quo. As Aliboni argues, to sustain the goals of 'regional nationalism', they will continue to divert resources towards military expenditure so as to make the basic conditions for a wider consensus more difficult or unlikely to emerge.[104] The collapse of the progressive pan-Arab regimes that, for the greater part of the 1980s managed to keep radical religious trends under control, witnessed a resurgence of a popular Islamic radicalism in the early 1990s. As the majority of these countries have no tradition of political pluralism, their respective governing regimes attempted to cope authoritatively with the problems just described through the employment of undemocratic practices, as in the cases of Algeria, Egypt and Turkey. But this kind of esoteric instability has serious external repercussions: since large numbers of immigrant workers from the southern Mediterranean reside in Europe, the possibility of turmoil spilling over to the northern Mediterranean rim is far from fictitious, if not it is already a living reality in major European capitals. If these alarming trends are followed by a deterioration of north–south relations along civilisational lines,[105] and no drastic socio-economic and political reforms are introduced, then the prospects for political stability, economic prosperity and social progress in the Mediterranean will remain particularly bleak. But let us turn to the contrasting interests and attitudes that characterise the major actors in the region.

Contrasting interests and attitudes

The Mediterranean between Europe and the US

For more than fifty years now, powers and forces that were either external or peripheral to the region have defined Mediterranean politics in mainly bipolar terms.[106] Since 1945, European policies towards the Middle East have been torn between, on the one hand, Europe's geographic contiguity, historical familiarity and privileged trade links with the Middle East and, on the other, Europe's ideological–strategic association with the US.[107] The end of the European era in the eastern Mediterranean begun in 1956 with the Suez debacle, sealing the fate of Europe's marginal role in Middle East politics. Through a series of crucial episodes,[108] the Europeans surrendered the Mediterranean basin to the competing American and Soviet spheres of influence. Thereafter, and throughout the 1970s, the swiftness with which the superpowers supported their Mediterranean allies further exposed the lack of a substantive European influence. But even in the 1980s, when Europe began to assert its role as an international (mainly economic) actor, it did not embark on a competitive tussle with the superpowers over the Mediterranean, a situation that tacitly suited everyone. Peters explains: 'By mirroring the stance taken by the Arabs, [the Community] effectively removed itself as a potential mediator between the two sides'.[109] As for Europe's 'civilian power' image, it also failed to project a common Mediterranean approach. By looking inwards to the strengthening of its internal arrangements,[110] the Community managed to play down security alliances in the region.

Although soon after the end of the Cold War the US and Europe had strikingly common global interests, such convergence began to fade by the mid-1990s. The US–EU dispute over the extraterritorial application of US laws – i.e. unilateral US sanctions against Libya, Iran and Cuba – is a good case in point.[111] According to Aliboni,

> the changing Mediterranean environment is *de facto* encapsulated by two different international contexts with different priorities, responsibilities and efficacies: on the one hand, the Mashreq, where the US is strongly committed both politically and militarily, with the EU playing only a secondary role in the economic field; on the other, the Maghreb, where the EU is the dominant, if not sole, actor.[112]

But, as Holmes argues, this arrangement is far from perfect, as it does not accurately reflect the interests and capabilities of both international actors.[113] Although transatlantic co-operation is central to Mediterranean stability, this does not necessarily apply in the case of the Middle East, where Europe and the US do not seem to pursue common strategies, as they do in the European theatre. As Khalilzad observes, the policies pursued by the transatlantic partners towards this unstable region are slipping close to rivalry, a situation that could not only hurt the US–European alliance itself, but could provide an opening for the rise of hostile regional powers like Iran.[114] On this issue, Marr warns that, if these differences are not handled carefully by the transatlantic partners, they could impair NATO's ability 'to take concerted out-of-area action when necessary … making diplomatic efforts increasingly contentious and ineffective'.[115]

Lesser defines three dimensions of US interest in the Mediterranean: a response to change and crisis in the region; an extension of the American commitment to European security; and a determination to lessen Middle East tensions.[116] But the US lacks an integrated view of the problems confronting the Mediterranean,[117] although its post-Cold War European objectives have displayed some continuity: to secure European support for US actions outside western Europe and to avoid increased financial and/or military obligations. Fiscal pressures in the US made the latter objective more important than before and have reinforced US interest in EU initiatives for greater burden sharing in defence. But US attitudes to an increased EU role in these areas have been ambivalent: the Americans are willing to see greater European co-operation in these fields, but are not keen to compromise NATO's role in the new European order.[118] It would be a mistake to believe that a safe alternative currently exists to the sustained US military capability to protect vital US (oil) interests in the Middle East. However, the fact that the US provided such a large number of troops in the Gulf War (and, recently, in Kosovo) is taken by Congress as an example of Europeans failing to pay their fair share.[119] The latter have argued that they do not wish to become the tail on an American dog wagged by American interests in the Middle East, and have complained that the US failed to consult them before expecting them to participate in operation 'Desert Storm'. In Nye's words: 'Americans complain about their allies seeking a free ride, but if Americans want others to pay full freight they will have to be more alert to the problems of discussion and consultation.'[120]

Currently, the EU faces significant difficulties in assuming a substantive security role in the Mediterranean, not least due to the evident US reluctance to share its regional initiatives, as in the Middle East Peace Process,[121] with European frustration growing not only by the lack of progress in the Arab–Israeli talks, but by Washington's near-monopoly position on diplomatic action.[122] US emphasis on Israel's strategic interests jeopardises concerted EU efforts towards the resolution of the Arab–Israeli conflict. As Köchler asserts, the EU plays no significant political role in Palestine, but is acting as paymaster for social and economic development projects in the Palestinian territories.[123] In Gordon's view, two scenarios seem possible. As long as the Arab–Israeli Peace Process is moving forward, the US is probably right that Europe's formal involvement in direct peace talks would not be helpful if such a role promotes policies different from those initiated by the US. But if the Peace Process stalls completely, it will be difficult for the US to justify a less active European role in the politics of the region.[124]

Regarding Europe's strategic interests in the Middle East, any political interference by the US – itself party to regional conflicts – is to say the least counterproductive. But leaving the Mediterranean entirely in European hands is too unrealistic an option, given the stakes involved.[125] As Hollis put it: 'Europe certainly lacks a distinct and unified military capability and in this respect cannot challenge the United State's role.'[126] Although the EU has furthered the scope and level of its political and economic integration, it still depends on US leadership, since it has so far proved delinquent in addressing effectively security and defence issues in the Mediterranean. At the same time, Holmes comments, the US 'will not escape the impact of negative consequences should that time bomb blow up'.[127] In any case, according to Snyder, a US exit from the Mediterranean would make practically impossible the crafting of a credible regional security structure.[128] Thus, Europe and its Atlantic partner should co-ordinate their Mediterranean policies. EU states should encourage littoral countries to adopt democratic policies and develop a strategy to address the deep roots of existing conflicts, while NATO must assume a role in creating military confidence by revising initiatives like the anti-ballistic missile project and modernisation plans that generate fear and mistrust in the Arab countries.[129] But a common US–EU approach towards the Mediterranean depends not only on the political willingness of the EU to assume greater international responsibilities, but also on the preparedness of the US to share leadership and join in a genuine partnership.[130]

North–south and south–south European dimensions

Gillespie suggests that the north–south European dimension must be considered in any analysis of EU Mediterranean policy, for it provides a potential fault-line along which European disunity could develop.[131] Post-1989 Euro-Mediterranean developments are followed closely by the EU's southern members, something that cannot be said of their northern partners. Intra-EU controversy is not about whether to have a Mediterranean policy, but about methods, priorities and interests.[132] The EU's economic interests in the southern Mediterranean are comparatively unimportant in relation to its interests in other geographical areas.[133] The EU's prospective enlargement has produced a set of dynamic policies toward its eastern periphery, in contradistinction to a vague Mediterranean orientation. As Kaminski notes, since a further Mediterranean enlargement will not be solving the regional 'security vacuum', the EU will keep concentrating on its eastern neighbours.[134]

The accession of Finland, Austria and Sweden has arguably increased pressures on the EU to direct its resources towards eastern Europe rather than the Mediterranean.[135] The reform process in eastern Europe, currently under severe financial stress, should be kept alive with EU budgetary constraints, as well as with EU attempts to support the newly introduced single currency. As Tovias's analysis has shown, in line with the north–south disagreement within the EU is the northern members' preference for the EU's Mediterranean policy to be based on trade concessions, in contradistinction to the southern members' emphasis on increased financial aid.[136] Indeed, over the last decade, there has been a substantial increase in financial assistance from France, Spain and Italy.[137] Southern European concerns became manifest in a joint statement produced by the Portuguese and Spanish Premiers in Seville in 1990. They argued that the redirection of EU interest eastwards could hinder the integration process of southern EU members, in terms of economic and social cohesion, in addition to purely economic concerns about an expected negative impact on foreign direct investment. But redirecting the EU's external focus is no easy task, given that its two largest members, Britain and Germany, are adamant that economic assistance should aim at the reconstruction of the central and eastern European economies to reinforce their accession process.[138] Whatever may be the endgame of the EU's eastward enlargement, simple geography dictates that the EU remains essentially a 'northern-central European entity', in which the Mediterranean states are in the minority.[139] For their part, many non-EU Mediterranean states worry that, as part of the single market programme, the massive transfer of resources to southern EU members further exacerbates an already widening Mediterranean north–south gap in terms of economic and developmental inequality. But as the globalising world economy moves towards greater liberalisation, a market economy can only bear fruits if the liberalisation process is assissted by the necessary economic and political infrastructure to sustain it. Central and eastern European countries seem to be in a better position to satisfy these requirements than are the non-EU Mediterranean countries.

A related issue that currently challenges the viability of the new European order is the absence of a homogeneous European political space linked to the maintenance of regional security: the EU lacks a common Mediterranean perspective, not least because different EU states have historically expressed interest in different parts of the region: France towards the Maghreb, Britain towards the Middle East and Germany towards Turkey and the Balkans. In addition to the above, a good part of European ambitions for a stable Mediterranean have been promoted outside the framework of the EU per se, in the form of different state-led initiatives for regional co-operation, like the CSCM and the Mediterranean Forum. Therefore, however attractive may be the thesis of the 'indivisibility' of security, Europe is not one, but many, in terms of the security-related status of its component parts.[140] It is also certain that in an enlarged and, hence, ever more diverse EU, the differences involved in the making of a common EU policy towards the Mediterranean will be made even more acute. After enlargement, one of the tasks of the Common Foreign and Security Policy (CFSP) will be to develop policies that will not create a sense of exclusion among the EU's peripheries. The EU's geopolitical role will much depend on whether it will maintain its 'civilian'[141] character as an open and peaceful power, or whether it will project an image of a closed and hostile club.[142]

But different perceptions of interest concerning the EU's relations with the Mediterranean persist among its southern members themselves. Although the southern EU states have some identifiable elements of a common identity, these are not strong enough to be reflected in a permanent and structured political solidarity.[143] As Constas rather sceptically observes, southern EU members have not yet formed a cohesive block in relation to the EU's eastward enlargement, even less so in relation to the future of the EU itself.[144] France, Spain and Italy, especially, bring Mediterranean issues to the fore of the EU's agenda, for they traditionally maintain a plethora of strong ties with the countries of the region. As Veremis put it, the proximity of Portugal, Spain and Italy to North Africa, and the common borders of Greece and Italy with the troubled Balkans, help explain each country's regional line of work.[145] Although France is generally seen as the 'champion' of EU Mediterranean interests,[146] it has displayed a rather 'inchoate strategy' towards parts of the Mediterranean (e.g. Algeria).[147] Moreover, countries like Spain and Italy are not willing to accept a French leadership in the formulation of the EU's Mediterranean policy.[148] Another contradiction is that, while those three countries play an active role in setting the EU's Mediterranean agenda, smaller countries like Greece face in a more direct manner the potential tidal waves of regional instability.[149]

The effectiveness of EU security policy depends on striking a balance between the competing visions its members have of European security itself. Accordingly, a co-ordinated pressure by all the Mediterranean actors will prove decisive if issues of Mediterranean security are to become an integral part of the EU's integrative project. Although existing differences in the formulation of separate foreign policy initiatives reveal that southern EU states and applicant countries have not yet found a reliable *modus operandi* for strengthening the EU's Mediterranean dimension, the geographical diversity of preferences among EU states does not necessarily mean that no such cohesive position can emerge. For instance, Tanner asserts that 'the fate of the Mediterranean Pact will heavily depend on the EU members' capability to take a common stance with regard to the Mediterranean'.[150] Such a stance should not be based merely on common strategic orientations, but actually on the development of mutual trust among the partners.

Having examined the essential elements of Mediterranean complexity, we can now turn to investigate the patterns of relations in the emerging Euro-Mediterranean regime by taking into account those European policies towards the Mediterranean that preceded the launching of the Barcelona Process in November 1995. Chapter 4 will then consider the structure and evolution of the EMP, the extent to which it represents a 'breaking with the past' and the nature of its basket-based arrangements.

Notes

1 B. Russet, 'International Regions and the International System', in R. A. Falk and S. H. Mendlovitz (eds), *Regional Politics and World Order* (San Francisco, W. H. Freeman, 1973), p. 83.
2 A. Siegfried, The Mediterranean (London, Jonathan Cape, 1984), p. 29.
3 See also P. Gould and R. White, *Mental Maps* (Harmondsworth, Penguin, 1974); and A. K. Henrikson, 'The Geographical "Mental Maps" of American Policy-Makers', *International Political Science Review*, 1: 4 (1980), 495–530.
4 W. Wallace, *The Transformation of Western Europe* (London, Pinter, 1990), p. 8.

5 G. de Marco, 'The Mediterranean Roots of Europe', Paper presented at the seminar 'Europe After 1992: Which Europe?', organised by the European Christian Democrats of Malta, 23–6 September 1992.

6 D. Alexander and P. Alexander, *The Lion Handbook to the Bible* (London, Lion, 1983), pp. 30–1.

7 T. Couloumbis and T. Veremis, 'Introduction: The Mediterranean in Perspective', in S. Stavridis *et al.* (eds), *The Foreign Policies of the European Union's Mediterranean States and Applicant Countries in the 1990s* (London, Macmillan, 1999), p. 1.

8 H. Köchler, ' Muslim–Christian Ties in Europe: Past, Present and Future', Second International Seminar on 'Civilizational Dialogue: Japan, Islam and the West', Kuala Lumpur, 2–3 September 1996, p. 1.

9 C. Spencer, 'The Mediterranean Region', Paper presented at the 23rd Annual Conference of the British International Studies Association, University of Sussex, 14–16 December 1998.

10 A. Tovias, 'The EC's Contribution to Peace and Prosperity in the Mediterranean and the Middle East', *Jerusalem Journal of International Relations*, 14: 2 (1992), 212.

11 S. Ulrich, 'The Mediterranean Challenge: Europe and North Africa', *Libertas Europaische Zeitschrift*, 1–2, Stuttgard, 1992.

12 N. Waites and S. Stavridis, 'The EU and Mediterranean Member States', in Stavridis *et al.* (eds), *The Foreign Policies*, p. 29.

13 See S. C. Calleya, *Navigating Regional Dynamics in the Post-Cold War World: Patterns of Relations in the Mediterranean Area* (Aldershot, Dartmouth, 1997), especially pp. 89–140.

14 D. Fenech, 'Ways and Means of Security Around the Mediterranean Sea: A Euro-Mediterranean Partnership', Fondation Méditerranéenne des Etudes Stratégiques, Séminaire de la Tour Blanche, Toulon, 21–4 June 1995.

15 Niblock takes this view in relation to the development of overarching regional co-operation. See T. Niblock, 'The Realms Within which Integrated Communities Approach Could Be Fostered', in G. Nonneman (ed.), *The Middle East and Europe: An Integrated Communities Approach* (London, Federal Trust, 1992), p. 49.

16 W. Weidenfeld and J. Janning, 'Challenges in the Mediterranean: Strategy Options for Europe', in W. Weidenfeld and J. Janning (eds), *Europe in Global Change* (Gutersloh, Bertelsmann Foundation, 1993), p. 237.

17 See F. Braudel, *The Mediterranean and the Mediterranean World in the Age of Philip II*, vols I–II, 5th edn (London: Fontana Press, 1987).

18 See R. Aliboni, 'The Mediterranean Dimension', in W. Wallace (ed.), *The Dynamics of European Integration* (London, Pinter, 1990), pp. 155–67.

19 M. Lister, *The European Union and the South: Relations with Developing Countries* (London, Routledge, 1997), p. 72.

20 *Ibid.*

21 A. Ounais, 'Security Trends in the Mediterranean: A Perspective from North Africa', in F. Tanner (ed.), *Arms Control, Confidence-Building and Security Cooperation in the Mediterranean, North Africa and the Middle East* (Malta, MEDAC, 1994).

22 See P. Balta, 'La Méditerranée en tant que zone de conflits', *Revista CIDOB d'Afers Internacionals*, 37 (1997).

23 C. Spencer, 'Rethinking or Reorienting Europe's Mediterranean Security Focus', in W. Park and G. Wyn Rees (eds), *Rethinking Security in Post-Cold War Europe* (London, Longman, 1998), p. 139.

24 I. O. Lesser, 'Growth and Change in Southern Europe', in J. W. Holmes (ed.), *Maelstrom: The United States, Southern Europe, and the Challenges in the Mediterranean* (Cambridge, MA, World Peace Foundation, 1995), pp. 11–30.

25 D. P. Calleo, 'The United States and Security in the New Europe', in W. Weidenfield and J. Janning (eds), *Global Responsibilities: Europe in Tomorrow's World* (Gutersloh,

Bertelsmann Foundation, 1991), p. 172. See also W. H Taft, 'European Security: Lessons Learned from the Gulf War', *NATO Review*, 39: 3 (1991), 7–11.

26 J. P. Zanders, 'A New Security (Dis)Order for the Gulf', *POLE Papers*, 1, Centrum voor Polemologie, Vrije Universiteit Brussel, 1995.

27 In a speech delivered on 11 September 1990 before a joint session of Congress, President Bush stated: 'Out of these troubled times, our … objective – a new world order – can emerge … Today, that new world is struggling to be born, a world quite different from the one we have known …'. Quoted in B. R. Kessler, 'Bush's New World Order: The Meaning Behind the Words', *Research Paper*, Department of Air Command and Staff College, 1997, p. 1.

28 N. Gnesotto, 'Lessons of Yugoslavia', *Chaillot Papers*, 14, WEU Institute for Security Studies, Paris, 1994, p. 1.

29 F. Halliday, 'The Gulf War and its Aftermath: First Reflections', *International Affairs*, 67: 2 (1991), 223–4.

30 See T. Dokos, 'Security Problems in the Mediterranean', *ELIAMEP Occasional Papers*, OP97/04, Hellenic Foundation for European and Foreign Policy, Athens, 1997.

31 See I. O. Lesser and A. J. Tellis, *Strategic Exposure: Proliferation Around the Mediterranean* (Santa Monica, CA, RAND, 1996); T. Couloumbis and T. Dokos (eds), *Arms Control and Security in the Middle East and the CIS Republics* (Athens, Hellenic Foundation for European and Foreign Policy, 1995); and J. C. Snyder, 'Arms and Security in the Mediterranean Region', in R. Aliboni, G. Joffé and T. Niblock (eds), *Security Challenges in the Mediterranean Region* (London, Frank Cass, 1996), pp. 139–60.

32 R. Jervis, *Perception and Misperception in International Politics* (Princeton, NJ, Princeton University Press, 1976).

33 P. Moya, *Frameworks for Cooperation in the Mediterranean*, North Atlantic Assembly, Civilian Affairs Committee, Sub-Committee on the Mediterranean Basin, AM 259, 7 October 1995, p. 12.

34 Spencer, 'The Mediterranean Region'.

35 See J. Farley, 'Mediterranean – Southern Threats to Northern Shores', *The World Today*, 50: 2 (1994), 33–6. On Libya's exceptionalism, Faria and Vasconcelos note: 'Only Libya is still doomed to ostracism, seemingly wishing to manage its largely intentional isolation through alternating signs of enmity (for instance by expelling immigrants, in particular Palestinians) and offers to use its good offices (to assist the Sudan regime).' See F. Faria and A. de Vasconcelos, 'Security in Northern Africa: Ambiguity and Reality', *Chaillot Papers*, 25, WEU Institute for Security Studies, Paris, 1996. Cf. D. Sammut, 'Libya and the Islamic Threat', *The World Today*, 50: 10 (1994), 198–200.

36 R. Aliboni, 'Introduction', in Aliboni, Joffé and Niblock (eds), *Security Challenges*, p. 10.

37 Faria and Vasconcelos, 'Security in Northern Africa', p. 11.

38 K. Chater, 'Mediterranean Security: The Tunisian Viewpoint', in Aliboni, Joffé and Niblock (eds), *Security Challenges*, p. 65.

39 G. Joffé, 'Southern Attitudes Towards an Integrated Mediterranean Region', *Mediterranean Politics*, 2: 1 (1997), 18.

40 See T. Greenwood, 'US and NATO Force Structure and Military operations in the Mediterranean', *McNair Papers*, 14, Institute for National Strategic Studies, National Defence University, 1993.

41 N. de Santis, 'The Future of NATO's Mediterranean Initiative', *NATO Review*, 46: 1 (1998), 32–5.

42 E. Mortimer, 'Europe and the Mediterranean: The Security Dimension', in P. Ludlow (ed.), *Europe and the Mediterranean* (London, Brassey's, 1994), p. 106.

43 P. Cuco, *The Eastern Mediterranean*, Report submitted on behalf of the Defence Committee, Assembly of Western European Union, Document 1465, 24 May (1995).

44 Quoted in Faria and Vasconcelos, 'Security in Northern Africa', p. 1.

45 First, he projected himself as the Arab leader who stood up against the West and particularly the US. Second, he elevated his struggle to a holy war against the West and its allies in the Middle East. Third, he brought Israel and, by extension, the Palestinian issue into the conflict, thus offering Arab nationalism and Islamism a common cause. See K. Matthews, *The Gulf Conflict and International Relations* (London, Routledge, 1993), p. 21; and, A Ehteshami and G. Noneman, *War and Peace in the Gulf: Domestic Politics and Regional Relations into the 1990s* (Reading, Ithaca Press, 1991), pp. 19–44.

46 Fukuyama sees the end of the Cold War as evidence of the triumph of liberalism over communism; the former reigning triumphant as the only remaining ideological perspective. While he admits that certain internal conflicts exist within liberalism such as the economic conflict among classes, he dismisses these conflicts as manageable. Conflict is central to Fukuyama's view of the future of world politics; its most important sources being ideological. He posits two possible ideological challenges to liberalism: religion and nationalism. But he dismisses the threat posed by religion by claiming that religion is ill-suited to the realm of politics, while suggesting that the liberal political process may help to resolve nationalistic tensions. In both cases, Fukuyama's faith in liberalism is overly optimistic. Both Huntington (see below) and Fukuyama see religion as threatening either 'Western civilisation' or 'liberalism', although each seems to be taking a different approach: the former rejects ideology and focuses on culture, whereas the latter emphasises ideology. The fact that these apparently different perspectives lead to similar insights is not coincidental since both theorists find religion an inherently non-rational pre-modern phenomenon. See F. Fukuyama, *The End of History and the Last Man* (New York, Free Press, 1992).

47 For Huntington, much of the future of world politics and a good part of its past can be understood as conflict among differing civilisations. He admits to the emergence of non-state actors on the global scene but holds that nation states 'will remain the most powerful actors in world affairs'. He also claims that conflict will continue to occur within civilisations, but maintains that the most dangerous conflicts will occur on the faultlines between civilisations. Finally, he sees conflict occurring at both the level of individuals as 'adjacent groups along the fault lines between civilizations struggle, often violently, over the control of territory and each other' and at the level of structure as 'states from different civilizations compete for relative military and economic power, struggle over the control of international institutions and third parties, and competitively promote their particular political and religious values'. Although there are important differences within it, a civilisation shares general values, customs, ways of life, and, crucially, religion – all the items that make up a culture: 'Civilizations are the biggest "we" within which we feel culturally at home as distinguished from all the other "thems" out there.' This leads to conflict, because people have psychological and political needs for enemies, in part to mark their own identities. See by S. P. Huntington, 'The Clash of Civilizations?', *Foreign Affairs* 72: 3 (1993), 22–49; and *The Clash of Civilizations and the Remaking of World Order* (London, Touchstone, 1996); Cf. T. Couloumbis and T. Veremis, 'In Search of New Barbarians: Samuel P. Huntington and the Clash of Civilizations', *Mediterranean Quarterly*, 5: 1 (1994) 36–44; and D. A. Welch, 'The "Clash of Civilizations" Thesis as an Argument and as a Phenomenon', *Security Studies*, 6: 4 (1997), 197–216.

48 A. Sachedina, 'Religion and Global Affairs: Islamic Religion and Political Order', *SAIS Review*, 18: 2 (1998), 59–64.

49 See G. E. Fuller and I. O. Lesser, *A Sense of Siege: The Geopolitics of Islam and the West* (Boulder, CO, Westview Press, 1995).

50 M. J. Shapiro, *Violent Cartographies: Mapping Cultures of War* (Minneapolis, University of Minnesota Press, 1997).

51 M. Blunden, 'Insecurity in Europe's Southern Flank', *Survival*, 36: 2 (1994), 137.

52 B. Buzan, *People, States and Fear: The National Security Problem in International Relations* (Brighton, Wheatsheaf Books, 1983), p. 228.
53 N. Ayubi, 'Farms, Factories and … Walls: Which Way for European/Middle Eastern Relations?', in N. Ayubi (ed.), *Distant Neighbors: The Political Economy of Relations between Europe and the Middle East/North Africa* (Reading, Ithaka Press, 1995), p. 7.
54 T. W. Lippman, *Understanding Islam* (New York, Penguin Group, 1990), p. 70.
55 E. Said, *Orientalism* (New York, Vintage, 1979), p. 310.
56 E. Said, *Covering Islam: How the Media and the Experts Determine How We See the Rest of the World* (London, Routledge, 1981), p. 31.
57 *Ibid.*
58 J. L. Espozito, *Islam and Politics*, 4th edn (Syracuse, NY, Syracuse University Press, 1998).
59 B. A. Roberson, 'Islam and Europe: An Enigma or a Myth?', in B. A. Roberson (ed.), *The Middle East and Europe: The Power Deficit* (London, Routledge, 1998), p. 120.
60 I. M. Lapidus, 'Beyond the Unipolar Moment: A Sober Survey of the Islamic World', *Orbis*, 40: 3 (1996), 393.
61 See C. E. Black, *The Dynamics of Modernization: A Study in Comparative History* (New York, Harper & Row, 1966).
62 See G. A. G. Soltan, 'State Building, Modernization and Political Islam: The Search for Political Community(s) in the Middle East', *Revista CIDOB d'Afers Internacionals*, 37 (1997).
63 See E. Gellner, 'Up from Imperialism', *The New Republic*, 22 May (1989), 35–6.
64 P. G. Vatikiotis, *Islam and the State* (in Greek) (Athens, Hellenic Foundation for Eurpean and Foreign Policy, 1991).
65 S. P. Huntington, 'Democracy's Third Wave', in L. Diamond and M. F. Plattner (eds), *The Global Resurgence of Democracy* (Baltimore, MD, Johns Hopkins University Press, 1993), p. 19. Cf. S. Humphreys, 'Islam and Political Values in Saudi Arabia, Egypt and Syria', *Middle East Journal*, 33 (1979) 6–7.
66 R. Aliboni, 'Factors Affecting Mediterranean Security', in Tanner (ed.), *Arms Control.*
67 S. P. Huntington, 'Democracy's Third Wave', in Diamond and Plattner (eds), *The Global Resurgence of Democracy*, p. 19. For a different view see E. Mortimer, 'The Party of God', *Prospects*, 42: June (1999), 36–40; B. Khader and V. Legrand, 'Democratization in the Arab–Muslim World', *ELIAMEP Occasional Papers*, OP 98/09, Hellenic Foundation for European and Foreign Policy, Athens, 1998.
68 J. Diamond, J. Linz and S. M. Lipset (eds), *Democracy in Developing Countries* (Boulder, CO, Lynne Rienner, 1989), p. xx; quoted in D. Pool, 'Staying at Home With the Wife: Democratization and its Limits in the Middle East', in G. Parry and M. Morran (eds), *Democracy and Democratization* (London, Routledge, 1994), p. 197.
69 Pool, 'Staying at Home With the Wife', p. 198.
70 D. G. Curdy, 'Security and Peace in the Middle East: Experiments with Democracy in an Islamic World', *Maxwell Papers*, 4, Air War College, 1996, p. 4.
71 Pool, 'Staying at Home With the Wife', p. 215.
72 Lapidus, 'Beyond the Unipolar Moment', p. 404.
73 Quoted in H. A. Jawad, 'Islam and the West: How Fundamental Is the Threat?', *RUSI Journal*, 140: 4 (1995) 37.
74 H. Köchler, 'Philosophical Foundations of Civlizational Dialogue: The Hermeneutics of Cultural Self-comprehension Versus the Paradigm of Civilizational Conflict', *Occasional Papers Series*, 3, International Progress Organization, 1998.
75 See also D. Farrar-Hockley, 'Future Instability in the Mediterranean', *European Security*, 3: 1 (1994), 58–81.
76 I. O. Lesser, *Future Vision 2010: Mediterranean Europe and Turkey* (Santa Monica, CA, RAND, 1997), p. 9.
77 A. Bin, 'Strengthening Cooperation in the Mediterranean: NATO's Contribution', *NATO*

Review, 46: 4 (1998), 25.

78 World Bank, *Dept Tables 1994*, Washington, DC, pp. 200–1.

79 P. R. Ireland, 'Europe's Rio Grande? The Mediterranean Basin, Islam and the EU's Southern Strategy', Paper presented at the Fifth Biennial ECSA–USA Conference, Seattle, W, May 1997, p. 6.

80 M. Grenon and M. Batisse (eds), *Futures for the Mediterranean Basin: The Blue Plan* (Oxford, Oxford University Press, 1989).

81 J. C. Renaud, 'Security and Energy in the Post-Crisis Period', *NATO Review*, 39: 1 (1991), 22.

82 A. Toukan, 'A Plan for Euro-Med Conflict Prevention', in *How Can Europe Prevent Conflicts? Discussion Papers*, 14, Philip Morris Institute for Public Policy and Research, 1997, p. 89.

83 See G. Luciani, 'Euro-Arab Co-operation and Conflict in the Areas of Oil and Gas', in N. Ayubi (ed.), *Distant Neigbours*, pp. 65–88; and P. Stevens, 'Oil and Energy Cooperation', in G. Nonneman (ed.), *The Middle East and Europe*, pp. 83–94.

84 G. Joffé, 'Integration and Peripheral Dependence: The Dilemma facing the South Mediterranean States', Paper presented at the MEDAC Conference on 'Prospects after Barcelona', Malta, March 1996.

85 See analysis provided by H. Gunder Brauch, 'Energy Interdependence in the Western Mediterranean', *Politics*, 1: 3 (1996), 295–319.

86 G. Joffé *et al.*, 'The Mediterranean: Risks and Challenges', *International Spectator*, 28: 3 (1993), 36.

87 For a detailed analysis of these factors see M. Benyaklef, 'Socio-Economic Disparities in the Mediterranean', *Mediterranean Politics*, 2: 1 (1997), 110.

88 Couloumbis and Veremis, 'Introduction', in S. Stavridis *et al.* (eds), *The Foreign Policies*, p. 3. For a useful analysis of statistics on the north–south gap, see R. Aliboni *et al.*, 'Co-operation and Stability in the Mediterranean: An Agenda for Partnership', *International Spectator*, 29: 3 (1994), 5–20. For statistical data see Eurostat, 'Euro-Mediterranean Statistics', *General Short-Term Statistics*, 2, Luxembourg, 1998.

89 See A. de Vasconcelos, 'The New Europe and the Western Mediterranean', *NATO Review*, 39: 5 (1991), 27–31.

90 The effect of the windfall on oil producers was equivalent to a 50 per cent increase in their national incomes. The spillovers for the rest of the region were equivalent to a 3,540 per cent increase in GDP!

91 See B. Khader, 'Europe–Arab Economic Relations: Balance of a Quarter Century 1973–1997', *Revista CIDOB d'Afers Internacionals*, 37 (1997).

92 This has been particularly true not only for the major oil-producing countries, but for minor producers like Egypt, as well as those non oil-producing countries that benefited from the increase of oil wealth through migration and exports to Europe, and through direct investment flows from the latter.

93 World Bank Report, 'Claiming the Future: Choosing Prosperity in the Middle East and North Africa' (1995). See also N. Shafik, *Economic Challenges Facing Middle Eastern and North African Countries: Alternative Futures* (Basingstoke, Macmillan, 1998).

94 Joffé, 'Integration and Peripheral Dependence'.

95 For a detailed analysis of figures and trends in Mediterranean demographics, see R. King and M. Donati, 'The "Divided" Mediterranean: Re-defining European Relationships', in R. Hudson and A. M. Williams (eds), *Divided Europe: Society and Territory* (London, Sage, 1999), especially pp. 142–7.

96 S. E. Ibrahim, 'The Demographic Factors in the Security of the Mediterranean: From the Battle of Tours to the Battle of Algiers', Fondation Méditerranéenne d'Etudes Stratégiques, Séminaire de la Tour Blanche, Toulon, 21–4 June 1995.

97 Inter-Parliamentary Union, 'Employment is Key to Stability in the Mediterranean,

CSCM Meeting Concludes', Press release of the Inter-Parliamentary Union, No. 2, Monte Carlo/Geneva, 4 July 1997.

98 S. Collinson, 'Migration and Security in the Mediterranean: A Complex Relationship', Paper presented at the Conference 'Non-Military Aspects of Security in Southern Europe: Migration, Employment and Labour Market', organised by the Institute of International Economic Relations and Regional Network on Southern European Societies, Santorini, 19–21 September 1997.

99 See S. Spencer (ed.), *Immigration as an Economic Asset: The German Experience*, (Staffordshire, Trentham Books, 1994).

100 A new title has been inserted in the Treaty of Amsterdam concerning the 'free movement of persons, asylum and immigration'. It consists of nine Articles and several Declarations to the Final Act. According to Article A of the new Title, within a five-year period measures aimed at ensuring the free movement of persons, measures in the fields of asylum and immigration, and to safeguard the rights of third-country nationals (as well as measures in the field of judicial co-operation in civil matters, and police and judicial co-operation in criminal matters) will be introduced. These measures will provide the same level of security as in the Schengen Convention, according to a Declaration attached to the new Treaty. Article B provides legal authorisation for the adoption of measures that will ensure the free movement of persons for the citizens of the Union, the same treatment of nationals from third countries when crossing the frontiers of the Union, including the regime governing the issuing of visas. This Article, though, is followed by a Protocol and a Declaration to the Final Act on Article B(2)(b), by which the application of Article B(2)(b) seems to be negotiated in so far it is provided that 'due consideration shall be taken in the application of the said article of the general foreign policy considerations of the member states' and that its application will be 'without prejudice to the negotiation or conclusion (by individual member states) of agreements on related maters …'. Furthermore, according to Article C, within five years of the Treaty's coming into force, the Council of Ministers, acting unanimously (and through the co-decision procedure after the five years) will introduce sets of minimum requirements on asylum, measures on refugees and displaced persons and measures on immigration policy (issuing of long-term visas and residence permits, steps to curb illegal immigration and illegal residence) and measures defining the rights and conditions under which nationals of third countries who are legally residing in one member state may reside in another member state. With a Declaration attached to the Final At on Article C(3)(a), member states may negotiate and conclude agreements with third countries in the domains of the said article as long as such agreements respect Community Law. Moreover, measures by individual member states are foreseen in the event that they are confronted by an emergency situation characterised by a sudden inflow of refugees. In such cases Article D(2) stipulates that the Council of Ministers, on a proposal from the European Commission, may adopt temporary measures (not more than six months) for the benefits of the member states concerned. For more on the Amsterdam reforms, see D. N. Chryssochoou, M. J. Tsinisizelis, S. Stavridis and K. Ifantis, *Theory and reform in the European Union* (Manchester and New York, Manchester University Press, 1999), especially pp. 75–80.

101 See Aliboni *et al.*, 'Co-operation and Stability in the Mediterranean'.

102 S. Collinson, *Shore to Shore: The Politics of Migration in Euro-Maghreb Relations* (London, Royal Institute of International Affairs, 1997).

103 N. Fahmy, 'After Madrid and Barcelona: Prospects for Mediterranean Security', Paper presented at the MEDAC Conference on 'Prospects after Barcelona', Malta, March (1996).

104 R. Aliboni, 'European Security Across the Mediterranean', *Chaillot Papers*, 2, WEU Institute for Security Studies, Paris, 1991.

105 See E. Mortimer, 'New Fault Lines: Is North–South Confrontation in Security Terms?', in *New Dimensions in International Security*, *Adelphi Papers*, 266, International Institute for Strategic Studies, London, 1991–92.

106 Syria, Libya and the Balkan countries were supported by the Soviet Union, while US support was directed toward Israel, Lebanon, Jordan, Morocco and Tunisia, with both the US and the Soviet Union competing to support Egypt and Algeria, while the Europeans were supporting Turkey, Malta and Cyprus.

107 G. Salame, 'Torn Between the Atlantic and the Mediterranean: Europe and the Middle East in the Post-Cold Era', in Roberson (ed.), *The Middle East and Europe*, p. 20.

108 In the late 1970s and early 1980s, a disunity of regional alignments in the wider Mediterranean region through a series of events, including the change of regime in Iran, the Soviet invasion of Afghanistan and the beginning of the Iran–Iraq war, deeply influenced the European public opinion. However, none had the impact of the Algerian war for independence in 1962.

109 J. Peters, 'Europe and the Middle East Peace Process: Emerging from the Sidelines', in Stavridis *et al.* (eds), *Foreign Policies*, p. 300.

110 This process culminated in the signing of the Single European Act in February 1986, which represented the first formal revision of the original treaties.

111 H. Köchler, 'US–European Relations After the End of the East–West Conflict: Implications for Euro-Mediterranean Co-operation', *Occasional Papers Series*, 1, International Progress Organization, 1997.

112 R. Aliboni, 'Collective Political Co-operation in the Mediterranean', in Aliboni, Joffé and Niblock (eds), *Security Challenges*, p. 57.

113 J. W. Holmes, 'US Interests and Policy Options', in Holmes (ed.), *Maelstrom*, p. 224.

114 Z. Khalilzad, 'Challenges in the Greater Middle East', in D. C. Gompert and S. F. Larrabee (eds), *America and Europe: A Partnership for a New Era* (Cambridge, Cambridge University Press, 1997).

115 P. Marr, 'The United States, Europe and the Middle East: Cooperation, Co-optation or Confrontation?', in Roberson (ed.), *The Middle East and Europe*, p. 96.

116 For a more analytical accpunt, see I. O. Lesser, 'Southern Europe and the Maghreb: US Interests and Policy Perspectives', *Mediterranean Politics*, 1: 2 (1996), 231–42.

117 E. Laipson, 'Thinking About the Mediterranean', *Mediterranean Quarterly*, 1: 1 (1990) 50–65.

118 F. Carr and K. Ifantis, *NATO in the New European Order* (London, Macmillan, 1996).

119 It is noteworthy that the European share of the security budget in Operation Desert Storm was less than 10 per cent.

120 J. S. Nye, Jr, 'Patrons and Clients: New Roles in the Post-Cold War Order', in H. Haftendorn and C. Tuschoff (eds), *America and Europe in an Era of Change* (Boulder, CO, Westview Press, 1993), p. 95.

121 Joffé, 'Southern Attitudes', p. 18.

122 For more details, see 'The Middle East Peace Process and the Role of the European Union', *Euromed Special Features*, 7, 23 April 1999.

123 See Köchler, 'US–European Relations'.

124 P. H. Gordon, 'The Transatlantic Allies and the Changing Middle East', *Adelphi Papers*, 322, International Institute for Strategic Studies, London, 1998.

125 C. Gaspar, 'Europe and the Middle East: At the Crossroads', *NATO Review*, 42: 5 (1994) 26–30.

126 R. Hollis, 'Europe and the Middle East: Power by Stealth?', *International Affairs*, 73: 1 (1997) 29.

127 J. N. Holmes, US Interests and Policy Options', in Holmes (ed), *Maelstrom*, p. 225.

128 J. C. Snyder, 'Proliferation Threats to Security in NATO's Southern Region', *Mediterranean Quarterly*, 4: 1 (1993), 110.

129 M. Aguirre, 'NATO Needs a New Approach to the Mediterranean', *Summit Briefing Paper*, 97/4, Berlin Information Centre for Transatlantic Security, July 1997.
130 D. C. Gompert and S. F. Larrabee (eds), *America and Europe: A Partnership for a New Era* (Cambridge, Cambridge University Press, 1997).
131 See R. Gillespie, 'Northern European Perceptions of the Barcelona Process', *Revista CIDOB d'Afers Internacionals*, 37 (1997).
132 A. Jünemann, 'Europe's Interrelations with North Africa in the New Framework of Euro-Mediterranean Partnership – A Provisional Assessment of the Barcelona Concept', Paper presented at the Third ECSA–World Conference, 19–20 September 1996.
133 T. Niblock, 'North–South Socio-Economic Relations in the Mediterranean', in Aliboni, Joffé and Niblock (eds), *Security Challenges*, p. 116.
134 A. Kaminski, 'The Geostrategic Implications of Enlargement', Paper presented at the Second Meeting of the Working Group on the Eastern Enlargement of the European Union, Robert Schuman Centre, European University Institute, Brussels, October 1997, p. 1.
135 Calleya, *Navigating Regional Dynamics*, p. 205.
136 A. Tovias, 'The EU's Mediterranean Policies Under Pressure', in R. Gillespie (ed.), *Mediterranean Politics*, vol. II (London, Pinter, 1996), pp. 9–25.
137 J. Marks, 'High Hopes and Low Motives: The New Euro-Mediterranean Partnership Initiative', *Mediterranean Politics*, 1: 1 (1996), 11.
138 D. Allen, 'Conclusions', in C. Hill (ed.), *The Actors in Europe's Foreign Policy* (London, Routledge, 1996), p. 301.
139 R. Pace, 'Peace, Stability, Security and Prosperity in the Mediterranean Region', in A. Bin (ed.) *Co-operation and Security in the Mediterranean* (Malta, MEDAC, 1996), p. 110.
140 See V. Baranovsky, 'An Understanding of Europe's Overlapping Political Realities', *Revista CIDOB d'Afers Internacionals*, 38/39 (1997).
141 This term draws from C. Hill, 'European Foreign Policy: Power Bloc, Civilian Model – or Flop?', in R. Rummel (ed.), *The Evolution of an International Actor: Western Europe's New Assertiveness* (Boulder, CO, Westview Press, 1990).
142 H. Miall, 'Wider Europe, Fortress Europe, Fragmented Europe', in H. Miall (ed.), *Redefining Europe. New Patterns of Conflict and Co-operation* (London, Pinter, 1994), pp. 1–16.
143 R. Aliboni, 'Southern European Security: Perceptions and Problems', in R. Aliboni (ed.), *Southern European Security in the 1990s* (London, Pinter, 1992), p. 2.
144 D. Constas, 'Southern European Countries in the European Community', in Holmes (ed.), *Maelstrom*, pp. 127–50.
145 T. Veremis, 'International Relations in Southern Europe', in J. Loughlin (ed.), *Southern European Studies Guide* (London, Bauker-Saur, 1993), pp. 207–10.
146 Calleya, *Navigating Regional Dynamics*, p. 178.
147 See J. Howorth, 'France and the Mediterranean in 1995: From Tactical Ambiguity to Inchoate Strategy?', *Mediterranean Politics*, 1: 2 (1996), 157–75; N. Waites, 'France and the Post-Colonial Mediterranean Region', *Occasional Papers*, 33, University of Reading (September 1994); and L. Meyrede, 'France's Foreign Policy in the Mediterranean', in Stavridis *et al.*, *Foreign Policies*, pp. 40–72.
148 For comprehensive analyses of Spain's increasing role in the Mediterranean, see by R. Gillespie, *Spain and the Mediterranean: Developing a European Policy Towards the South* (London, Macmillan, 1999); 'Spanish Protagonismo and the Euro-Mediterranean Partnership', *Mediterranean Politics*, 2: 1 (1997), 33–48; 'Spain and the Mediterranean: Southern Sensitivity, European Aspirations', *Mediterranean Politics*, 1: 2 (1996), 193–211. On Italy, see J. W. Holmes, 'Italy: In the Mediterranean, but *of* it?', *Mediterranean Politics*, 1: 2 (1996), 176–92; and R. Aliboni, 'Italy and the Mediterranean in the 1990s', in Stavridis *et al.* (eds), *Foreign Policies*, pp. 73–97.

149 Greece has been reserved about assuming a more active Mediterranean role, mainly due to the Greco-Turkish dispute, with the exception of promoting EU–Cyprus relations. See C. Tsardanides, 'The Southern EU Member States' Policy towards the Mediterranean: Regional or Global Co-operation', *Journal of Area Studies*, 9: 3 (1996), 65; and D. K. Xenakis, 'Euro-Mediterranean Formations and the Emerging European System: The Role of Cyprus', *The Cyprus Review*, 11: 1 (1999), 59–82.

150 F. Tanner, 'An Emerging Security Agenda for the Mediterranean', *Mediterranean Politics*, 1: 3 (1996), 293.

PART II

Policy and process

3

European policies towards the Mediterranean

An overview

Signs of a common European interest in Mediterranean affairs were first recorded in the mid-1970s with the beginning of the Euro-Arab dialogue, then in the early and mid-1980s with the accession of Greece and the Iberian nations to the Community, and again after the Gulf War, in the early 1990s. Euro-Mediterranean relations have always been highly politicised as a result of geographical proximity, the nature and level of regional interdependence, and the role that earlier European policies had come to play in the region. Until 1972, no explicit policy governed the EC's Mediterranean approach. Despite Europe's good intentions, the results had been disappointing, or at least such was the general feeling among the Mediterranean countries. Since then, the Community has become increasingly aware of the need to transform Euro-Mediterranean relations – embodied until that time in ad hoc and/or à la carte agreements – into a more consistent and uniform pattern of mutually rewarding interactions. It was in 1972 also that the Community adopted a 'global' approach, with a more comprehensive Mediterranean policy, offering free entry to its markets for manufactures. During the early 1970s, most Mediterranean countries re-negotiated their Co-operation Agreements with the Community, with the Commission claiming that each agreement would be tailored to the needs of the partner countries concerned.[1] With minor differences, however, they all shared the same general characteristics. Most of these agreements entered into force from 1977 onwards, inaugurating a new phase in Euro-Mediterranean relations. The new phase brought with it a series of protocols to broaden the scope of existing preferential agreements, which until then had been confined mainly to trade issues, and it was decided that more weight should be given to financial and technical co-operation. The need for such protocols emerged during the 1970s, as most Mediterranean countries were particularly vulnerable to the international economic environment. Aid was thus to become, in however modest terms, an integral part of the so-called 'protocol phase'.[2]

The signing of the first Association Agreements with Spain and Israel in 1969 inaugurated a period of relative inactivity on the part of the Community towards the Mediterranean that extended throughout the 1980s. The reason was that the Community occupied itself primarily with a series of internal and external concerns, including the completion of the single-market programme, the accession of the Iberian nations, negotiations with the countries of the European Free Trade Area (EFTA) for the creation of the European Economic Area (EEA), the negotiations of the Uruguay Round and, post-1989, developments in central and eastern Europe.[3] Until 1989, the Community's external relations with southern Mediterranean states took the form of bilateral agreements that were, paradoxically, of a similar content. This largely undifferentiated approach resulted in two types of Association Agreement: those concerning prospective Community members and closer economic associates, namely Cyprus, Malta and Turkey, and those relating to the rest of the littoral states that loom in the wider framework of the Community's Mediterranean policy. By that time, the Global Mediterranean Policy (GMP: see below) had become a complex juxtaposition of ad hoc measures, rather than a co-ordinated policy approach.[4]

After the Community's Mediterranean enlargements in the early and mid-1980s, the interdependencies between the two Mediterranean shores became more acute and the new members pleaded for more activism in the area. In addition, the majority of the southern Mediterranean countries (especially the Maghreb) showed an interest in revitalising co-operation with the Community, to the extent that Morocco applied to join the Community in 1987. By the late 1980s, the revolutionary events in the East had provoked fears among European and non-European Mediterranean countries of a shift in emphasis eastwards. The Renovated Mediterranean Policy (RMP) (see below) that began in 1991 tripled the financial commitment of the Community to the region. The bulk of aid was transmitted through financial protocols covering the period 1992–96, but two additional incentive budget lines were set to support economic reforms and regional co-operation.

The EC's Mediterranean policy in the 1970s and 1980s was patterned primarily on the following triptych: trade concessions; financial co-operation; and project aid. But these actions have proved insufficient to sustain regional economic progress. Similarly, all pre-1989 Community efforts to promote political dialogue and horizontal regional co-operation failed. Euro-Mediterranean relations lacked a formal and comprehensive political dialogue component, due to their largely bilateral nature. A reflection of this was that the Joint Councils, that were supposed to meet twice a year on a *de facto* basis, hardly ever met. Moreover, political tensions were often reported, resulting, on at least three occasions, in the European Parliament (EP) blocking the financial protocols with Israel (1988), Morocco and Syria (1992) because of the domestic political scene in those countries.

Today, Euro-Mediterranean relations are in transition towards a new post-bipolar order, in which factors relating to political and economic multilateralism co-exist. But attempts to create a multilateral framework of co-operation in the Euro-Mediterranean space are not entirely new. Their roots date back to the inception of the GMP in the early 1970s. However, today's attempts at multilateralism mark a clear step forward, by tracing a set of partly overlapping circles, a kind of variable geometry characterised by a small common subset or core.[5] In contrast to previous European approaches, post-1995 Euro-Mediterranean relations are based not only on a lasting multilateralism, but on reciprocity, political dialogue, gradual (albeit controlled) political and economic liberalisation, respect for diversity and political pluralism, and conditionality. These innovative elements, in both structural and functional terms, are to be found in the 1995 Barcelona Declaration and the agreements already signed with Tunisia (July 1995), Israel (November 1995), Morocco (February 1995), the West Bank and the Gaza Strip (February 1997), Jordan (April 1997), and the Customs Union signed with Turkey (March 1996). The new agreements focused on trade liberalisation (eliminating tariffs on the basis of reciprocity and not on a preferential basis), the encouragement of foreign direct investment and economic co-operation, as well as the strengthening of political, social and cultural ties. Further, a series of decentralised co-operation programmes were put in place, including Med-Invest, Med-Campus, Med-Media, and Med-Urb, to reinforce co-operation between (civil) societies north and south of the Mediterranean. These programmes are open to non-state actors and should involve at least two southern Mediterranean and two EU countries to be eligible for finance. Yet, they did not result in any significant increase in the scale and intensity of intra-regional exchanges. To reach a better understanding of the current state of Euro-Mediterranean relations and place it in a historical context, we now draw attention to the earlier European policies towards the region. These policies are generally divided into four distinct but interrelated phases.

The European 'rapprochement' (1961–72)

Europe has always been associated in one way or another with Mediterranean countries, not least because of their strategic geographic location. The early impetus dates back to post-colonial French efforts to preserve relations with North African states.[6] In his analysis, Ginsberg argues that the logic of European integration explains much of the initial – pre-1973 – European interest in the Mediterranean basin.[7] From the then dominant economic perspective of the 1950s, the formation of the Community affected the economies of most Mediterranean countries negatively, in that the latter relied heavily on west European markets for trade. Most of these countries competed directly with France and Italy (the only Mediterranean EC members at the time) in the sale of olive oil, citrus and vegetables. Already in 1957, these countries began to lobby the Community to negotiate trade accords in order to protect their historical market shares in Europe and to minimise anticipated losses in the new regional trade bloc. According to Ginsberg, what effectively emerged from these bilateral negotiations was a patchwork of unrelated EC preferential trade agreements, as opposed to a common policy.[8] These agreements were of limited duration and, more importantly perhaps, lacked any clearly defined regional objectives. Weidenfeld has termed this first phase the Community's 'rapprochement' with the Mediterranean, a phase which extended throughout the 1960s.[9]

The Community itself was passive, and its activities were initiated mainly by the countries of the Mediterranean in an attempt to gain a preferential position and free access to the Common Market. Gradually, bilateral agreements with different incentives came into force with Mediterranean countries that wanted closer links with Europe.[10] On the other hand, Association Agreements were signed with two littoral countries located at the most strategic part of the region, namely Greece (1962) and Turkey (1964). The Athens Agreement was by far the most comprehensive of those which the Community had already signed with third (Mediterranean) countries.[11] The rationale behind the association of these two countries with the Community was that the latter's Mediterranean policy was designed largely to stabilise political regimes against possible Communist penetrations to the eastern Mediterranean.[12] But the Greek and Turkish experiments were not to be repeated. Other littoral Mediterranean countries did not sign agreements that were intended to act as a prelude to full EC membership. Rather, their agreements were limited to trade issues, sustaining free access for industrial goods and providing specific concessions for particular agricultural products. South European Mediterranean states pressed the Community for tariff preferences and other concessions that discriminated against them. The Community's response was to conclude the so-called 'first wave' of trade agreements with Mediterranean states. In 1969, the Community agreed to offer Spain and Israel preferential access for their citrus fruits. These prototype agreements led the Community to negotiate a series of similar arrangements with Lebanon, Jordan, Syria, Egypt, Malta and Cyprus.

Despite the references to the Mediterranean in the Treaty of Rome (1957), the Community was far from having a coherent Mediterranean policy by the late 1960s.[13] Grilli argues that the Community attempted to adopt a regional approach that was largely reflecting the design of the Lomé Conventions with the African, Caribbean and Pacific countries (ACP).[14] Tovias notes: 'The Maghreb/Mashreq agreements … still had more to do with the idea of development aid than with trade in the proper sense'.[15] A possible exception to the above pattern was the Community's agreement with Israel, in that it was closer to the free-trade agreements that were signed between the Community and the EFTA countries. Moreover, the agreements with the former French colonies in sub-Saharan Africa, based in Part IV of the Treaty of Rome, had a more harmonious character than those signed between the Community and Mediterranean states, which were more of a 're-active' than 'pro-active' nature.[16]

It is worth pointing out that, in contrast to the economic context relating to the anticipated rapid development of the Third World, Mediterranean states were regarded as having considerable advantages over most ACP countries. Still, though, EC trade and aid arrangements with Mediterranean states remained more modest and defensive than those under the Lomé Convention that came to include the STABEX[17] and SYSMIN[18] financial programmes. In Edwards and Philippart's words: 'The Mediterranean states refused the symbolism of Lomé, conscious, perhaps, not only of their proximity to the EC but also … of the EC's willingness to enter into political dialogue ….'[19] Overall, it is rather naive to believe that any kind of 'unique conditions for regional integration' existed in the Mediterranean in the late 1960s, and that the Community's regime would have adopted a common approach towards the newly de-colonised states of the region.

The Global Mediterranean Policy (1972–89)

The beginning of this phase was characterised by an attempt on the part of the Community to formulate an overall Mediterranean policy – hence the term 'global'. There were several reasons for such an ambitious approach: the first enlargement of the Community in 1973, leading to the accession of the UK, Denmark and Ireland; the French-led anxiety for new and more advanced agreements with North African countries, especially Morocco and Tunisia; the desire of some non-EC Mediterranean countries, like Israel, to be included in the European tariff system;[20] the necessity for a commercial arrangement, on the one hand, with the UK and, on the other, with Spain and Israel due to their market orientation towards the UK; the identification of the exigency that the Community's Mediterranean relations had regional and not bilateral correlation; and the potential danger of antagonism among Community members as a result of isolated bilateral relations with non-EC Mediterranean countries.

In 1972 the Community announced its GMP, at the heart of which was free access to European markets for Mediterranean manufactured exports. This was justified as the only possible step towards a free trade area, since developing Mediterranean countries were not strong enough to reciprocate by opening up their domestic markets.[21] The GMP was built out of the Association and Co-operation Agreements that were signed during the 1960s. But their co-ordination was described as an 'unplanned accident' resulting, in Promfred's words, from 'a fit of absence of mind'.[22] As Waites argues, the GMP produced disorderly economic relations with non-EC Mediterranean members, offering incremental adjustments to trade and aid.[23] Like most other analysts at the time, Schlaim and Yannopoulos accepted that such an approach lacked internal coherence:

> Given the stakes involved and the existence of unique conditions for regional co-operation, the apparently random and almost absent-minded manner in which the

> Community's policy toward the Mediterranean evolved is most striking. Indeed, the importance of these problems was almost matched by the incoherence of the policies.[24]

The Community established trade restrictions with a view to protecting its sensitive sectors, mainly textiles and agricultural products, thus breaking its previous promises. As a result, it lost some of its credibility to its Mediterranean partners. The GMP posed a serious dilemma to all southern European states: although the Mediterranean region represents an essential market for their industrial products, it is also a competitive market for specific agricultural and textile products. Changes in the Community's Mediterranean policy, especially after its Iberian enlargement and the consequent reorientation of its geopolitics, raised the question not only of the relative success or failure of its previous and largely uncoordinated regime of bilateral (trade) relations, but of an appropriate policy design for a 'global' approach to emerge and bear fruits.[25]

In overall terms, the GMP has had a positive effect on non-EC Mediterranean countries, for it maintained their traditional exports to European markets, in part by increasing the level of regional economic interdependence. A fair line of criticism here is that such an approach was largely a codification of previous practices, rather than an attempt at institutionalising a comprehensive regime. In the 1970s, when Europe found itself in serious economic difficulties due to the successive oil crises and the collapse of the Bretton Woods system, it turned protectionist. This policy stance, combined with supply-side problems on the part of third Mediterranean countries, led to disgruntlement with the GMP.[26] As Duchene *et al.* point out, the Community's economic performance, far from sustaining growth as in the heady 1960s, had become constricted and a source of anxiety for development planners in the region.[27] In addition, the increasing overlap between political and economic interests in the management of European integration forced the Community to perceive the normalisation of its Mediterranean relations as an extension of its unification process.[28] But such a climate of optimism was soon shaken by the Middle East eruption, followed by the first oil crisis of 1973–4. In December 1973 the Arab states informed the Community that they wished to end their co-operation in all fields. The trade and aid agreements with the Maghreb and Mashreq countries had to be re-negotiated, and they also had to be subjected to non-tariff barriers (calendar restrictions and quotas) to take account of the Community's protectionist strategy in a period of global economic recession. However, trade and financial protocol agreements under the GMP were eventually concluded with these countries in 1976–7, while Association Agreements were signed with Cyprus and Malta in 1978–9.

In the first half of the 1980s, the Community operated through a system of import controls on sensitive agricultural products, following preparations for the entry of Greece, Spain and Portugal.[29] But their accession complicated the operational aspects of EC trade agreements with Mediterranean countries, whose products were subjected both to quotas and various other limitations, while less 'sensitive' products were subjected to reference quantities and to a system of minimum prices established under the protectionist regime of the Common Agricultural Policy (CAP).[30] These categories were measured in reference to Maghreb exports between 1980 and 1984 which, in the words of Joffé, 'were years of drought'![31] Products like olive oil, wine and some fruits were put under specific trade regimes. The third wave of trade and financial protocols with Mediterranean states (ECU 1.6 billion from 1986 to 1991) was designed to offer them the opportunity to enter into open competition with the newly admitted EC members.

The democratic transitions in Greece, Portugal and Spain in the mid-1970s following the collapse of the their respective dictatorial regimes, along with the rapid transformation of their economies,[32] paved the way for the Community's Mediterranean enlargement. This in itself made it imperative for the Community to further develop its Mediterranean policy, not least because the combined impact of the democratisation and accession of these countries to the Community changed the geopolitical map of the region. In Ginsberg's words: 'The EC scored a major political coup by helping stabilise nascent democracies in southern Europe through the lure of EC membership and the acceptance stamp of approval that membership entails.'[33] The Community thus grabbed the opportunity to make the point that it is not simply an 'economic confederation',[34] but also a political entity committed to democratic norms, principles and values.

Under the terms of the GMP, and after its successive Mediterranean enlargements, the Community somewhat consolidated its relations with third Mediterranean countries, by continuing to approach them on a unilateral basis. Even until the end of the 1980s, its Mediterranean policy followed the traditional pattern of combining trade concessions with financial co-operation, operating, in the words of the Commission, 'largely through conventional aid arrangements'.[35] Despite the Community's attempts to 'globalise' its Mediterranean policy and further the Euro-Arab dialogue, Euro-Mediterranean relations remained bilateral throughout the 1970s and 1980s. The institutionalisation of the Euro-Arab dialogue began prior to and continued after the 1973 crisis and, hence, the GMP did not result in the interruption of oil flows from the region; its motivation was primarily economic. Therefore, the global approach was less a response to growing European anxieties and more a reflection of an international economic environment deteriorating sufficiently rapidly as to have prompted a protectionist line. As Waites rightly points out, the co-ordination of the Community's Mediterranean agreements was a hesitant and haphazard process,[36] but the GMP and its subsequent adjustments 'were purposeful responses to EC requirements stemming from successive Community enlargements and evolving ambitions to have harmonious and beneficial relations with Non-Member Mediterranean states'.[37] Although considerably less than 'global' in both content and outlook, the GMP aimed at creating an industrial free trade area between the Community and those Mediterranean states that were not eligible for EC membership.[38]

The Renovated Mediterranean Policy (1989–95)

By the late 1980s the Community was firmly enough established as a collective entity to have formed an important part in the political and economic life of the Mediterranean.[39] But, despite some gradual improvements, the efficacy of its Mediterranean policy was still limited, with modest results in the economic performance and level of external protectionism of its Mediterranean neighbours. While its members remained reluctant to open their agricultural markets to external competition, the apparent lack of economic liberalisation in the southern Mediterranean countries prevented trade diversification from a north–south to a south–south scale to offset the structural deficit in trade. Moreover, the political dialogue foreseen by the Community's Mediterranean approach up to the late 1980s lacked a strategic vision – i.e. it failed to perceive the Mediterranean as a single space – crafting, instead, distinct approaches for the Maghreb, the Mashreq and other sub-regional groupings. It was largely against this background that the Community started to plan a substantial overhaul of its approach to post-Cold War Mediterranean reality.

The anxieties of the new era were reflected in demands for increased financial and political support from France, Spain and Italy towards the Middle East and North Africa (MENA), including Iran.[40] These southern European countries were most disturbed by post-1989 developments in the region. Although they initiated a number of multilateral schemes, in the end, they failed to deal with the complex challenges of the day.[41] As Tsardanides states, not only did such a diffused strategy prove ineffective,[42] but it caused considerable friction to other EC members. For instance, the joint Spanish–Italian proposal for a CSCM in 1990 – to parallel the CSCE project – was halted mainly due to French disagreements over which states should be included. Similar problems also obstructed the 'Five plus Five' initiative, which had not been intended to touch upon pressing eastern Mediterranean problems like the Greek–Turkish dispute.[43] More importantly, although these initiatives managed to foster some economic and political co-operation, they all failed to establish an efficient regional regime to accommodate, and even transcend, post-1989 international change. By the end of the Cold War, the whole range of Euro-Mediterranean relations was once more under scrutiny. The first attempt to assess the Community's Mediterranean policy came in 1990 with a Commission document addressed to the Council and the EP under the title 'Redirecting the Community's Mediterranean Policy'.[44] Apart from stressing the importance of the region's socio-economic development to European security, it focused on horizontal rather than strictly bilateral co-operation in transport, energy and telecommunications. In December 1990, the Rome European Council reviewed the Community's Mediterranean policy and proposed the intensification of Euro-Mediterranean relations through the RMP.

The Community was now forced to redirect its Mediterranean policy towards sustainable economic agreements, since, by that time, the countries of central and eastern Europe had already attracted the interest of northern EC members. Aiming at structural (horizontal) reform of the Mediterranean economy, the Community approved extra financial support, as the third in a series of five-year protocols was about to expire. The rationale behind the RMP was, in Weidenfeld's words,

> to back up the process of economic reform; to support private investment activity; to increase bilateral and Community financial aid; to maintain and improve access to the Community market; to integrate the Mediterranean countries in the Community's progress towards the single market; and finally, to strengthen where possible the economic and political dialogue at the regional level.[45]

Europe's southern and south-eastern regions were now to include the countries of the Gulf Co-operation Council (GCC),[46] for which new trade arrangements had been proposed, but were never finalised. This approach was closely linked to a 'policy of geographic proximity' through which the Community aspired to play a greater role in the transformations that were under way in its southern periphery. The 'global' approach was soon abandoned.[47]

The policy options facing the Community were either to allow for wider socio-economic gaps between itself and its Mediterranean neighbours, or to minimise the danger of instability on its proximity.[48] The rationale of the RMP was no longer reflective of past military or energy security threats, but rather of new anxieties that were mainly of a socio-economic nature.[49] Intra-regional income differences, currently standing at 1:12, would increase to 1:20 by 2010 without any measures to support the economic development of southern Mediterranean countries, whose population, at 220 million in 1995, will reach 300 million by 2010. Thus, the RMP provided a substantial increase in financial aid, including the introduction of finance for cross-border projects with particular reference to loans from the European Investment Bank (EIB). The size of the whole aid package amounted to ECU 4,405 million and was subdivided as follows:

- ECU 2,075 million for the fourth financial protocols (with Egypt, Morocco, Algeria, Tunisia, Syria, Jordan, Israel and Lebanon) which ran from 1 November 1991 to 31 October 1996; ECU 2030 million for more broadly based financial co-operation outside the protocols (including regional and environmental co-operation);
- and ECU 300 million to provide back-up for economic reform.[50]

Although the assistance offered by the Community increased considerably under the new financial framework and was geared towards structural adjustments, economic reform, health care and education, it remained inadequate relative to the financial needs of a heavily indebted south.[51]

A second Commission communication on future relations between the Community and the Maghreb followed in 1992.[52] It proposed that, on the expiration of the latest financial protocols, in 1996, a new regional framework with the littoral countries should be set up, leading to a 'Euro-Maghreb partnership' based on a free trade area. As Marks asserts, Europe's more dynamic contribution 'would be the opening up of the Maghreb's under-performing economies to its own competitive market'.[53] Indeed, the Community's long-term objective was now the acceleration of economic and social development in the once-neglected region of the Maghreb. The next step in the Community's RMP came with the Euro-Maghreb Document being agreed at the June 1992 Lisbon Summit. In that document the Community linked for the first time in explicit terms economic and financial issues with human rights and political liberalisation.[54] Under the new CFSP provisions, the Maghreb was now declared a geographical area of 'common interest'. Edwards and Philippart note that the importance of this linkage was that it presupposed a degree of consensus among southern and northern EU members on the overall lines of a Mediterranean policy (whose implementation now allowed for some majority voting as part of the CFSP).[55] Although limited to North African countries, the partnership proposals were extended and, as a result, the Mashreq was dealt with by two further Commission papers in 1993: the first envisaged regional co-operation and the creation of a free trade area; the second proposed the Community's reactivation within the multilateral efforts of the Middle East Peace Process.[56] Later in the same year, after an arduous ratification process, the Treaty on European Union came into effect and the EU continued to work on the basis of the guidelines agreed by the Lisbon Summit.

It should be recalled that during the two-year preparatory phase of the RMP, the Yugoslav Crisis had diverted the Community's attention. In addition, the difficulties in adopting a 'common' European foreign and security policy impacted negatively on the formulation of a new Mediterranean approach. It was around that time that EU policy makers discovered that the development of the CFSP was deviating from the Maastricht rhetoric. Also, the EU's approach to post-Communist central and eastern Europe offered the opportunity of a policy design that could form a useful analogy if applied to the Mediterranean. In the end, however, no such development occurred. Instead, the third enlargement of the EU, this time extended towards the EFTA countries, together with an earlier Community decision to support the reconstruction of the central and eastern European economies, created an imbalance in the EU's Mediterranean orientation. Against the background of these developments, the EU finally attempted to strike a balance between its growing interest in central and eastern Europe and the making of a more viable Mediterranean order.

In 1993 the EU's 'renewed' Mediterranean policy was hijacked by a wave of increased interest in the countries of former-Yugoslavia[57] and by new trends in the Arab–Israeli Peace Process that led to the endorsement of an agreement between Israel and the Palestinian Authority. Although the EU was represented at the signing ceremony of the latter agreement (on 13 November 1993 in Washington) by Commission President Delors and European Council President Claes, the major European participant in the peace negotiations was the Norwegian Foreign Minister. The EU was now able to upgrade its 1975 agreement with Israel.[58] The new objective was support for political dialogue, the expansion of the previous trade agreements and the development of closer co-operation in the areas of banking, research, technology, energy and industrial property. Also, in June 1993, the Commission delivered its opinion on the application of Cyprus and Malta for EU membership. Despite some obvious problems, a favourable view was taken on both accounts.[59] The June 1993 Copenhagen European Council welcomed the Commission's positive opinion and added an acknowledement of the need to develop closer relations with Turkey.[60] The Commission also promoted the idea of involving Israel with the Mashreq countries in a process of regional co-operation. The object was to underpin the Arab–Israeli Peace Process with the creation of a free trade area accompanied by more interactive patterns of institutionalised co-operation in the wider context of a triangular partnership between the Commission, Israel and the Mashreq. But it was the 1994 Corfu European Council that provided the initial impetus towards a new 'partnership' within the Mediterranean space. In this meeting, EU leaders asked the Commission to evaluate the existing Euro-Mediterranean policy and make proposals for its future evolution. The Commission responded to this request with its October 1994 and March 1995 proposals for a 'Euro-Mediterranean partnership' based on two overriding objectives: to underpin political reforms and secure human rights and freedom of expression; and to support economic and political reform with a view to boosting growth rates and, hence, living standards and employment. It also proposed to support programmes of economic transition towards a more equitable socio-economic regional space, including civil society formation. Later, at the Essen and Cannes European Councils, in December 1994 and June 1995 respectively, EU leaders endorsed these recommendations and increased the budget resources for the proposed partnership.

From a Mediterranean perspective, among the decisions taken at the Essen Summit the following are worth noting:

- a request on the part of the EU to speed up the pace of individual country partnership negotiations;
- the conclusion of negotiations with Turkey for a Customs Union; and
- a confirmation that 'the next phase of enlargement of the Union will involve Cyprus and Malta'.[61]

The EU, however, was rather puzzled as to the best course of action. Once again, a certain degree of tension arose out of the divergent interests of EU members regarding the form of support appropriate for their Mediterranean partners, with the northern EU states favouring trade concessions and the southern states being in favour of direct aid. At Essen, approval was also given to an ambitious plan proposed by the Commission for a Euro-Mediterranean Economic Area by the year 2010. Although this was patterned along the lines of the EEA, it was clear from the outset that southern Mediterranean countries were not to be considered for full EU membership. The Foreign Affairs Council met again on

18 July 1994 and requested the Commission to prepare a draft plan for strengthening the EU's Mediterranean policy. The Commission's response was a policy recommendation that constituted a milestone in Euro-Mediterranean relations. It is worth quoting at some length:

> Progress towards a Euro-Mediterranean zone of peace and stability would be initiated through close political dialogue based on respect for democracy, good governance and human rights. The dialogue should be extended to security issues, leading to the introduction of measures to consolidate peace. In the economic sphere the Community should promote, in the framework of the WTO, free trade with individual Mediterranean partner countries, which would require the countries to embark on a process of modernisation of their economies and increased competitiveness. This process would require a long transition and the willingness of the Community to offer help, particularly in terms of aid for structural adjustment and economic restructuring. In the long term, this would lead to the establishment of the largest free trade area in the world ... Beyond free trade, the Community should be prepared to enter into wide-ranging areas of co-operation with Mediterranean countries, to be defined jointly with them. These would cover industrial co-operation, energy, environment, information and communication technologies, service, capital, science and technology, decentralised co-operation, drug traffic, illegal immigration, tourism.[62]

At the same time, however, the EU continued to negotiate new bilateral agreements with Israel, Tunisia and Morocco. Arrangements with Israel proved difficult, despite the rather generous trade concessions by the EU on a number of products, and an agreement to allow Israel to participate in its Research and Development Programme.[63] The deal was complicated by Israel's request for a greater recognition of its role in the Middle East Peace Process and its dissatisfaction with EU project-funding action towards the Palestinian Authority.[64] These problems were further compounded when, in November 1994, the EU announced its decision to grant ECU 100 million in EIB loans to the Occupied Territories.

As far as EU–Turkish relations are concerned, they got off to an uncertain start in 1994.[65] In December 1995, a year after the EU Foreign Ministers decided to delay the Customs Union agreement, the EP gave its final approval. On 1 January 1996 Turkey joined the Customs Union, thus accepting EU trade-related legislation and a common external tariff. Turkey was to receive a total of ECU 355 million in financial aid and EIB loans, and ECU 1.5 billion in allowances for the assorted loss of custom taxes. The EU's anxiety to find an acceptable formula with Turkey owes much to the fact that, had it rejected the deal, the Islamic opposition parties in Turkey could have posed a serious challenge to the secular government of the day in the elections of December 1995.[66]

The last act of the previous phase of Euro-Mediterranean relations was played at the 1995 Cannes summit, concluding that 'the countries of the European Union and their Mediterranean partners must act together to a greater extent to ensure that the Mediterranean becomes, more so than at present, an area of exchange and dialogue guaranteeing peace, stability and the well-being of those who live around it'.[67] The latter objectives became the framework of the founding Euro-Mediterranean Conference that was held in Barcelona on 27–8 November 1995. Although the Cannes summit put together a rather modest financial budget for the southern Mediterranean partners,[68] it proved a difficult agreement as the credibility of the process was shaken by northern-led criticisms of the Franco-Spanish proposal to increase the aid package to ECU 5,500 million as compared to ECU 7,000 million for the reconstruction of the central and eastern European economies. Northern EU members preferred to stick to the old ratio of 5:1 in favour of the latter economies and only to trade concessions to southern Mediterranean countries. After strong Franco-Spanish pressures, the aid ratio was raised to 5:3.5.[69] With this in mind, we now turn to the structure and evolution of the Barcelona Process.

Notes

1 S. A. Al-Mani', *The Euro-Arab Dialogue: A Study in Associative Diplomacy* (London, Pinter, 1983), p. 82.

2 Protocols lasted for five-year periods and specified which sectors should receive aid. The first protocol period lasted until 1981, the second from 1981/82 to 1986 and the third from 1986/87 to 1991.

3 R. Pace, 'Peace, Stability, Security and Prosperity in the Mediterranean Region', in A. Bin (ed.), *Co-operation and Security in the Mediterranean* (Malta, MEDAC, 1996).

4 F. Serre, 'The Community's Mediterranean Policy After the Second Enlargement', *Journal of Common Market Studies* 19: 4 (1981) 377–87.

5 A major implication from this problematic transition to new multilateralism is that the Mediterranean is not yet able to generate a multilateral framework from within, but rather has to accept or reject frameworks proposed from extra-regional actors. See G. Luciani, 'Where to Start with Multilaterism – An Agenda for Cooperation Between Europe, the Middle East and North Africa', *Working Papers*, Research Group on European Affairs, University of Munich, August 1996.

6 See N. Waites, 'France and the Post-Colonial Mediterranean Region', *Occasional Papers*, 33, University of Reading, 1994.

7 R. H. Ginsberg, *Foreign Policy Actions of the European Community: The Politics of Scale* (London, Adamandine Press, 1989), p. 117.

8 *Ibid.*, p. 120.

9 W. Weidenfeld, *Challenges in the Mediterranean: The European Response* (Gutersloh, Bertelsman, 1991).

10 For example, when Morocco and Tunisia signed their first Association Agreements in 1969 their products were given preferential access to the European market. The market for industrial product imports into the European Economic Area was made almost totally open, which was not a major concession at the time given the nature of production in Morocco and Tunisia. Agriculture already represented the most contentious issue and the 1969 agreements gave preferential access to the Community only for certain Moroccan and Tunisian products. Algeria's agreement with the Community gave the country a duty-free access to the French market zone. It was not until January 1973, however, that Algeria was given the 'third country' management utilised by the Community, thus doing away with any preferential treatment.

11 L. Tsoukalis, 'The EEC and the Mediterranean: Is "Global" Policy a Misnomer', *International Affairs*, 53: 3 (1977), 425.

12 G. Vanhaeverbeke, 'Survey of Europe's Mediterranean Policy: Where it Comes From – Where it Stands Today – Where it Is Likely to Go', Euro-Med Training and Information Programme for Diplomats, Mediterranean Academy of Diplomatic Studies, University of Malta, 15–17 March 1997, p. 1.

13 The signatories of the Treaty of Rome mentioned the term 'relations with the Mediterranean'. In Article 237 EC, they declared their eagerness to conclude economic Association Agreements with Morocco and Tunisia, within the 'franc zone'. In Article 16 EC, they declared that the French colonial states were qualified to receive Community aid. It is worth mentioning here that in one of its communications the Commission unveiled the 'tentative' character of 'relations with the Mediterranean', but also referred to Article 16 EC as evidence of the Community's interest in the region. See European Commission, *The Europe–South Dialogue*, Brussels, 1988, p. 40.

14 E. Grilli, *The EC and Developing Countries* (Cambridge, Cambridge University Press, 1993), p. 198.

15. Tovias, 'The Mediterranean Challenge III: EEC Enlargement – the Southern Neighbours', *Sussex European Papers*, 5, European Research Centre, University of Sussex, 1979, p. 26.

16 M. Lister, *The European Community and the Developing World* (Aldershot, Avebury, 1988).

17 STABEX was the first north–south system to break the traditional commercial rules such as classic preferential agreements. This mechanism deals with agriculture, and covers a total of forty-nine agricultural and fishing products. Its purpose is to compensate by direct financial aid for losses of earning by ACP states. STABEX aid focuses on a small number of key products. Between 40 and 60 per cent of the funds are paid out in favour of a dozen products, including coffee, cocoa, cotton, tea, peanuts, oil-producing plants and bananas.

18 Following the example of STABEX, Lomé II created SYSMIN to take account of the difficulties of ACP countries dependent on earnings from mineral exports to the Community. The list of products (product groups) covered by this mechanism is limited to bauxite/aluminium, copper/cobalt, iron, tin, phosphates and manganese. Aid is granted to states requesting it as a special reimbursable loan if their financial dependence threshold in relation to the mineral exports concerned reaches at least 15 per cent (10 per cent for the LDC). Initially, SYSMIN aimed at re-establishing the economic viability of mining undertakings, normally in the public sector in situations of temporary crisis. Lomé IV enlarged and simplified its operation (a seventh product – uranium – was added to the restricted list), and henceforth aid was to be accorded in the form of grants. The fund is also better endowed: ECU 480 million as compared to ECU 253 million in the sixth European Development Fund. See European Commission, *EU–ACP Co-operation* (special issue), Directorate General for Development, Brussels, April 1994.

19 G. Edwards and Eric Philippart, '*Mare Nostrum* – the European Union and the Mediterranean in the 1990s and Beyond', paper presented at the Fifth Biennial ESCA–USA Conference, Seattle 29 May–1 June (1997), p. 4.

20 C. Tsardanides, *The Renewed Mediterranean Policy of the European Community and Greece* (in Greek) (Athens, Papazisis, 1992), p. 16.

21 F. Duchene *et al.*, *The European Community and the Mediterranean Basin*, Commission of the European Communities, Luxembourg (1984), p. 32.

22 R. Promfred, *The Mediterranean Policy of the European Community* (London, Macmillan, 1986), p. 18.

23 N. Waites, 'Dynamics of EU Mediterranean Policy', Paper presented at the ELIAMEP Halki International Seminar 'The European Union and the Mediterranean Region', Hel-

lenic Foundation for European and Foreign Policy, Halki Island, Greece, September 1996, p. 1.

24 A. Schlaim and G. N. Yannopoulos, 'Introduction', in A. Schlaim and G. N. Yannopoulos (eds), *The EEC and the Mediterranean Countries* (Cambridge, Cambridge University Press, 1976), p. 4.

25 R. Taylor, *Implications for the Southern Mediterranean Countries of the Second Enlargement of the European Community* (Brussels, Commission of the European Communities, 1980).

26 See Pace, 'Peace, Stability, Security'.

27 Duchene *et al.*, *The European Community*, p. 20.

28 European Commission, *The Europe–South Dialogue*, Brussels, 1988, p. 41.

29 The negotiations between the Community and the Greek Government were completed on 4 April 1979 and the Accession Treaty was signed in Athens on 28 May 1979, with Greece becoming the tenth member of the Community on 1 January 1981. The accession of Spain and Portugal completed the second Mediterranean enlargement of the Community in 1986.

30 Duchene, *et al.*, *The European Community*, p. 16.

31 G. Joffé, 'Integration or Peripheral Dependence: The Dilemma Facing the South Mediterranean States', Paper presented at the MEDAC Conference 'Prospects After Barcelona', Malta, March 1996.

32 L. Tsoukalis, *The European Community and its Mediterranean Enlargement* (London, George Allen & Unwin, 1981), p. 242.

33 Ginsberg, *Foreign Policy Action*, p. 124.

34 See M. Forsyth, *Unions of States: The Theory and Practice of Confederation* (Leicester, Leicester University Press, 1981).

35 Commission of the European Communities, Communication to the Council, *Strengthening the Mediterranean Policy of the European Union: Establishing A Euro-Mediterranean Partnership*, COM(94) 427 final, 19 October 1994, p. 20.

36 The conclusion of the Association Agreements within the GMP was prolonged due to the difficulty of reaching agreement among EC members and less because of the need to accommodate their interests with those of southern Mediterranean agricultural producers. N. Waites, *European Community Mediterranean Policy and Agricultural Problems of the Maghreb: A View from Northern Europe* (Reading, University of Reading, 1988), p. 1.

37 Waites, 'Dynamics of EU Mediterranean Policy', p. 1.

38 Edwards and Philippart, '*Mare Nostrum*', p. 4.

39 N. Waites and S. Stavridis, 'The European Union and the Mediterranean Member States', in S. Stavridis *et al.* (eds), *The Foreign Policies of the European Union's Mediterranean States and Applicant Countries in the 1990s* (London, Macmillan, 1999), p. 36.

40 J. Marks, 'High Hopes and Low Motives: The New Euro-Mediterranean Partnership Initiative', in *Mediterranean Politics*, 1: 1 (1996), 11.

41 For a detailed account of Mediterranean initiatives see S. C. Calleya, *Navigating Regional Dynamics in the Post-Cold War World: Patterns of Relations in the Mediterranean Area* (Dartmouth, Aldershot, 1997), pp. 141–57; and V. Y. Ghebali, 'Toward a Mediterranean Helsinki-Type Process', *Mediterranean Quarterly*, 4: 1 (1993), 92-101.

42 C. Tsardanides, 'The Southern EU Member States' Policy towards the Mediterranean: Regional or Global Co-operation', *Journal of Area Studies*, 9: 3 (1996), 53–69.

43 Tsardanides, *The Renewed Mediterranean Policy*, p. 94.

44 Commission document, SEC(90) 812, 1 June 1990.

45 Weidenfeld, *Challenges in the Mediterranean*, p. 26.

46 E. Rein, 'Agreement with the Gulf Cooperation Council: A Promising if Difficult Beginning', in Edwards and Regelsberger (eds), *Europe's Global Links: The European Community and Inter-Regional Cooperation* (London, Pinter, 1990), p. 112.

47 Weidenfeld, *Challenges in the Mediterranean*, p. 26.
48 European Community, *European Community and the Mediterranean*, Luxembourg, 1991, p. 6.
49 Vanhaeverbeke, 'Survey of Europe's Mediterranean Policy', p. 2.
50 European Community, *European Community and the Mediterranean*, p. 2.
51 Vanhaeverbeke, 'Survey of Europe's Mediterranean Policy', p. 3.
52 Commission document, SEC(92) 401, 30 April 1992.
53 Marks, 'High Hopes and Low Motives', p. 12.
54 T. Melasuo, 'The Mediterranean Revisited', *Research Report*, 57, TAPRI, 1994, 117.
55 Edwards and Philippart, '*Mare Nostrum*', p. 6.
56 Commission documents, SEC(93) 375, 8 September 1993, and SEC(93) 458, 29 September 1993.
57 For example, the Economic and Trade Co-operation Agreement between the EU and Slovenia came into force in September 1993. Once Slovenia had an agreement with the EU, the logical next phase would be an application for full membership. As for the other newly independent republics, the EU extended its injunction against Serbia (with the exemption of Greece) and Montenegro to include the Serb-occupied territories in Bosnia, raised some of its sanctions-related barriers on exports from Croatia and FYROM, and adjoined it in the list of PHARE recipients.
58 In the short term the EU was able to grant a further ECU 20 million to the Occupied Territories to help establish administrative structures in the Gaza Strip and Jericho (raising the total EU contribution to the Palestinian Authority in 1993 to circa ECU 90 million). At the macro-level, the Commission announced that it intended to grant the Occupied Territories ECU 500 million for the period 1994–98; half of this sum was to come from the EU's financial budget and the other half from long-term EIB loans.
59 See Official Journal of the European Communities, *The European Community and Economic Co-operation in the Middle East*, C73, Brussels, 15 March 1993; Commission of the European Communities, Communication to the Commission, *Future Relations and Co-operation Between the Community and the Middle East*, COM(93) 375 final, Brussels, 1993; and Commission of the European Communities, *EC Support to Middle East Peace Process*, COM(93) 458 final, Brussels, 1993.
60 Relations with Turkey were made more complex by Turkish concerns over the EU's fiasco to assist the Muslim populations in Bosnia and by EU concerns, expressed mainly by the EP, about the violation of human rights *vis-à-vis* the Kurds. In addition, the kidnapping of European tourists in Kurd-controlled areas became yet another thorny issue in EU–Turkish relations.
61 European Council at Essen, *Presidency Conclusions*, 9–10 December 1994, SN 300/94, p. 15.
62 See Commission of the European Communities, Communication to the Council, *Strengthening the Mediterranean Policy of the European Union.*
63 D. Allen and M. Smith, 'External Policy Developments', Annual Review of Activities, *Journal of Common Market Studies* (1995), 80.
64 The EU contributed ECU 500 million and technical assistance to the West Bank and Gaza for the period 1994–98 (mainly on health and education projects). Such aid came in addition to the annual support of ECU 30 million from the UN Relief and Works Agency (UNWRA) Convention.
65 UK and Germany opposed the Greek Presidency's proposals and paid a joint visit to Turkey to express their support for the Customs Union agreement. Relations were aggravated later in July by a decision of the European Court of Justice to block direct exports from the so-called 'Turkish Republic of Northern Cyprus' to the EU, but matters significantly worsened in 1995 when eight Turkish parliamentarians of Kurdish origin were imprisoned. After its rejection by the EP, and aware of a possible Greek veto, EU Foreign Ministers finally decided to suspend the Customs Union.

66 EU concerns about democratisation and human rights violations persist, as do anti-Western sentiments in large sections of Turkish society. The latter trend was confirmed in the 1995 elections, where the fundamentalists performed strongly despite the approval of the Customs Union. It is worth noting that the Greek Government's consent to the latter agreement came only after the EU had set a negotiations' agenda for Cyprus and Malta's accession. The EU was assured that the expectation of a Cypriot accession, along with the development of a working relationship with Turkey through the Customs Union, would help to break the protracted deadlock in inter-communal negotiations following the 1974 Turkish invasion.

67 European Council at Cannes, Presidency Conclusions, 26–7 June 1994, SN 211/95.

68 Between 1995 and 1999, ECU 4,700 million was topped up with EIB loans: ECU 2,100 million to support the creation of a Euro-Mediterranean free trade zone by 2010, to encourage European investment in the region, and to develop the private sector and the economic infrastructure of Mediterranean states; ECU 2,100 million to strengthen social equality; and ECU 500 million for regional integration projects.

69 E. Barbé, 'The Barcelona Conference: Launching Pad of a Process', *Mediterranean Politics*, 1: 1 (1996), 32.

4

The Barcelona Process: structure and evolution

Launching the partnership

On 27–8 November 1995, at the Conference in Barcelona organised by the Spanish Presidency of the EU, the European Commission, the Foreign Ministers of the fifteen EU member states and the twelve Mediterranean partners (Algeria, Morocco, Tunisia, Egypt, Israel, Jordan, Syria, Lebanon, Turkey, Palestinian Authority, Cyprus and Malta) reached a complex agreement designed to promote peace, stability and prosperity in the region. All of the southern EU states were particularly active, but at the supranational level it was the Commission that influenced the agenda, the EP having only limited agenda-setting powers.[1] It is worth noting that the EU's position at the Barcelona Conference was in marked contrast to the other states of the region, which lacked a common position.[2]

The political aims of the EMP were not extensively discussed, in order to avoid drawing attention to the democratic deficit in the Middle East.[3] 'For the moment, we provide the only forum where the Arab countries and Israel can sit together and discuss their different problems', said an EU diplomat, adding that 'there is great value in being able to do that'. Others, like Dumont, the Secretary-General of the Parliamentary Association for Euro-Arab Co-operation, were more critical: 'When you talk about issues like security, it makes no sense to leave out Libya.'[4] Libya was excluded from the Conference because of the UN sanctions over the Lockerbie affair. According to Köchler, 'this has unfortunately led to a situation in which the Maghreb "remains unintegrated and disintegrated when facing the European Union [and] the Barcelona process"'.[5] It is a well-established fact that the majority of EU members are in favour of normalising their relations with Libya, whose exclusion from the EMP is yet another proof of the overwhelming US influence on both regional and global EU policies, although during the preparation of the Conference the EU did all it could to prevent its transatlantic partner from participating. The USA saw the

EU's involvement in the region as a direct invasion by European diplomacy of an area firmly located within its traditional sphere of influence. But all the participants in Barcelona stressed that, while the new initiative was not to replace other regional projects, it would undoubtedly contribute to their success. In the end, no operational role was foreseen for the EMP in the ongoing Middle East Peace Process, although it was hoped that it could make a positive impact at a general economic level.

The founding Euro-Mediterranean Conference managed to bring Israeli and Syrian representatives to the same table, arguably something that had been inconceivable for any previous Mediterranean initiative. As was suggested at the time, the participation of the two Arab countries gave the meeting a degree of political legitimacy that the MENA did not seem to enjoy. A contributing factor was the euphoria that stemmed from the significant progress made in the Oslo peace talks during the Middle East multilateral negotiations.[6] In an atmosphere of 'high hopes and low motives',[7] the Barcelona Conference became the 'launching pad'[8] for a genuine regional process aimed at the preservation of peace and stability, the setting up of a shared zone of prosperity through the creation of a free trade area, and the promotion of structured dialogue among the distinct culturally defined and politically organised states and societies of the region. Although one could argue that the Barcelona Declaration does not in itself represent a historical turning point in Euro-Mediterranean relations – in so far as its main objective was not one of regional integration – it did introduce a new co-operative spirit in three areas: political and security; economic and financial; and socio-cultural. These fields were structured into three respective 'baskets', resembling the 1975 Helsinki Final Act. Much like the latter, the Barcelona Declaration contained a follow-up procedure, while it stated that the participants were 'resolved to establish a multilateral and lasting framework of relations based on a spirit of partnership, with due regard for the characteristics, values and distinguishing features peculiar to each of the participants'.[9]

The political basket

According to Jünemann, although the political basket specifies measures for enhancing regional peace and stability, 'it avoids concrete commitments in political and security co-operation' due to the divergence of interests between the EU and its southern Mediterranean partners.[10] Yet, all partners involved stressed their conviction that Mediterranean peace, stability and security are common assets that should be promoted and strengthened 'by all means at their disposal'. They have also agreed to respect human rights, fundamental freedoms, diversity, pluralism and the rule of law, recognising 'the right of each of them to choose and freely develop its own political, socio-cultural, economic and judicial system'. To that end, they agreed to conduct a political dialogue at regular intervals based on observance of the essential principles of international law and reaffirmed various common objectives in matters of internal and external stability.[11] In a declaration of principles, the partners undertook a range of commitments that, given Mediterranean complexity, seem far-reaching:

> To act in accordance with the United Nations Charter and the Universal Declaration of Human Rights, as well as other obligations under international law, in particular those arising out of regional and international instruments to which they are party;
>
> To develop the rule of law and democracy in their political systems, while recognising in this framework the right of each of them to choose and freely develop its own political, socio-cultural, economic and judicial system;
>
> To respect human rights and fundamental freedoms and guarantee the effective legitimate exercise of such rights and freedoms, including freedom of expression, freedom of association for peaceful purposes and freedom of thought, conscience and religion, both individually and together with other members of the same group, without any discrimination on grounds of race, nationality, language, religion or sex;
>
> To give favourable consideration, through dialogue between the parties, to exchanges of information on matters relating to human rights, fundamental freedoms, racism and xenophobia;
>
> To respect and ensure respect for diversity and pluralism in their societies, promote tolerance between different groups in society and combat manifestations of intolerance, racism and xenophobia. The participants stress the importance of proper education in the matter of human rights and fundamental freedoms;
>
> To respect their sovereign equality and all rights inherent in their sovereignty, and fulfil in good faith the obligations they have assumed under international law;
>
> To respect the equal rights of peoples and their right to self-determination, acting at all times in conformity with the purposes and principles of the Charter of the United Nations and with the relevant norms of international law, including those relating to territorial integrity of States, as reflected in agreements between relevant parties;
>
> To refrain, in accordance with the rules of international law, from any direct or indirect intervention in the internal affairs of another partner; respect the territorial integrity and unity of each of the other partners;
>
> To settle their disputes by peaceful means, call upon all participants to renounce recourse to the threat or use of force against the territorial integrity of another participant, including the acquisition of territory by force, and reaffirm the right to fully exercise sovereignty by legitimate means in accordance with the UN Charter and international law;
>
> To strengthen their cooperation in preventing and combating terrorism, in particular by ratifying and applying the international instruments they have signed, by acceding to such instruments and by taking any other appropriate measure;
>
> To fight together against the expansion and diversification of organized crime and combat the drugs problem in all its aspects;
>
> To promote regional security by acting, inter alia, in favour of nuclear, chemical and biological non-proliferation through adherence to and compliance with a combination of international and regional non-proliferation regimes, and arms control and disarmament agreements such as NPT, CWC, BWC, CTBT and/or regional arrangements such as weapons free zones including their verification regimes, as well as by fulfilling in good faith their commitments under arms control, disarmament and non-proliferation conventions.

> To pursue a mutually and effectively verifiable Middle East Zone free of weapons of mass destruction, nuclear, chemical and biological, and their delivery systems.[12]

Furthermore, within this first basket the participants considered practical steps to prevent the proliferation of nuclear, chemical and biological weapons, as well as the excessive accumulation of conventional arms in the region. They have also agreed to refrain from developing military capabilities beyond their legitimate defence requirements in an attempt to build mutual confidence. However, some southern European countries tried to ensure that the Barcelona Declaration would not venture into the deep Mediterranean waters of 'hard' security. Linked to that is the need to promote and sustain good-neighbourly relations. The basket also contained a mandate for a regional security arrangement to consider confidence and security-building measures (CSBMs) as means for the creation of an 'Area of Peace and Stability', including the long-term objective of adopting a Euro-Mediterranean Charter. Both France and Malta tabled proposals to that end during the Barcelona Conference.

The French proposal, by drawing from the Stability Pact as originated in the Balladur Plan and adopted as a Joint Action under the CFSP, sees the envisaged Charter as an exercise in preventive diplomacy, providing a framework for a political and security-related dialogue. The proposal does not represent an arrangement dealing with current conflicts in the region, but is rather the basis for a future regional security architecture: designed to promote voluntary and politically binding commitments, it did not foresee the creation of new mechanisms and institutions, but aimed to build on the experience of existing organisations. For its part, the Maltese proposal highlighted the need to create a pan-Mediterranean security system to promote regional political dialogue, including the creation of operational mechanisms for crisis management and conflict prevention. As Tanner observes, both proposals reflected the need to give a clearer framework of action to the ambitious objectives of the first basket.[13]

The political and security dialogue launched in Barcelona is one of the EMP's most promising elements, representing a new experiment in Euro-Mediterranean relations. As Aliboni asserts, the first basket is an innovative and light mechanism, in that it is not linked to specific objectives, but is instead directed to the broad task of political consultation.[14] But the envisaged security partnership is no easy task, for it has to reconcile long-term goals with the contingencies of everyday politics in a fragmented and volatile region.[15] Added to that, the EMP does not presently offer the institutions necessary to deal with regional complexity. Important problems remain like its 'EU-centric character' and the fact that it has not been endowed with its own Secretariat. Rather, it is the Commission that *de facto* performs that role. Besides, the Senior Officials' Committee is chaired by the EU Presidency itself. As Edwards and Philippart note, the non-institutionalisation of the dialogue among the Senior Officials 'has been surrounded by an air of deliberative vagueness, largely because of sensitivities created by the Arab–Israeli conflict and the peace process'.[16] Such arrangements exacerbate the southern partners' sense of estrangement from the EMP by confirming that it is less attuned to their security needs than it is to those of the EU.[17]

The Barcelona document sought to encourage the application of the principles of good governance – e.g., the encouragement of democratic values, respect for universal human rights norms etc. – and the promotion of collective security arrangements through partnership-building measures (PBMs). Although democratic principles are crucial to the Barcelona Process, PBMs have received greater attention.[18] But the complexity of protracted conflicts like the Arab–Israeli one, and the misperception of threats at both sides of the Mediterranean, constrain the implementation of PBMs in 'hard' security issues. The same goes for conflict-prevention mechanisms with a minimal capacity to intervene in real conflict situations. Thus, the 'confidence-building process of the Partnership and its attendant CBMs [confidence-building measures] must have a prevailingly non-military nature and, whenever related in some way to military factors, they must have a slowly- or non-evolutive character'.[19] To borrow again from Tanner: 'the only chance of the Mediterranean Pact to assume an effective role is to focus on soft security co-operation and to pursue an incremental policy of crisis prevention that is closely linked to the economic Euro-Med partnership'.[20] As Echeverria argues, however, the principle that the EMP is indivisible – i.e. a full partnership – constitutes a CBM in itself, since recognition of parity has never existed among the partners.[21]

The economic basket

The economic and financial basket of the Barcelona Declaration was the most detailed basket of the Barcelona document. In it, the partners fixed three long-term objectives:

- to speed sustainable social and economic development;
- to improve living conditions by increasing employment and closing the development gap in the region; and
- to promote co-operation and regional integration.

But the major issue agreed by the partners was to set up a target date for the establishment of the Mediterranean Free Trade Area (MEFTA) by the year 2010.[22] The latter objective, which was considered as the main drive of the EU's initiative, is to be achieved through a process of economic transition and financial assistance from the EU to relieve the southern Mediterranean countries of their debt burden and to develop the private sectors. The document also called for the liberalisation of manufactured products through the elimination of quantitative and qualitative trade barriers. Such a liberalisation strategy is expected to lead to an increased awareness of market potential among the partners.

The MEFTA is not an end in itself, but rather a means intended to diminish socio-economic disparities, promote regional co-operation, accelerate sustainable development and facilitate the integration of southern Mediterranean economies into the global economy. In an attempt to reduce the socio-economic gap between the two Mediterranean shores, Commission proposals included the improvement of social services, especially in urban areas, the harmonious development of rural areas, the development of fisheries and environmental protection. In the same context, the Commission will take steps to the development of human resources. One of the key issues here is technical assistance to reduce illegal immigration. The Commission also intends to offer its expertise to combat the new forms of insecurity, most notably drug trafficking, terrorism and international crime. With regard to regional integration, the Commission promised to supply appropriate technical assistance for the creation of co-operative structures and to finance the development of infrastructures for increased intra-regional trade, especially in transportation, communications and energy.

The economic rationale behind the MEFTA, which, once in place, will consist of approximately 700 million people, is relatively easy to state: the EU, a large unit of some 400 million inhabitants, can only progress and prosper within a stable Euro-Mediterranean space, within which prosperity can be shared. Southern Mediterranean countries are in urgent need of substantial institutional policy reforms and public capital flows to boost their economic performance at both regional and world levels. In that respect, integration is imperative for these counties to face the challenges of globalisation. But an obvious asymmetry exists between EU policies towards central and eastern Europe and toward the Mediterranean, where sub-regional integration and intra-regional co-operation depend not only on the success of structural economic reforms and asserted socio-economic adjustments, but on the development of the Arab–Israeli peace negotiations. At the same time, however, the southern Mediterranean states have been engaged in a sensitive but necessary process of domestic political reform.

It was also agreed that the EU would negotiate with most Mediterranean partners new Association Agreements with a view to establishing, albeit on a bilateral basis, an industrial free trade area within a time-specific framework. The rationale underlying such an objective is the need to improve the synergy of economic competition across the Euro-Mediterranean space. This is why Jünemann has claimed that the notion of multilateralism in the Barcelona Declaration was merely added to the traditional 'bilateral concept' of Euro-Mediterranean relations.[23] As Minasi has put it:

> the new system is not really *multilateral*, rather it is *bi-multilateral*, whereas it is negotiated between a multilateral entity – the EU – and single partner countries, encouraging fragmentation. Considering that trade among partner countries is a mere 5% of their total external trade, the unusual fact is going to happen that there will be a free trade area based on bilateral rather than multilateral exchanges, and where intense North–South exchanges are not matched by relevant South–South trade.[24]

According to the Declaration, trade in agriculture will be liberalised only 'as far as the various agricultural policies allow'. In practical terms, this means that real free trade in the region might have to wait until the EU reforms its largely protectionist and cash-draining CAP system of domestic subsidies. As Tsoukalis highlights, 'free access to industrial exports does not mean a great deal if there is little to export, as it is the case for most of the Mediterranean partners'.[25] This view is fully in accord with Wolf's depiction of the EU's approach to Euro-Mediterranean economic integration as 'Janus-faced', for it combines 'liberalism within and mercantilism without'.[26]

The two key components of the new Association Agreements are the gradual introduction of free trade in the remarkably short period of fifteen years (in order to hasten the growth of competitiveness), and the parallel financial and technical support necessary to economic reform (as means towards institutional and policy reform). The point here is that the twelve non-EU Mediterranean countries should not be left alone to deal with the consequences of the envisaged regional economic transformation. Flexible patterns of economic support are available from the EU, in what is often referred to as 'the tool box approach'. By this is meant that there is no compulsion to use all of the policy instruments, but only those that are thought to be best suited to a country's needs.[27] The year 2010 was decided upon for the completion of such individual free trade agreements. Each Association Agreement is a specific case, and thus individual timetables leading to free trade should not, for the purpose of being accepted by the WTO (an absolute requirement on the part of the EU), exceed twelve years. Thus, complete free trade will only be achieved when the last transitional period of the last agreement to have come into force is terminated. By that time, however, trade barriers among the twelve southern Mediterranean partners would make no sense and a strong incentive would have been established among them for direct free trade arrangements.

Due to the considerable economic strains of meeting the MEFTA objective,[28] the southern Mediterranean economies would have to undergo a lengthy transition period. Any partner entering this process will have to deal with the necessary fiscal reforms (less revenue from tariff duties and more from related value-added taxes), the need for a strong economic environment conducive to private investment (a functioning financial sector, an adequate legislative environment for business, a proper judicial system as well as patent laws), and the need for an efficient class of entrepreneurs and businesses (given the quality requirements and the competitiveness of the European market).[29] These countries will have to create a leaner and more efficient state so that they are able to deal promptly with the kinds of social requirements characteristic of any modern polity. This means that some inefficient public sectors should be restructured or even phased out. Similarly, their agricultural sectors would have to undergo some serious restructuring, not least in order to comply with the EU's quality standards like product quality, packaging norms, etc.

The regulatory package of the MEFTA implies that the partners have to make a pragmatic judgement whether the benefits in the short and medium term outweigh the drawbacks, and whether their future option is to remain free from collective market regulation or, conversely, to participate in the making of a regional trading space.[30] In a 1997 EuroMeSCo report it was predicted that the medium- and long-term effects of creating the MEFTA would be positive, as they will trigger economic growth and active integration into the international trade system, thus boosting the job market. In the short term, however, measures to lower the social cost of the transition period will have to be taken. The general conclusion is that, without substantive measures, the creation of the MEFTA will have adverse short-term effects on the states' budgets and their social situation, due to the immediacy of adjustment costs.[31] Although the MEFTA objective has been largely conceived without fully considering its long-term socio-economic consequences, and although it presently restricts free trade to specific products, it may well encourage growth on both shores of the Mediterranean, provided that the EU is adequately involved in the funding of structural change in the south, and that the partner countries agree to improve their domestic policies and to integrate their economies reciprocally.[32] In line with the above Khader claims that the economic basket makes the EMP's success an absolute necessity, otherwise the southern Mediterranean partners will either be left in economic isolation and impoverishment, or have to struggle in a disorganised way with savage economic restructuring.[33]

Overall European support for economic transition currently represents an active pipeline of over ECU 650 million, to which should be added the loans secured by the EIB. On an average-commitment basis, EU finance in the Mediterranean amounts to ECU 1,700 million per year from the Community budget and the EIB's resources. The MEDA programme is the principal EU financial instrument for the implementation of the EMP.[34] It accounts for ECU 3,424.5 million out of a total ECU 4,685 million for the period 1995–99. Webb defines the funding priorities for the MEDA programme as follows:

- support to economic transition (to prepare for the implementation of free trade by increasing competitiveness so as to achieve sustainable economic growth through the development of the private sector);
- strengthening the socio-economic balance (to alleviate the short-term costs of economic transition through appropriate measures in the field of social policy; and
- regional co-operation (to complement existing bilateral activities through measures to increase exchanges at regional level).

The economic agenda, particularly the MEFTA objective, poses serious challenges to the southern Mediterranean partners, for it will expose them to EU standards of competition without providing any additional significant market. As Aliboni has put it, 'one may wonder why they accepted it'. The answer is threefold.

1 Forces of both globalisation and liberalisation of the world economy today confront all countries in an organised and orderly manner. In the age of

'casino capitalism', sound macro-economic policies and industrial competitiveness are the factors that most determine the overall performance, economic or otherwise, of any country.[35] These are issues that the Mediterranean countries would have to come to terms with irrespective of the EMP.

2 If any Mediterranean partner wishes to reinforce its economic strength, mobilise national savings and attract foreign investment and technological know-how then it must prepare itself for tough competition with other parts of the globe that also aim at a better share of the European market. To compete, the Mediterranean states must implement far-reaching liberalisation, privatisation and deregulation.[36]

3 Any littoral state which accepts that some form of institutional and policy reform is necessary, will be well advised to do so with the assistance of the EU that already constitutes its major economic partner, rather than by itself in an uncontrolled manner burdened by additional external economic constraints.

The socio-cultural basket

Anne-Charlotte Bournoville, the Commission official in charge of culture, audio-visual and information within the EMP, described the nature of the third basket thus:

> although the Mediterranean's foremost product over thousands of years has been culture, cultural co-operation at Euro-Mediterranean level was a ground-breaker for the Barcelona Conference. Therefore, the fact that culture was included among the areas of co-operation is a mini-revolution in itself. In practice, this means that in 1995 people were not used to working together at the Euro-Mediterranean level and there was little experience at the Community level of dealing with issues of this nature.[37]

The aim of the socio-cultural basket is wide-ranging and ambitious, granting non-governmental organisations (NGOs) and civil society representatives a significant role in EMP affairs. As Colas has argued: 'The incorporation of civil society into the Barcelona process is a clear case of international regime formation, which seeks to respond to changes of intergovernmental elitism.'[38] Linkages and networks between civil societies on both Mediterranean shores may lay the foundation for knowledge, understanding and mutual confidence, which are vital for the construction of a common Euro-Mediterranean space. Co-operation among northern and southern Mediterranean civil societies should not take the form of assistance or the imposition of the Western model. Rather, it should incorporate the component civil societies in political decision making and also take into account their respective particularities.

The Barcelona Declaration underlined that 'the reinforcement of democracy and respect for human rights are indeed the essential elements of the entire project. But co-operation in these areas is also the most sensitive dimension of the partnership, not least because the debate on democracy and human rights in the Mediterranean, among other principles that fall within the wider remit of good governance, is linked to the debate on identity and civilisational interaction. Certain sectors of North African and Middle Eastern public opinion suspect that the West wants to impose on them its civilisation and hegemony under the guise of universal democratic principles, while in the North, in parallel to the rise of racism and xenophobia, the preconceived idea that there is an intrinsic incompatibility between Islam and democracy has developed at both grassroots and elite levels.[39] As Fahmy points out, potential differences may emerge in the various conceptions of democracy and human rights, and the only way for their resolution is through a cultural dialogue to reconcile the contending interpretations.[40] The EMP aims to bring the peoples of Europe and the Mediterranean closer, to promote shared understandings, to eliminate discomforting stereotypes and to project positive images. Arguably, such a 'pro-active' approach challenges the Islamophobic 'clash of civilisations' thesis. The means for bringing the partners closer together with a view to creating a 'new cultural order'[41] rest on an inter-cultural hermeneutical dialogue in a wide range of areas like cultural heritage, media, inter-faith communication, etc.

The third basket highlights common roots (as part of a common experience), as well as Mediterranean cultural diversity, doing away with negative preconceptions. But building the cultural partnership is a delicate process due to the difficulties involved in sustaining a constructive dialogue among different civilisations, especially if such dialogue aims at transcending images from the region's colonial past, feelings of intolerance and xenophobia, as well as a narrow view of national identity. An additional obstacle may be that any cultural dialogue implies an openness to cultural exchange and mobility that is not always easy to achieve in the southern rim. In light of the above, what is needed is a new hermeneutics of north–south perceptions together with the inclusion of religious and cultural rights in the debate on democracy and modernity. Although the socio-cultural dimension is often projected as being of secondary importance to the politico-economic dimensions of the EMP, the view taken here is that it is potentially the most revolutionary outcome of the regional process. It is a recognition that trade, investment and economic assistance are part of an evolutionary and purposeful process that incorporates a substantive human dimension. After making obligatory references to 'dialogue and respect among cultures and religions' as 'a necessary precondition for bringing peoples closer', the socio-cultural basket goes on to identify the need for a programme of human exchanges between the two Mediterranean shores, while including the utilisation and development of human resources in the region. In addition, it touches upon the sensitive issues of illegal immigration,[42] organised crime and drugs trafficking, and on co-operation between local government authorities, trade unions, interest associations, as well as public and private companies. Finally, the Declaration recognises the future challenges posed by demographic trends in the southern Mediterranean and declares that these trends should be counterbalanced by appropriate policy measures to advance social and economic development.

The follow-up mechanism

The Barcelona Declaration includes an appendix that offers a follow-up procedure, in various sectors and at different levels, for implementation purposes. Progress towards its declared aims, and the definition of new aims and activities, are governed by the annual meetings of Foreign Affairs Ministers. The Barcelona Process also consists of Ad Hoc Ministerial Conferences for different portfolios (industry, energy, etc.) and thematic fields (the information society, local management of water, etc.). Conferences are also arranged on an ad hoc basis for senior officials, experts, civil society agents and parliamentarians. A Euro-Mediterranean Committee was thus set up, consisting of officials from the EU Troika (the previous, current and next Council Presidencies) and of representatives of all southern Mediterranean states. The Committee should meet regularly and report to the Foreign Affairs Ministers who are also to meet periodically to review progress on the implementation of agreed principles and to reach consensus on actions that would promote the objectives of the EMP. As Waites and Stavridis put it: 'This was a substantial advance on earlier experiments in Mediterranean cooperation which had little follow up and depended for progress on constant ministerial action.'[43] But as Edwards and Philippart rightly point out, no 'Barcelona Secretariat' as such was established. They explain:

> The Barcelona Declaration designated 'the Commission departments' to undertake the 'appropriate' preparatory and follow-up work for meetings resulting from the Barcelona Work Programme and from the conclusions of the Euro-Med Committee – a somewhat odd designation given the fairly general use of the term directorates-general and even, perhaps, suggestive of a degree of fragmentation or segmentation within the Commission.[44]

The inclusion of a follow-up procedure provides assurance for the 'continuity' of the process, so positioning the partnership that it can be considered a pragmatic mechanism for co-operation. But both structural and institutional analyses of its decision-making procedures lead to an important conclusion: the term 'partnership' does not reflect the substance of the actual Euro-Mediterranean relationship. Aliboni makes the point well by claiming that the EMP is not really a partnership among equals, but is rather the aggregation of the non-EU Mediterranean partners to the EU's institutions of political co-operation in a satellite status.[45] Or, as Monar argues, the EMP suffers from the gap that exists between its potential to act and its actual performance, and this is explained in part by the particular institutional and procedural constraints of the EU's '"dual" system of foreign affairs'.[46] But let us now examine the evolution of the Barcelona Process and its uneasy relationship with the Middle East Peace Process.

The evolution of the Barcelona Process

Within the Work Programme of the Barcelona Declaration it was decided that the Senior Officials would meet periodically, starting with the first quarter of 1996, to conduct a political and security dialogue, and to examine appropriate means for implementing the Barcelona principles. In this context, five meetings were held in 1996. Although the results were somewhat weak, *grosso modo*, progress was steady despite numerous political problems, especially in the Middle East Peace Process. Progress was achieved in three areas, where the Senior Officials decided to set up:

- a list of PBMs such as the network of foreign policy institutes (EuroMeSco),[47] and a mechanism for co-operation in the event of natural and human disasters;[48]
- a regularly updated Action Plan as a blueprint for the group's work, covering six sectors of activity: strengthening democracy, preventive diplomacy, security and CBMs, disarmament, terrorism and organised crime; and
- a Euro-Mediterranean Charter for Peace and Stability to serve as an institutional mechanism for dialogue and crisis prevention, and to enhance co-operation in the political basket.[49]

But as EuroMeSco itself recognised, for these tasks to be accomplished, efficient decision-making mechanisms are needed.[50]

In its communication to the Council and the EP, the Commission indicated the priorities of the Second Euro-Mediterranean Conference of Foreign Ministers, to take place in 1997. After reviewing the first fifteen months of the EMP and the state of negotiations in the Association Agreements with the twelve Mediterranean partners, the Commission suggested several objectives for future co-operation.[51] More specifically, it proposed a Euro-Mediterranean Charter for Peace and Stability to endorse the achievements of the political and security dialogue, while on the economic and financial front it considered measures to encourage free trade. On the question of socio-cultural affairs, the Commission reported that efforts had already begun in the spheres of cultural heritage, promotion of human rights, education and dialogue among civil societies, and that these efforts should be further intensified along with the introduction of measures to combat drug trafficking and organised crime.

After the Barcelona Declaration, the whole process moved forward by a series of new Euro-Mediterranean Association Agreements that updated and enhanced the previous bilateral arrangements under the GMP and the RMP. In addition to the Customs Union with Turkey, new Association Agreements were signed with Jordan, Israel, the Palestinian Authority, Morocco and Tunisia,[52] while close to completion were agreements with Egypt and Algeria. Licari argues that 'the agreements are likely to need a serious reappraisal by the fourth or fifth year of their life'; otherwise, 'two-way trade will probably increase to the EU's advantage'.[53] But these were not genuine free trade area agreements of the kind enjoyed by Israel or Turkey, nor did they resemble the common economic space arrangements of the EFTA countries. Also, the idea of using the Barcelona Process as a springboard for strengthening co-operation among the southern partners did not prove particularly profitable, mainly due to the deterioration of Arab–Israeli relations and the upheaval among the Arabs following Netanyahu's election in June 1996. To increase external pressure on Israel and the US, some Arab states, in a manner reminiscent of the Euro-Arab dialogue, have pushed during the Malta Conference for a European track of the Middle East Peace Process.

Although a certain commonality of interests exists between Europe and the US, the Middle East Peace Process and the Barcelona Process can be interpreted as competitive projects.[54] The exclusion of the US from the EMP, thus giving the EU a predominant role in the Barcelona Process, prompted Washington to consider the EU's initiative as irrelevant in the construction of regional peace in the Middle East. Accordingly, US policy makers placed their trust in the Middle East Peace Process – as initiated in Madrid in 1991 and as modified by the Oslo Accords in 1993 – and in the concomitant Middle East and North Africa economic summit process that begun in Rabat in 1994.[55] But keeping the US out of the EMP was of importance, given the previous experience of containing the US presence in Europe (e.g., Bosnia).[56] On the other hand, this mutual exclusion between the transatlantic partners may be regarded as a potentially significant problem that can obstruct the Barcelona Process from bearing full fruit. This is clearly reflected in the negative results of the 1997 Malta Review Ministerial Conference, illustrating the existence of a causal relationship between progress in the Barcelona Process and the Middle East Peace Process. It was the task of the Malta Conference, coming as it did at a most critical phase in Middle East politics, to sustain the political dynamic of the partnership. As Tanner records, however, such hopes were dashed by the Arab–Israeli disagreement, to an extent that prevented the Malta Conference from adopting a concluding document.[57] Senior Officials agreed to meet in Brussels in early May 1997 to put together a text whose content had little relevance to the reality of what had actually occurred in Malta.

The main task of the Second Euro-Mediterranean Ministerial Conference in Malta was to elaborate more specifically on the implementation of the partnership programme and to set up short-term action plans for the advancement of tangible co-operative ventures. Its results provided, in Calleya's words, a 'reality check' on what had been the main issues at stake in the first two years of the Barcelona Process.[58] Apart from the problems relating to the Middle East Peace Process, the Malta Conference revealed some difficulties in the economic dimension of the partnership. So far, the economic basket has shown mixed results, some of which – 'more by accident than by design' – allow for some degree of optimism. All in all, the proposed new agreements were hardly as generous or as optimistic as the Barcelona Declaration had implied.[59] The Turkish Foreign Minister stayed away from the Malta Conference due to the EU's apparent inability to disburse the $500 million pledged to Turkey under the

Customs Union agreement, while Egypt's Foreign Minister publicly announced his frustration regarding the protracted negotiations with Brussels on the Association Agreement.[60]

The Malta *communiqué* reported serious disagreements over language used in referring to human rights, and referred only *in passu* to 'the rule of law, democracy and human rights' as commonly shared objectives. During 1997, many EU governments took up ratification of the new Euro-Mediterranean Association Agreements that the EU had earlier initiated with Tunisia, Israel and Morocco. During the ratification process, parliamentarians and others raised questions of human rights compliance, particularly with reference to Israel, as specified in Article 2 of the Agreements. Several EU governments indicated that they would seek to have the Commission set up a human rights monitoring mechanism as part of the implementation process. But no EU member demanded human rights' improvements of Israel, Tunisia or Morocco as a condition for ratifying the respective Association Agreements. In 1997 the EU signed an interim Association Agreement with the Palestinian Authority and was scheduled to sign one with Jordan in November of the same year. Negotiations continued with Egypt and Algeria. As EU and Syrian officials were about to open negotiations, the Council of Ministers continued to suppress a November 1995 report on human rights in Syria that the EP had mandated as prerequisite for economic assistance.

At the top of the agenda in Malta was the endorsement of a Euro-Mediterranean Charter. But, as Calleya notes, the Malta Declaration indicates that very little has been achieved to that end.[61] Equally important was the need for a renewed commitment to ensure a close balance between the three baskets, although some partners felt that progress in the political basket was overtaking progress in the remaining two. The Malta Conclusions partially redressed this imbalance, by indirectly slowing down progress on the first basket.[62] The vagueness of the Conclusions was indicative of the lack of progress in the creation of a region-wide security arrangement.[63] Joffé argues that both the French and the Maltese proposals raised Arab suspicions of European hegemony, and at the Malta Review Conference both were pushed aside by EU attempts to rescue the Middle East Peace Process.[64] In general, the Malta Conference was unsuccessful in revitalising the latter process and in reviewing progress in the implementation of the Barcelona provisions. But at a rhetoric level, the First Euro-Mediterranean Review Conference stressed that the EMP is an 'irreversible process', albeit not particularly well equipped to confront the challenges of a turbulent region. The disappearance of both the MENA summits and the multilateral component of the Middle East Peace Process left the Barcelona Process as the only vehicle for economic development in the southern Mediterranean, whatever regional security structure was to emerge.[65]

After the Malta Conference, the atmosphere continued to deteriorate with an unsuccessful attempt to hold a meeting on terrorism and a last-minute cancellation by Morocco under Syrian pressure of the Industrial Ministers' meeting that was to be held in Rabat in October 1997.[66] As the Palermo meeting approached, the deadlock in the Oslo Process intensified, fuelling debate about a perceived 'contamination' of the Barcelona Process by US initiatives, as well as the possibility of a corresponding boycott by most Arab countries. But in the June 1998 Ad Hoc Ministerial Meeting in Palermo, Arab–Israeli co-operation managed to keep the temperature low on first-basket issues, thus setting the scene for a constructive discussion of the two remaining baskets. In the Concluding Document the participants

> reaffirmed their commitment to the Partnership, to which all Partners continue to attach the highest importance;
>
> reviewed the substantive results already achieved;
>
> improved their understanding of the reasons why progress in some areas
>
> has been less rapid than in others;
>
> agreed on broad priorities for the year ahead;
>
> stressed their desire to work for a successful third Euro-Mediterranean Ministerial Conference in Stuttgart in April 1999.[67]

The partners also confirmed their shared commitment to work on issues of substance, including the objective of 'global stability' and the increased importance of developing common perceptions on matters that may endanger progress in the Barcelona Process. Such an attitude was expected to contribute to the drafting and adoption of a Euro-Mediterranean Charter for Peace and Stability as foreseen in the Barcelona Declaration. Senior Officials were once again assigned the task of taking this matter forward by means of special Ad Hoc Meetings. In particular, their task was to achieve progress on this issue before the next meeting, in Stuttgart the following year.

At the Experts' Meeting on the Euro-Mediterranean Economic Area in Brussels on 27–8 April 1998 it was confirmed that the MEFTA would comprise three elements: establishment of free trade; reforms towards economic transition; and action to encourage private investment. It was agreed that support from the MEDA framework should be diversified and focus on institutional and policy reforms on a range of instruments to address the partners' specific needs, with local and international financial markets as the main source of capital.[68] In addition, the thematic sessions of the Experts' Meeting focused on the different aspects of the economic basket. The key message was that free trade would not be pursued on its own: it would be accompanied by supporting measures. On the establishment of free trade, the southern Mediterranean partners were critical of the fact that free trade was not envisaged in agriculture, given the latter's relative importance to their socio-economic structures. They even questioned whether it was at all appropriate to use the term 'free trade',[69] despite the EU's promise to reconsider its agricultural policy after the year 2005. Once again, the Experts' Meeting in Brussels underlined the need for integration among southern Mediterranean partners in view of the MEFTA objective.

Cultural relations and mutual understanding have been subject to extensive scrutiny due to the absence of any visible progress in this field since the signing of the Barcelona Declaration.[70] In this context, however, it is fair to suggest that, post-1995, there has been a strongly stated political commitment to place the socio-cultural dimension on an equal footing with the other two.[71] The 1998 Rhodes Ministerial Conference confirmed the priorities of the cultural partnership. This strategy, outlined also in Stockholm and Palermo, is based on three pillars:

- focusing activities on a small number of thematic framework programmes (heritage, audio-visual and humanities);
- increasing public involvement (particularly by women and young people); and
- encouraging the establishment of networks of cultural operators at the regional level to foster exchanges of experience and further develop joint endeavours.

The Barcelona Declaration was adopted after the signing of the Oslo Accords, and it was agreed that the EMP would not intrude on other peace processes in the region, but would contribute to them. By the end of the 1990s, however, a very different political atmosphere started to prevail in the Middle East. The Third Euro-Mediterranean Ministerial Conference in Stuttgart was crucial, for it was held three weeks before the end of the five-year period of the Oslo Accords. At the Berlin European Council on 24–5 March 1999, EU leaders remained concerned at 'the current deadlock in the Middle East' and called for 'an early resumption of negotiations on an accelerated basis'. Three weeks later in Stuttgart, the partners reiterated their firm commitment to the realisation of a just, comprehensive and lasting peace in the Middle East based on faithful implementation of the UN Security Council Resolutions 242 and 338 and the terms of reference of the Madrid Peace Conference, the Oslo Accords and the Wye River Memorandum.[72] Furthermore, the 1999 EuroMeSCo report concluded that negotiations on the Euro-Mediterranean Charter for Peace and Stability had failed

> because the priorities and contents assumed by the Political and Security Partnership are incongruous with respect to objective political conditions; and also because the organisational and institutional structure of the EMP itself is unbalanced, thus preventing the 12 Mediterranean partners from being fully and more actively involved. For the Charter to become acceptable, the security and political dimension of EMP must take Mediterranean diversities into consideration and be re-set accordingly. This would concern two main aspects: the structure of political dialogue and decision-making, and the objectives or contents of the Partnership.[73]

The Stuttgart Conference demonstrated that, 'three and half years after the inaugural conference in Barcelona, the EMP has developed considerably and has given clear proof of its viability in sometimes complex circumstances'.[74] The main aim of the Conference was to provide additional impetus to the EMP and more clearly confirm the goals set out in the Barcelona Declaration. The participants recalled the priority accorded in the EMP for the protection and promotion of human rights and agreed to focus their action on priority areas, increase the involvement of actors outside central government and make the EMP more 'action-oriented' and 'visible'. They also emphasised the need for intra-regional and sub-regional co- operation in all baskets, endorsing the guidelines set out at the 1999 Valencia Conference on future co-operative arrangements, and calling for a 'systematic evaluation' of the Barcelona Process and for a 'concrete follow-up'.[75]

Having looked at the patterns of interaction that characterise the evolving Euro-Mediterranean process and the extent to which the latter represents a break with pre-1995 European policies towards the region, let us move on to the theoretical study of the EMP with a view to capturing the nature of its emerging governance structures and the prospects for its qualitative transformation 'from policy to regime'.

Notes

1 A. Jünemann, 'Europe's Interrelations with North Africa in the New Framework of Euro-Mediterranean Partnership – A Provisional Assessment of the Barcelona Concept', in *Conference Proceedings: The European Union in a Changing World*, Brussels, 1998, p. 365.

2 R. Whitman, 'The EU and the Mediterranean: Looking Towards the Millennium', *CMS Occasional Papers*, 18, Centre for Mediterranean Studies, University of Bristol, 1998, p. 10.

3 See R. Gillespie, 'Northern European Perceptions of the Barcelona Process', *Revista CIDOB d'Afers Internacionals*, 37 (1997).

4 Mauritania was also excluded for not being considered a Mediterranean country by the EU. Yet, the constituent session of the Euro-Mediterranean Parliamentary Forum adopted a Declaration recommending the participation of both Libya and Mauritania in the Barcelona Process.

5 H. Köchler, 'US–European Relations After the End of the East–West Conflict: Implications for Euro-Mediterranean Co-operation', *Occasional Papers Series*, 1, International Progress Organization, 1997.

6 See J. Peters, *Pathways to Peace: The Multilateral Arab–Israeli Peace Talks* (London, Royal Institute of International Affairs, 1996).

7 See J. Marks, 'High Hopes and Low Motives: The New Euro-Mediterranean Partnership Initiative', in *Mediterranean Politics*, 1:1 (1996), 1–24.

8 See E. Barbé, 'The Barcelona Conference: Launching Pad of a Process', *Mediterranean Politics*, 1: 1 (1996), 25–42.

9 Commission of the European Communities, *Barcelona Declaration Adopted at the Euro-Mediterranean Conference*, final version, Barcelona, 28 November 1995.

10 Jünemann, 'Europe's Interrelations with North Africa', p. 369.

11 Commission of the European Communities, *Barcelona Declaration*, p. 2.

12 *Ibid.*

13 F. Tanner, 'An Emerging Security Agenda for the Mediterranean', *Mediterranean Politics*, 1: 3 (1996), especially pp. 282–5.

14 R. Aliboni, 'The Euro-Mediterranean Partnership: An Interpretation from Italy', Paper presented at the MEDAC Conference 'Prospects After Barcelona', Malta, March 1996.

15 N. Kliot, 'Politics and Society in the Mediterranean Basin', in R. King, L. Proudfoot and B. Smith (eds), *The Mediterranean: Environment and Society* (London, Arnold, 1997), pp. 108–25.

16 G. Edwards and Eric Philippart, '*Mare Nostrum* – The European Union and the Mediterranean in the 1990s and Beyond', paper presented at the Fifth Biennial ESCA–USA Conference, Seattle, 29 May–1 June 1997, p. 15.

17 See R. Aliboni, 'Re-Setting the Euro-Mediterranean Security Agenda', *The International Spectator*, 33: 4 (1998).

18 As Joffé notes, this may occur despite rather than because of the recommendations for 'good governance'. See G. Joffé, 'The Euro-Mediterranean Partnership: Two Years After Barcelona', *Briefing Papers*, 44, Royal Institute of International Affairs, London, 1998.

19 EuroMeSCo, Working Group on Confidence-Building, Arms Control and Conflict Prevention, EuroMeSCo Network, April 1997. In order to establish functions of conflict prevention, it is also argued in the report, the EMP should combine short- and long-term action (systemic, structural and diplomatic preventive actions) with a highly pragmatic approach in intra-conflict and post-conflict situations. The report argues that this may become acceptable if a strong mechanism for information (whose scope should not be subjected to significant limitations) and communication without intervention is firmly established.

20 Tanner, 'An Emerging Security Agenda for the Mediterranean', p. 292.

21 C. J. Echeverria, 'Euro-Mediterranean Political Relations: Confidence- and Security-Building Measures', *ELIAMEP Occasional Papers*, OP97/07, Hellenic Foundation for European and Foreign Policy, Athens, 1997.

22 Similar to the 1992 single-market programme, the date set for the MEFTA objective is a target date rather than a legal date. This allows for higher levels of flexibility for the necessary adjustments.

23 Jünemann, 'Europe's interrelations with North Africa', p. 370.

24 N. Minasi, 'The Euro-Mediterranean Free Trade Area and its Impact on the Economies Involved', *Jean Monnet Working Papers in Comparative and International Politics*, 16, University of Catania, 1998.

25 L. Tsoukalis, 'The EU in Search of a Mediterranean Policy', *European Expression: A Quarterly Edition on European Issues* (in Greek), 28 (1998), 37.

26 M. Wolf, 'Cooperation or Conflict? The European Union in a Liberal Global Economy', *International Affairs*, 71: 3 (1995) 333.

27 See Euromed Internet Forum, 'The Euro-Mediterranean Economic Area', *Euromed Special Feature*, 2, November 1998.

28 An early EU study has suggested that during the transition EU competition could bankrupt some 2,000 companies in Tunisia alone, and that even with funding the future of another 2,000 would be uncertain.

29 See Euromed Internet Forum, 'The Euro-Mediterranean Economic Area'.

30 See E. L. Hudgins, 'Regional and Multilateral Trade Agreements: Complementary Means to Open Markets', *Cato Journal*, 15: 2-3 (1995/96).

31 See EuroMeSCo, Working Group on 'Confidence-Building, Arms Control and Conflict Prevention'.

32 See Minasi, 'The Euro-Mediterranean Free Trade Area'.

33 B. Khader, 'Euro-Mediterranean Partnership (EMP): The Unaccomplished Tasks', *The IPTS Report* (special Euro-Mediterranean issue), 25, European Science an Technology Observatories Network, June 1998.

34 For more details see H. Schneider and H. Zomer, 'European Union and the Mediterranean (MEDA)', APRODEV Information Document, August 1997.

35 The term is borrowed from S. Strange, *Casino Capitalism* (Manchester and New York, Manchester University Press, 1997).

36 B. Hoekman, 'The World Trade Organization, the European Union, and the Arab World: Trade Policy Priorities and Pitfalls', *Working Papers in International Economics*, Private Sector Development Division, World Bank, September 1995.

37 Quoted in Euromed Internet Forum, 'The Euro-Mediterranean Cultural Partnership', *Euromed Special Feature*, 3, December 1998.

38 A. Colas, 'The Limits of Mediterranean Partnership: Civil Society and the Barcelona Conference of 1995', *Mediterranean Quarterly*, 8: 4 (1997) 75.

39 See A. de Vasconcelos, R. Aliboni and A. Monem Said Aly, EuroMeSCo Report 1997/98.

40 N. Fahmy, 'After Madrid and Barcelona: Prospects for Mediterranean Security', Paper presented in MEDAC Conference on 'Prospects after Barcelona', Malta, March 1996.

41 We borrow this term from His All Holiness Bartholomew I, Archbishop of Constantinople – New Rome and Ecumenical Patriarch. Speech delivered at the University of Exeter, 13 July 2000, on the occasion of the conferment of the degree of Doctor of Laws *Honoris Causa.*

42 To reduce migratory pressures, the partners stressed that overall responsibility for the re-admission of illegal immigrants to Europe ultimately rests with the southern Mediterranean countries.

43 N. Waites and S. Stavridis, 'The European Union and the Mediterranean Member States' in S. Stavridis *et al.* (eds), *The Foreign Policies of the European Union's Mediterranean States and Applicant Countries in the 1990s* (London, Macmillan, 1999), p. 33.

44 Edwards and Philippart, '*Mare Nostrum*', p. 10.

45 Aliboni explains that the EU gives its southern Mediterranean partners a limited co-management of its Mediterranean policy. In practice, what they can do is either 'corroborate' or 'oppose' EU decisions, as their initiative is strongly conditioned by EU mechanisms for reaching consensus or taking decisions in the CFSP framework. See Informal EuroMeSCo–Senior Officials' Seminar, 'Euro-Mediterranean Security Dialogue', Bonn, Ministry of Foreign Affairs, 20 March 1999; *EuroMeSCo News*, 5: April 1999.

46 J. Monar, 'Institutional Constraints of the European Union's Mediterranean Policy', *Mediterranean Politics*, 3: 2 (1998), 39-60.

47 The EuroMeSco network of Euro-Mediterranean foreign policy institutes was established in June 1996 at Sesimbra. It functions as a laboratory for ideas and methods in tackling sensitive but essential issues for the functioning of the EMP. Two working parties were formed. The first deals with political and security co-operation, which includes the issues of democratisation, social changes and the economic aspects of security; the second deals with confidence-building measures, disarmament and conflict prevention, and all aspects of preventive diplomacy. The network includes 34 member institutes and 7 observers. It has held several meetings of the working parties and two joint meetings with Senior Officials. The first was organised on 11 March 1997 at The Hague under the Netherlands Presidency and allowed for the development of political dialogue. The Annual Conference in Tunis on 30 September–1 October 1997 identified new work topics and welcomed new members to the network. A second informal joint meeting took place in Bonn on 20 March 1999. The Annual Conference in London in May 1998 decided to diversify the issues for reflection to include consideration of the Charter for Peace and Stability, as well as the political conditions for regional integration. See Euromed Internet Forum, 'EUROMESCO: The Network of Foreign Policy Institutes', *Information Note*, April 1999.

48 Among other issues that were raised but eventually deferred to future discussions were the creation of a network of defence institutes and the organisation of a seminar on the

deployment of armed forces for humanitarian work.

49 The Charter for Peace and Stability aims to establish a set of principles and instruments to enable partners to make and implement common decisions. It would thus create an institutional framework with a normative ambition: that partners should adopt a more coherent agenda to that put forward by the Action Plan.

50 Informal EuroMeSco-Senior Offiials' Seminar, 'Euro-Mediterranean Security Dialogue', Bonn, Ministry of Foreign Affairs, 20 March 1999; *EuroMeSco News*, 5: April 1999,

51 COM(97) 68, 'Commission Communication on the Progress of the Euro-Mediterranean Partnership and Preparations for the Second Ministerial Conference', 19 February 1997, *Bulletin*, 11–1995.

52 See A. Jbili and K. Enders, 'The Association Agreement Between Tunisia and the European Union', *Finance and Development*, 33: 3 (1996), 18-23.

53 J. Licari, 'The Euro-Mediterranean Partnership: Economic and Financial Aspects', *Mediterranean Politics*, 3: 3 (1998), 19.

54 H. Lindholm-Schulz and M. Schulz, 'The Middle East – Exception or Embryonic Regionalism?', *Politeia*, Department of Peace and Development Research, Göteborg University, (1998), 106.

55 In so far as they did accord it a role, the EU was to bankroll the bilateral part of the Middle East Peace Process. See Joffé, 'The Euro-Mediterranean Partnership'.

56 F. Attinà, 'Regional Cooperation in Global Perspective: The Case of the "Mediterranean" Regions', *Jean Monnet Working Papers in Comparative and International Politics*, 4, University of Catania, December 1996.

57 F. Tanner, 'The Malta Meeting Revisited: The Middle East Is Catching Up with the Barcelona Process', Editorial of Director on the Second Ministerial Meeting of the Barcelona Process held in Malta, 15–16 April 1997.

58 S. C. Calleya, 'The Euro-Mediterranean Process After Malta: What Prospects?', *Mediterranean Politics*, 2: 2 (1997), 1-22.

59 See Joffé, 'The Euro-Mediterranean Partnership'.

60 See Tanner, 'The Malta Meeting Revisited'.

61 S. C. Calleya, 'Providing New Dynamism to the Euro-Med Process', *Euro-Mediterranean Magazine*, 3, EuroMed Internet Forum, 1998.

62 Maltese Prime Minister's Closing Statement, Second Euro-Mediterranean Ministerial Conference, Malta, 16 April 1997.

63 The Malta Declaration states: 'The Participants take note of the work of Senior Officials on a Charter for Peace and Stability in the Euro-Mediterranean region, and instruct them to continue the preparatory work, taking due account of the exchanged documents, in order to submit an agreed text at a future Ministerial Meeting when political circumstances allow.'

64 See Joffé, 'The Euro-Mediterranean Partnershp'.

65 *Ibid.*

66 R. Edis, 'Does the Barcelona Process Matter?', *Mediterranean Politics*, 3: 3 (1998), 101.

67 Concluding Statement by Robin Cook, UK Presidency, Ad-Hoc Euro-Mediterranean Ministerial Meeting, Palermo, 3-4 June 1998.

68 Experts' Meeting on the Euro-Mediterranean Economic Area, Brussels, 27–8 April 1998.

69 They recognised the importance of an appropriate regime on rules of origin.

70 EuroMeSCo, Working Group on 'Confidence-Building, Arms Control and Conflict Prevention', EuroMeSCo Network, April 1997.

71 Since the Barcelona Conference, there have been four meetings on the socio-cultural dimension; two Ministerial Conferences, in Bologna in April 1996 and in Rhodes in September 1998; and two meetings of experts, the Thessaloniki Conference on audio-visual co-operation in November 1997 and the Stockholm Workshop on dialogue between cultures and civilisations in April 1998.

72 Euromed Internet Forum, 'The Middle East Peace Process and the Role of the European Union', *Euromed Special Features*, 7: 23 April 1999.

73 As reported by the Informal EuroMeSCo Senior Officials' Seminar, 'Euro-Mediterranean Security Dialogue', Bonn, Ministry of Foreign Affairs, 20 March 1999, *EuroMeSCo News*, 5: April 1999.

74 Chairman's Formal Conclusions, Third Euro-Mediterranean Conference of Foreign Ministers – Barcelona III, Stuttgart, Germany, 15–16 April 1999.

75 Euromed Internet Forum, 'Euro-Mediterranean Conference on Regional Cooperation' *Euro-Med Special Features*, 5: 5 February 1999.

PART III

Theorising sea-change

5

Conceptualising Euro-Mediterranean governance

The theoretical setting

Reflections on theory and method

Theorising in the social sciences can be defined as the art of organising the production of knowledge about the constitution of social activity. It is about the systematic study of the conditions, structure and evolution of that constitution, by means of explaining, interpreting, understanding and, where possible, predicting individual small- or large-scale social action. Although some theories direct their *foci* on one, more, or even all of the above categories, what they all have in common is the quest for reliable answers and, at times, questions too. Theories entail different notions of knowledge, relying on different cognitive resources for the development of working conceptions. Thus they differ in the methods of knowledge acquisition, application, evaluation and critique. In short, theories allow room for a variety of methodologies and lines of social inquiry to be pursued, the biases and particularistic concerns of the researcher notwithstanding.

According to Mjøset, there exist four different understandings of social science theory: law-oriented, idealising, constructivist and critical. The first, by avoiding the search for truly universal laws as in the natural sciences, focuses on 'regularities that apply only within specific contexts', with theory itself becoming 'a collection of "lawlike regularities" or "quasilaws"'; the second, by accepting that social science 'laws' are 'ideal types', centers 'on the conditions which establish the *ideal* situation', with theory being capable of yielding predictions in an idealised world; the third questions 'any foundation for the social sciences', implying that no alternative ethical foundations can be found', with theory taking the form of 'contextual understanding of interacting motives'; the fourth rests on an 'internal linkage between theoretical and ethical reflection', with theory focusing 'more on ethical foundations and less on concrete paradigms involved in the explanatory efforts of applied social sciences'.[1] In summary, the first notion of theory focuses on 'theory testing, the second on modelling, the third on theory formation and the fourth on ethical reflection'.[2]

A much debated issue in the social sciences concerns the 'scientific' nature of their explanations, for they lack 'the axiomatic quality of mathematics' as the variables in their equations are human beings whose very uniqueness prevents their reduction to 'scientific law'.[3] Indeed, how can we accept that a given social phenomenon can only be subject to a single pattern of systematic inquiry resulting in an impersonal form of knowledge, in turn, driven by the explanatory power of formal rationality? As problems of recognition, classification and definition have not been solved in the social sciences, their theories are defined by their ability not to 'prove' but rather to 'illustrate'. At the same time, though, 'crass positivism' is equally untenable in the social sciences, for the meanings and our understanding of the concepts themselves are affected by the cultural context of both the researcher and the social phenomenon being studied.[4] And, given the difficulties in applying a tightly controlled experimental design to study complex social phenomena as well as in establishing causal links among variables that are consistent and generalised across time and space, explanation is but one element of the feasible end of social inquiry. Also, it is highly doubtful whether too much 'social sciency' can help uncover the alleged coherence that underlies the apparent chaos of contemporary social and political life through the operations of deductive logic and modelling.

The point advanced in this chapter is that a useful theoretical enterprise has to incorporate a sense of understanding as a valued element in the pursuit of unravelling the puzzling features of complex social processes, organisations, episodes or system-steering events, and even that it should allow for 'an intuitive organization of perception'.[5] At the same time, such an intellectual strategy should also be able to draw attention to schemes for understanding the evolutionary nature of complex processes as constitutive of wider social phenomena, by tracing the broader intellectual environment within which concepts and assumptions are used to facilitate the production of explanatory patterns, and attempting to make advances in the realm of social inquiry by taking risks as well as being prepared to accept criticisms from competing research programmes in the framing of hypotheses that state the general conditions of the social phenomenon under investigation.

The centrality of theory in the conduct of social science research has been justified on several grounds. Indeed, familiarity with theory helps to test our analytical tools and appreciate their relevance in real-life situations. As Taylor has put it: 'Each theory … leads to unique insights which are valid starting points for the purpose of comparison and evaluation'.[6] Or, as Keohane and Hoffmann have asserted: 'Attempts to avoid theory … not only miss interesting questions but rely on a framework for analysis that remains unexamined precisely because it is implicit'.[7] Similarly, Church observes that 'awareness of theory is a necessary ground-clearing measure'.[8] To borrow from Rosamond:

'Theorizing intellectualizes perceptions. It is not that theory just helps us to identify that which is significant.'[9] Finally, in addition to being 'an intellectual mapping exercise', theory is a means of linking 'the order of ideas' to 'the order of events'.[10]

But what is the appropriate theoretical path to the study of Euro-Mediterranean governance? The first point to make is that this subject requires a transcending of purely narrative approaches about the form and functions of the emerging system. This exercise is informed by 'structured ways of understanding changing patterns of interaction',[11] free from the inherently narrow boundaries of micro-analysis. The aim is to project a macroscopic view of Euro-Mediterranean relations based on systematic conceptual explanation. As Church notes: 'We need to be aware of the conceptions we use since they determine our perception of things.'[12] After all, 'one cannot get at reality except from within some system of concepts'.[13] Groom makes the point well:

> Our conceptualization does ... give a context to the activities of practitioners and provides them with an opportunity of learning from the experience of others ... And different projections show us different worlds so that we may find what we are looking for in the sense that we impose meaning on 'facts' rather than speaking for themselves. There is a sense in which one can be pragmatic, but behind every 'pragmatic' approach lies a theory of conceptualization – no matter how inchoate. All social activity requires choice and that choice cannot be exercised without some criteria for judgement – in short, a theory, a conception, a framework.[14]

This methodological pathway to the study of Euro-Mediterranean politics offers the necessary conceptual infrastructure from which a 'hierarchy of realities' is enabled to emerge. The hypothesis here is that a continuum of accessible knowledge domains might bridge the gap from the study of specialised issue areas to the understanding of collective conduct. In this way, important connections are established between knowledge acquisition and knowledge evaluation in the process of theorising the regional partnership: theory thus becomes a system of interconnected principles and ideas, concepts and practices, as well as links between wholes and parts, or between totalities and substructures. But there is considerable variation in the way in which scholars ascribe different meanings to concepts, the study of which is crucial for understanding a given social phenomenon. Also, some scholars are interested in the larger picture, others in capturing only part of the overall image, others again in the relationship among different realities and still others in the process of theorising itself. In any case, Rosamond is right to assert that '[t]heories are necessary if we are to produce ordered observations of social phenomena'.[15] This view accords with Stoker's view that in the social sciences, '[t]heories are of value precisely because they structure all observations'.[16]

The above reflections on theory and method are not intended as a negation of disciplined, empirically-oriented social inquiry. They are simply to suggest that 'the value of theory is not determined by any rigid criteria',[17] and that narrow training and the employment of an overly 'scientific' method resting on the illusion of ethical neutrality are not the most appropriate methodological blueprints for enriching our understanding of Euro-Mediterranean governance. All the more so, if one looks at the possibilities the latter offers in collective norm-setting, large-scale social engineering, internationalised economic governance, civil society formation, etc. Theorising the Euro-Mediterranean condition is as much about explaining the causality of multiple interactions as it is about developing feelings for the play of regional governance arrangements and the inevitable normative and ethical questions to which they give rise. Normative as these claims are, it seems that the highest purpose the theoretical study of complex social phenomena can serve is to venture for a deeper and more penetrating understanding of the conditions of human association, the forces that shape the range and depth of societal interactions and the possibilities of improving the quality of debate about such self-inquiring matters as 'where we are now, from where we have come and to where we might go'.[18]

Theorising international governance

After 1945, numerous international organisations were set up, most notably the UN and its specialised agencies, to give the world democratic instruments for international governance. At that time, international organisations and international regimes were two sides of the same coin. The former focused on structural or institutional arrangements and the latter on the norms and principles that were laid down by these organisations. International regimes are a sub-group of international institutions, of which international organisations is a more formalised and bureaucratic sub-class. Young distinguishes not only between organisations and institutions, but between orders and regimes: organisations are 'material entities possessing physical locations (or seats), offices, personnel, equipment, and budgets … generally possess[ing] legal personality',[19] whereas institutions are 'social practices consisting of easily recognised roles coupled with clusters of rules or conventions governing relations among the occupants of these roles'.[20] International orders are broad structures governing the diverse activities of most actors in the international system and international society – i.e. the economic order – and international regimes are more specific structures governing 'well-defined activities, resources, or geographical areas of only some actors'.[21] Although a distinction is made between 'regime' and 'order', the two are not mutually exclusive. Regimes can have orders associated with them, and vice versa. As Keohane writes, orders are embedded within tregimes. Hence, they are coterminous in practice: 'much of what they do is to monitor, manage, and modify the operation of regimes'.[22] Important to this study, and in this respect a departure from others, is that the EMP combines both regime and order aspects: although it sets up a specific framework of activities, the area within which they apply is not well defined, while it involves only a sub-set of states.

The term 'international regime' was introduced as early as 1975 by Ruggie to signify 'a set of mutual expectations, rules and regulations, plans, organizational energies and financial commitments, which have been accepted by a group of states'.[23] In a seminal collection of essays published in 1983, Krasner argued that international regimes appear 'when there are clearly understood principles, norms, rules and decision-making procedures around which decision-makers' expectations converge in a given area of international relations'.[24] A somewhat different account, however, is offered by Young, who defines regimes as 'social institutions governing the actions of those involved in specific activities or set of activities'.[25] The emphasis here is on rules that are translated into 'well-defined guides to action' and on compliance mechanisms with the rules governing the regime. There is a certain procedural bias in this view, in terms of the actors' expected actions 'under appropriate circumstances'.[26] But the regularisation of behaviour means the creation of patterns – patterns of procedure, patterns of compliance to norms and rules, and above all, patterns of expectations: 'What these arrangements have in common is that they are designed not to implement centralized enforcement of agreements, but to establish stable mutual expectations about others' patterns of behavior.'[27] Norms and principles have a major psychological component in that policy makers feel they should act in certain ways because they are expected to (and expect others to), whether or not a rule has been formalised by a treaty framework.

Governing arrangements relate to various issue areas in international relations. Issue areas may be functional and, hence, be very wide or narrow, paralleling the structure of functional organisations. Young notes: 'We live in a world of international regimes'; their concerns range from monetary issues to trade issues, to the management of natural resources, to armament control, to the management of power, to the management of outer space and the seabed.[28] Although the literature on international regimes has been influenced largely by American-led international relations research programmes, especially from the mid-1970s to the early 1980s, the concept remained conveniently vague, embracing a plethora of different manifestations about the management of complex interdependencies. To enter a small parenthesis here with regard to the latter: although some scholars emphasise the relationship between positive linkages among national interests, others, like Keohane and Nye, stress the costs or constraints imposed on states: 'the reciprocal (although not necessarily symmetrical) costly effects of transactions'.[29] These authors tend to accept the organising principles of the *Gesellschaft* model of society, in that they are more concerned with procedures for realising interests that are thought to be separately defined by the competing actors, 'rather than the question of whether interests are compatible, or reflect a consensus, which would be central in the alternative *Gemeinschaft* approach'.[30] In the latter case, interdependence is expected to act as a learning process, with the realisation of mutual interests preceding the procedural arrangements: states may learn to identify common interests and act collectively upon them. In the *Gesellschaft*-oriented pluralist accounts, 'interdependence is to be tested in the opportunities it creates to exert power by exploiting the "sensitivity" or "vulnerability" of partners'.[31] Here, the strength of the partnership is tested in relation to one actor's vulnerability against another actor's threat. From this perspective also, the following useful parallelism is drawn:

> the interdependence theorists are the most recent intellectual heirs of Thomas Hobbes. The modern equivalent of the Leviathan, however, is not a superior international power which compels the citizens in their own interest to refrain from war, but rather a procedural device such as the 'régime'. Subjects are seen to accept the rules of the régime because it is only by doing this that they obtain their separate interests, as Hobbes' citizens accepted the Leviathan, so that they could establish order which was otherwise unobtainable.[32]

Revisiting the conceptual vagueness of 'international regimes', one may venture to claim that almost every aspect of international co-operation, whether stemming directly from a formal treaty-based mandate or from 'extra-treaty' – i.e. politically rather than legally binding – arrangements, can be classified as a one type of international regime or another. Cox's definition of regimes illustrates this point well: '[Regimes] are … recognized patterns of practice that define the rules of the game'.[33] Since then, there has been much discussion on the 'consensus definition' of international regimes and, more generally, about the usefulness of the theory itself. The latter has been criticised as imprecise and value-based, for over-emphasising the static, and for being narrow-minded, a 'fad'.[34]

Neoliberal institutionalists view international institutions and regimes as stemming from attempts by individual actors to achieve control and counteract the inadequacy of their own resources. Fluctuations in their number or strength reflect the calculations of self-interested actors trying to resolve collective-action problems and gain efficiency through voluntary exchanges, contracts and treaties. Outcomes largely depend on the ability to find and implement Pareto-improvements, counteract market-failures, reduce transaction costs and, crucially, overcome conflicts of interest. A core question here is how alternative institutions and regimes affect the chances of discovering mutual benefits.[35] Realist studies, on the other hand, portray states as being more concerned with clashing interests, strategic interaction, alliances, coercion, relative power, distributional aspects and relative gains. Because such elements of order reflect the interests of powerful states, they are more likely when power is concentrated in the international system – i.e. when a hegemon or a stable coalition of powers perceives an institutional arrangement as maintaining or increasing its capacity to exercise power. As Keohane observes, changes in order result from changing powers and material capabilities.[36]

In contrast to the above, there has been a recent re-embrace of institutions: 'In part for descriptive purposes, and in part to find a venue for the previously-institutionless abstractions of formal theory, both area specialists and formal modelers have avidly turned to study the institutions of Europe.'[37] The point here is that institutions impact on the behaviour of actors and become important venues for the resolution of conflicts. This 'new institutionalism' goes beyond descriptive empiricism, placing institutions 'in a context which allows differentiation between formal political institutions, informal conventions and the norms and beliefs embedded within those institutions'.[38] The gist of the thesis is that 'institutions matter' in the organisation of public life and 'political struggles are mediated by prevailing institutional arrangements'.[39] Also, they are seen as instruments going 'beyond the formal organs of government' to include 'standard operating procedures, so-called soft-law, norms and conventions of behaviour'.[40] Rosamond writes: 'Rather than being simple and passive vessels within which politics occurs, institutions provide contexts [or venues] where actors can conduct a relatively higher proportion of positive sum bargains.'[41] Although the new institutionalism is not a coherent body of thought, a common underlying assumption is that institutions shape behaviour, influence the formation of preferences and impact on the pursuit of interests. The renewed interest in institutions has also explored their impact on those working within their structures. Olsen and Peters explain: 'Institutions contain some sort of governmental DNA and tend to transmit that genetic code to the individuals who take up roles within them.'[42] To that, a layer of theorising can be added which focuses on the emergence of norms and rules that impinge upon various domains of policy action.

In general terms, institutions facilitate the exchange of information, provide the possibility of informal contacts, assist the internalization of norms, enhance the quality of communicative action, promote patterns of co-operative behaviour (even consensus) and act as real testing grounds for the building of trust. But perhaps one of the most crucial services they perform as non-neutral arenas of governance is that they offer alternative ways of mapping the expectations of actors on issues of change. In Olsen's words, institutions 'are seen as having the potential to form and transform actors, their mentality and identity and change logics of actions, e.g. from expected utility calculation to identity based rule-oriented behaviour'.[43] He adds: 'Institutions authorise and enable, as well as constrain, change. Therefore, there is a need for understanding how institutions may transform, modify, redirect and integrate, and not only aggregate, the demands, interests, and powers of societal actors and forces.'[44] Whether or not scholars perceive institutions as purposive agents of systemic change, they do play an important role in structuring 'the access of political forces to the political process',[45] while offering a peaceful means for changing the rules of the game. Although new institutionalism raises challenging questions about the institutional dynamics of macro-political order building, the consequences of institutional form, the impact of norms on policy and performance, as well as the relationship between institutional affirmation and transformation, it is imperative that its central institutionalist tenet – that institutions matter – be further qualified. As Lane and Ersson succinctly put it: 'The crucial question in relation to the new institutionalism is: important – yes, but for what?'[46]

In a recent contribution to regime analysis, Hasenclever, Mayer and Rittberger have distinguished between power-based, interest-based and knowledge-based theories of international regimes.[47] Power-based theories can be described as 'realist' theories of international co-operation: power and the distribution of capabilities among states can explain both 'conflict' and 'co-operation'. Interest-based theories are mainstream theories of international regimes, emphasising 'the role of international regimes in helping states to realize common interests'.[48] In Clae's words: 'If the observed cooperation is explained by patterns of complementary interests and underlying distribution of power, regimes have no effect and thus, in such cases, theories of international regimes do not contribute to the explanation of cooperation.'[49] The focus here is on situations where the constellation of the actors' interests is such that they can only achieve mutually rewarding outcomes through institutionalised co-operation. Finally, knowledge-based theories stress ideas and knowledge as explanatory variables, and they also focus on the question of how causal and normative beliefs form perceptions of international problems and thus increase the demand for regimes.[50]

Different interpretations of international regimes come from authors who focus on the norms that regularise the behaviour of (mainly state) actors and guide their choices. Norms constitute 'standards of behaviour defined in terms of rights and obligations'.[51] Others have argued that norms carry social content and are often independent of power distributions: they provide agents/states with understandings of interests and, hence, do not merely constrain behaviour. In recent years, empirical work along these lines has convincingly demonstrated that norms can have such constitutive effects.[52] A related question here is whether norms can transcend possible sources of tension among regime actors stemming from the 'self-interests of governments'. If 'yes', then through what accommodationist mechanisms do actors reconsider their choices and decide to comply with certain patterns of behaviour that are acceptable to their partners? This is no ontological issue. Rather, it is about the flexibility of the regime in question, the way in which the participants value it as a purposeful structure capable of achieving intended outcomes, and the means by which norms can facilitate mutualism and reciprocity.

International regimes justify the separateness of states as constitutionally distinct entities. As Taylor put it: 'states do not cease to be states because they are members of a regime …'.[53] At the same time, regimes allow actors to 'socialise' with each other in a complex web of norms of behaviour, rules and decision-making procedures that are commonly, if not *ex ante*, agreed upon by the actors involved. Socialising, or its close synonyms like habitualisation, schooling, internalisation, depersonalisation and the rest, is a key mechanism linking international institutions and norms to states, or to groups and agents within them.[54] The emphasis is on informal routes of co-operative behaviour, patterned as much on specific political interests – although regimes imply 'a form of co-operation that is more than the following of short-run interests'[55] – as on a common tendency to achieve reciprocal objectives. Finally, regimes project both 'inclusive' and 'exclusive' frameworks of multiple and often complex interactions that reflect a given political reality.[56] What follows offers a general assessment of Euro-Mediterranean governance and examines its evolution through the conceptual lenses of regime theory.

Assessing the partnership

Jünemann defines the EMP as 'the climax of a political process that started shortly after the fall of the Berlin Wall, but more than that it marks the starting point of a new era of interregional relations'.[57] Keeping in mind Edwards and Philippart's view that the EMP has led to a process whose analysis and interpretation encompasses different theoretical possibilities,[58] its philosophy has been summarised by Derisbourg as non-paternalistic, based on a recognition of interdependencies, shared interests and the right to development and freedom, the need for decentralised co-operation, as well as the importance of the private sector and of a continuous dialogue at both intergovernmental and civil society levels.[59] A new phase in Euro-Mediterranean relations has thus emerged, consisting of openness, prior dialogue and work in common from policy design to implementation.

As Jünemann argues, however, 'the Barcelona concept aims at a careful westernisation of the Mediterranean, gradually converting it into an area of economic and political influence'.[60] Regarding the commitment to democracy and human rights, it seems that some non-EU partners will at some stage face the reality that the other participants, European or not, will actually insist on the preservation of the principles and norms agreed in Barcelona. But although the political conditionality underlying the economic and financial partnership 'allows the EU to suspend its commitments in cases of failure concerning democracy or respect of human rights, offering an apparently effective instrument to influence the process of democratisation … it exposes the MPCs to the good will of the Europeans, thus offending their demand for equal partnership'.[61]

As Fahmy notes, the EMP resolved the major question of whether regional security would be addressed within a strictly Mediterranean context or within a wider framework encompassing European security concerns.[62] Although the Barcelona Declaration did not linger over the meaning of security and stability, it produced a clearly Euro-centric perspective on the 'common threat'.[63] The EMP was a collective attempt to redefine European threat perceptions towards the Mediterranean by addressing issues of social unrest and economic underdevelopment, rather than by detecting a direct Arab military threat. Although the initial target date for the establishment of the MEFTA is the year 2010, EU states made no secret of the fact that the aid plan for the transition period was intended to contribute to the slowing of migratory flows to their respective societies. As Rifkind, the then British Foreign Secretary, stated: 'One of the most important ways in which we can achieve political stability is by economic growth, and by the countries of the EU helping those in North Africa and the Middle East develop their economic potential and economic infrastructure. Political stability will flow from that.'[64] The argument is that with trade growing, jobs will be created in Mediterranean countries and emigration will slow. From this view also, political change in the southern Mediterranean is expected to result from large-scale economic liberalisation. In this context, Kienle argues, this approach is a retouched version of the theory of markets as a democratising force.[65]

This 'automatic pilot' theory of the market is among the basic tenets of liberalism. For economists and political thinkers such as Adam Smith or Herbert Spencer social harmony is spontaneous. It does not require coercive force to be produced, or for that matter maintained. *Laissez-faire*, the argument goes, defined in the context of pursuing individual interests, is capable of producing co-operation in other fields automatically. But the proposition that this theory applies to international markets that consist only of independent agents trading on their own account and competing against each other is largely questionable. For it may well be that economic rationality, along the lines of an 'exchange *Gesellschaft*',[66] continues to play a central role in the economic governance of an ever globalising market economy, but this is not the case in the Mediterranean space, where elements of such economic rationality co-exist with a struggle for power. It is, therefore, highly unrealistic to suppose that a kind of automatic governance could spontaneously emerge from the approach adopted in Barcelona.

From a purely economic perspective, the Barcelona document does not represent a radical break with past European policies towards the Mediterranean; rather it is 'a deepening of past efforts',[67] in that it incorporates in its economic agenda more clearly defined global objectives.[68] In overall terms, the entire project was a sign of the EU's willingness to play an increasingly active economic role in bringing all partners closer together and in reducing political and social sources of conflict.[69] But building the MEFTA presupposes that partners will be able to understand each other and, gradually, to share the same practices. Since the Barcelona Declaration, any rigid distinction along economic, political and socio-cultural lines can only be made at the cost of avoiding the complexity of regional reality. Herein lies perhaps the most innovative aspect of the EU's Mediterranean approach post-1995: that in addition to the traditional economic pattern of intra-regional relations, there now appears to be an intrinsic link between the political (mainly security driven) and socio-cultural arenas (civil society oriented).

According to Marquina, no existing notion of security gives backbone to the EMP and the documents themselves contain incoherence and imprecision regarding the concepts of co-operative security, preventive diplomacy and 'good neighbourliness'.[70] He also claims that these principles remain under-explained in both conceptual and operative aspects. Despite such views, however, one could legitimately argue that there exists a degree of coherence, albeit not organisational symmetry, let alone isomorphism, within the EU's intention, in that economic problems can only be tackled once issues of political legitimacy are adequately addressed. Ultimately, most Mediterranean players seem to agree that institutionalised regional co-operation would have to involve, at least in terms of implementation, the private sector, business enterprises and individuals.[71] Aliboni argues that such an initiative is the result of a remarkable and successful effort by the EU to innovate and reinforce its Mediterranean policy, in that its efforts towards a 'structured strategy of regionalism' are now clearly marked by elements of change predicated on the establishment of the MEFTA and the search for a common area of peace and stability to provide security and support economic development.[72] But the MEFTA objective, which is to be met through a series of economic reforms, hides security risks since accelerated market liberalisation in the southern rim could produce greater waves of instability.[73] Moreover, the EMP has not yet utilised the mechanisms necessary to operationalise and regularise political co-operation, both of which may prove vital in the event of further economic recession in the southern rim. These mechanisms are cited in the Barcelona document (encouraging information exchanges and establishing dialogue mechanisms) and in the Action Plan that was set out at the beginning of the process.

Joffé makes the point that the EU, in seeking to employ a meaningful global and comprehensive approach, should provide the following set of mechanisms:

- support for responsive and participatory political processes sustained by the encouragement of economic transparency and accountability within a codified and independent legal structure;
- collective co-operative security alongside viable economic restructuring; and
- a financial commitment to the creation of a vital human and physical infrastructure that will make the economic refashioning of the region into a 'win–win situation for all'.[74]

In general, the EMP aims at correcting the structural deficiencies evident in past European policies, and can be seen, in Gillespie's words, to be 'emblematic of a process' being constituted from a set of dynamic international exchanges, but as still falling short of a meaningful partnership.[75] At the same time, it is a vital step in the process of animating some confident expectations about the emergence of a common 'Euro-Mediterranean consciousness', laying the groundwork for the creation of an international regime.[76]

The emerging Barcelona regime

From a systemic point of view, the EMP is a nascent and multidimensional regime that aims at establishing links between political (security), economic (MEFTA) and socio-cultural (human rights and civil society) arenas. The core claim here is that states obey the rules embodied in international regimes because of the functional benefits the latter provide. For the moment, however, the EMP represents a balance of separate national preferences, rather than a common Euro-Mediterranean interest per se. Although it sets up a system of flexible regional arrangements, the substantial differentiation of the ratio with the Community budget for the economic reconstruction of central and eastern Europe has been the major reason for attracting the interest of southern Mediterranean countries.[77] Indeed, the EMP is propelled by a certain 'economism' whose financial rather than trade implications are favourable to the non-EU partners. In return for the above, the EU linked issues of economic liberalisation to a set of political principles.

Keohane, in an influential study that straddled the lines of realist and neoliberalist thinking, suggested that international regimes are 'institutions with explicit rules, agreed upon governments that pertain to particular sets of issues in international relations'.[78] This is of particular importance, considering that Euro-Mediterranean politics combine both power-political considerations and questions of increased complex interdependence. Keohane's 'lean' definition of the term, as opposed to that advanced earlier by Krasner, has the advantage of relieving scholars of the burden of justifying their decision to call a given injunction a 'norm' rather than a 'rule'.[79] Such a definitional approach is helpful, since norms are not explicit in the complex framework of Euro-Mediterranean relations and since no substantive level of institutional autonomy characterises the operation of the newly formed regional mechanisms. Although the EMP offers some general rules, it remains weak in relation to the development of an identifiable set of norms. *Ceteris paribus*, it can be seen as an international regime *in statu nascendi*, albeit one that accords with Keohane's 'lean' definition of the term. Without a better or less nebulous definition offered by the *acquis académique*, such a claim remains valid.

A distinctive feature of international relations today is that power is becoming more widely dispersed, so that low politics acquire greater salience for scholars and policy makers. Developments in Euro-Mediterranean politics and attempts at institutionalising the EMP are no exceptions. The EMP, only a handful of years since its inception, remains *in limbo*, between a loose association of states and an international regime. The question is whether the partnership can sustain itself for any length of time without becoming first a system of patterned behaviour, generating a notion of rules of the game capable of guiding and, at a later stage, structuring international behaviour. From a linear projection of Euro-Mediterranean governance, the EMP could evolve into a full-fledged international regime with an institutional life of its own. At present, and given the rather discomforting empirical developments in the process, no such entity has fully come into being, in terms of complying with the basic analytic construct of international regimes.

On the other hand, the fascinating element in the evolving EMP is that, from a dynamic macro-political perspective, it may well prove capable of instrumentalising the principles and norms embedded in the Barcelona Declaration and of transforming them into concrete rules of the game based on shared beliefs, standards of behaviour and, crucially, decision-making procedures for implementing collective choice. Keeping in mind Olsen's point that '[w]riting rules for a large number of heterogeneous countries is no easy task',[80] especially with a view to making these rules fit the special conditions and particular situation of each country, implementation is central to the viability of international regime formation, for the latter process emphasises the need for institutionalisation and the development of an international culture to sustain co-operation. For it is the combined effects of institutionalisation, in the sense of 'learning one's place in a larger order',[81] and international culture, in terms of developing repertoires of shared understandings, that bring about a purposeful system of mutual governance. The idea here is to regularise a form of international co-operation that, in Jervis's words, 'is more than the following of short-term self-interest'.[82] Put another way, to go beyond ad hoc agreements based on short-term power maximisation.

But it would be wrong to equate in any deterministic fashion the end-result of the Barcelona Process with the formation of an international regime *per se*. For these constructs are not regarded, at least in Krasner's terms, as ends in themselves. Rather, '[o]nce in place they do affect related behaviour and outcomes. They are not merely epiphenomenal.'[83] From this angle, principles, norms, rules and decision-making procedures have an impact on policy outcomes and related behaviour, thus transcending 'structural orientations [that] conceptualise a world of rational self-seeking actors'.[84] In short, regimes make a difference, in that they often transcend a state-centred realist perspective that reflects primarily calculations of self-interest. The relationship between patterned behaviour and convergent expectations is a key to our understanding of international regimes: those two aspects create an environment of 'conditionalised behaviour' that in turn 'generates recognised norms' that transcend national boundaries and nurture a broader social space.[85] Contrary to structural arguments forwarded by realists, international regimes have an independent impact on behaviour and are a crucial part of patterned human interaction. The latter view is drawn from the Grotian tradition, where 'regimes are a pervasive and significant phenomenon in the international system'.[86]

In the case of the EMP, it could be argued that regime creation is directed at setting the limits of acceptable behaviour within a nascent and flexibly arranged structure of governance. Noteworthy in that respect is that the EMP addressed the post-Cold War Mediterranean reality as an overlap of different regions bringing together different dimensions.[87] The flexibility of the EMP sets the limits for 'consciousness raising' in issues of Euro-Mediterranean governance and in particular for the possibility of acquiring operational capabilities. In this context, its weak institutional structure makes it difficult for individual state actors to transcend the pursuit of short-term interests. Regimes also deploy a system of interconnectedness among different areas of co-operation that helps explain the nature and complexity of interdependence among the actors involved, who, in turn, are conscious of the need to achieve mutually rewarding outcomes in systems of institutionalised rule. But being a highly fragmented system of policy interactions, any future attempts to navigate the dynamics of the Euro-Mediterranean governance need to be differentiated according to the specific conditions of co-operation embedded within its structures. In particular, the EMP encompasses a multiplicity of norms of behaviour, especially when different procedures apply, determining the degree of involvement of the relevant actors. Further, a partial conceptualisation of its component baskets as separate pillars is not particularly helpful when assessing its cross-sectional, essentially political, properties – i.e. what defines it as a system with significant regime aspects.

But international regime theory may fail in this context to explicate the relationship between the politicisation of issues that regional co-operation might bring about and the strategy employed by particular state actors to exercise managerial or even other, more substantive, forms of control over the process of international regime formation. These deeper concerns have as much to do with the implied benefits of collective action or, alternatively, of regime maintenance, as they do with questions about what kind of co-operation the EMP is allowed, or indeed is prohibited from taking. Envisioning the EMP through the conceptual and analytic lenses of regime theory has the advantage of moving away from a formalistic approach to one of multilateralism, institutional linkages and the impact of domestic politics on regional affairs: it could set in train a process for the internationalisation of issues and their inclusion under a flexible management system.

As students of international relations put great emphasis on international regimes as institutional devices for collective problem solving, it is questionable how far the Euro-Mediterranean system can realise its 'co-operative objectives' under its currently weak institutional structures. That is to say, without investing further in concrete partnership-building measures on matters of substance, such as the need to develop a Charter for Peace and Stability in the region, accompanied however by proper mechanisms and procedures for monitoring its compliance.[88] The envisaged Charter will be an exercise in pre-emptive diplomacy and, crucially, will take the form of an institutionalised alliance. In addition, the Charter can provide the levels of transparency necessary for an ongoing and structured political dialogue among distinct socio-cultural settings, along with the necessary machinery for managing protracted and potentially unresolved crises.

Also, the emerging interparliamentary co-operation through the Parliamentary Forum will provide the EMP with an additional legitimising platform from which to promote peace and stability in this often troubled part of the globe. In this Forum, a structured and regular dialogue among the partners will no doubt engender awareness of common Euro-Mediterranean interests and contribute to the creation of symbiotic structures of governance. Both agenda-identification functions (the acknowledgement of legitimate claims by a partner) and agenda-setting functions (the way in which such claims are included) could be achieved through institutional interaction between the Parliamentary

Forum and the dominant decision-making authorities. A normative implication underpinning this dynamic, yet asymmetrical, relationship between the newly institutionalised Forum and the intergovernmental structures that have set up the institutional machinery of the EMP is the search for a legitimate form of mutual governance. Be that as it may, there is evidence to suggest that the proliferation of legitimate arenas will have an equally important domestic impact on the policy strategy of the partners, in that the latter would now have to direct their claims to, and via, additional institutional avenues. In any event, it would be interesting to evaluate the endorsement of a parliamentary structure for the workings of the EMP and assess the extent to which its mechanisms are capable of accommodating declared principles and particular national interests.

All the above raises the question of why states are bound by certain norms, principles, rules and decision-making procedures. Regime theory offers a plausible answer: whether international co-operation is an *a priori* objective of states, or whether it stems from a certain idealism about the management of pressing international affairs, states pursue their interests more effectively by being members of a larger association.

Notes

1 L. Mjøset, 'Understanding of Theory in the Social Sciences', *ARENA Working Papers*, 99/33, 1999.
2 *Ibid.*
3 H. J. Laski, *A Grammar of Politics* (London, Allen & Unwin, 1938).
4 D. Collier, 'The Comparative Method', in A. Finifter (ed.), *Political Science: The State of the Discipline* (Washington, DC, American Political Science Association, 1993), p. 113.
5 A. Rapopport, 'Various Meanings of "Theory"', *American Political Science Review*, 52 (1958), 981; quoted in R. J. Lieber, *Theory and World Politics* (London, Allen & Unwin, 1973), p. 8.
6 P. Taylor, *International Co-operation Today: The European and the Universal Patterns* (London, Elek, 1971), p. i.
7 R. O. Keohane and S. Hoffmann, 'Conclusions', in W. Wallace (ed.), *The Dynamics of European Integration* (London, Pinter, 1990), p. 284.
8 C. H. Church, *European Integration Theory in the 1990s*, European Dossier Series, 33 (London, University of North London, 1996), p. 8.
9 B. Rosamond, *Theories of European Integration* (Basingstoke, Macmillan, 2000), p. 5.
10 See R. M. Unger, *Knowledge and Politics* (New York, Free Press, 1975), pp. 12–16.
11 Church, *European Integration Theory*, p. 8.
12 *Ibid.*
13 D. W. Hamlyn, *Metaphysics* (Cambridge, Cambridge University Press, 1995), p. 31.
14 A. J. R. Groom, 'The Setting in World Society', in A. J. R. Groom and P. Taylor (eds), *Frameworks for International Co-operation* (London, Pinter, 1990), p. 3.
15 Rosamond, *Theories*, p. 4.
16 G. Stoker, 'Introduction', in D. Marsh and G. Stoker (eds), *Theory and Method in Political Science* (Basingstoke, Macmillan, 1995), p. 17; quoted in Rosamond, *Theories*, p. 4.
17 Lieber, *Theory and World Politics*, p. 9.
18 Groom, 'The Setting in World Society', in Groom and Taylor (eds), *Frameworks*, p. 3.

19 O. R. Young, *International Cooperation: Building Regimes for Natural Resources and the Environment* (Ithaca, NY, Cornell University Press, 1989), p. 32.
20 *Ibid.*
21 *Ibid.*, p. 13.
22 R. O. Keohane, 'Neoliberal Institutionalism: A Perspective on World Politics', in R. O. Keohane (ed.), *International Institutions and State Power: Essays in International Relations Theory* (Boulder, CO, Westview Press, 1989), p. 4.
23 J. Ruggie, 'International Responses to Technology: Concepts and Trends', *International Organization*, 29: 3 (1975), 557–84.
24 S. D. Krasner (ed.), *International Regimes* (Ithaca, NY, Cornell University Press, 1983), p. 2. In particular, Krasner defined principles as 'beliefs of fact, causation, and rectitude'; norms as 'standards of behaviour defined in terms of rights and obligations'; rules as 'prescriptions or proscriptions for action'; and decision-making procedures as 'prevailing practices for making and implementing collective choice'.
25 Young, *International Cooperation*, p. 12.
26 *Ibid.*, p. 16.
27 R. O. Keohane, *After Hegemony: Cooperation and Discord in the World Political Economy* (Princeton, NJ, Princeton University Press, 1984), p. 89.
28 O. R. Young, 'International Regimes: Problems of Concept Formation', *World Politics*, 32 (1980), 331–56.
29 R. O. Keohane and J. S. Nye, *Power and Interdependence: World Politics in Transition* (Boston, MA, Little, Brown, 1977), p. 9.
30 P. Taylor, 'Interdependence and Autonomy in the European Communities: The Case of the European Monetary System', *Journal of Common Market Studies*,18: 4 (1980), 372.
31 *Ibid.*
32 *Ibid.*
33 R. W. Cox, 'Social Forces, States and World Orders: Beyond International Relations Theory', *Millennium*, 10: 2 (1981), 128; quoted in R. Tooze, 'Regimes and International Co-operation', in Groom and Taylor (eds), *Frameworks*, p. 202.
34 On this, see further the analysis provided by S. Strange, '"*Cave! Hic Dragones*": A Critique of Regime Analysis', in Krasner (ed.), *International Regimes*, pp. 337–54.
35 See, among others, A. A. Stein, 'Coordination and Collaboration: Regimes in an Anarchic World', in S. D. Krasner (ed.), *International Regimes*, pp. 115–40; R. O. Keohane, *After Hegemony*; and O. R. Young, 'International Regimes: Toward a New Theory of Institutions', *World Politics*, 39 (1986), 104–22.
36 See, among others, R. O. Keohane, 'Neoliberal Institutionalism: A Perspective on World Politics', in R. O. Keohane (ed.), *International Institutions and State Power: Essays in International Relations Theory* (Boulder, CO, Westview, 1989), p. 8; and J. M. Grieco, 'Anarchy and the Limits of Cooperation: A Realist's Critique of the Newest Liberal Institutionalism', *International Organization*, 42 (1988), 485–507.
37 S. Tarrow, 'Building a Composite Polity: Popular Contention in the European Union', *Institute for European Studies Working Paper*, 98/3, Cornell University, 1998, p. 14.
38 S. Bulmer, 'The Governance of the European Union: A New Institutionalist Approach', *Journal of Public Policy*, 13: 4 (1993), 353.
39 *Ibid.*, p. 355.
40 *Ibid.*
41 Rosamond, *Theories*, p. 114.
42 J. P. Olsen and B. G. Peters, 'Learning from Experience', *ARENA Reprints*, 96/5, 1996, p. 28.
43 J. P. Olsen, 'Organising European Institutions of Governance: A Prelude to an Institutional Account of Political Integration', *ARENA Working Papers*, 00/2, 2000, p. 10.
44 *Ibid.*, p. 14.

45 S. Bulmer, 'New Institutionalism, the Single Market and EU Governance', *ARENA Working Papers*, 97/25, 1997, p. 7.

46 J.-E. Lane and S. Ersson, The New Institutional Politics: Performance and Outcomes (London, Routledge, 2000), p. 20.

47 A. Hasenclever, P. Mayer and V. Rittberger, *Theories of International Regimes* (Cambridge, Cambridge University Press, 1997).

48 Keohane, 'Neoliberal Institutionalism', in Keohane (ed.), *International Institutions*, p. 4.

49 D. H. Claes, 'What Do Theories of International Regimes Contribute to the Explanation of Cooperation (and Failure of Cooperation) among Oil-Producing Countries?', *ARENA Working Papers*, 99/12, 1999, p. 2.

50 Hasenclever, Mayer and Rittberger, *Theories*, p. 137.

51 S. D. Krasner, 'Structural Causes and Regime Consequences: Regimes as Intervening Variables', in Krasner (ed.), *International Regimes*, p. 2.

52 This strand in theorising international relations acknowledges the importance of a normatively informed research context, by systematically investigating the impact of constitutive norms and rules; the role of ideas and communicative action; the uses of language and deliberative processes; the interplay of routinised practices, socialisation, symbolism and institutional interaction; and the relationship between agent identity and interests. The whole exercise is meant to herald a 'constructivist turn' in international relations theory that stresses the impact of intersubjectivity and social context on international processes. The starting point here is to incorporate into the process of understanding complex social reality 'human consciousness' and 'ideational factors' with a normative as well as instrumental dimension. Keeping in mind that there is both a realist and an idealist component in constructivist thought, constructivism is, above all, a social theory with a strong interdisciplinary reach, straddling the lines between the various sub-fields of social science research. The core conclusion to be drawn from constructivist research is that norms may achieve strong structuring power and that norm construction and rule following are mutually constitutive. Although it is difficult to reach an authoritative conclusion on the overall contribution of constructivist theorising to the study of international relations, it seems that a multitude of useful epistemological and analytic insights can be drawn from constructivist work, placing metatheoretical thinking at the centre of understanding the social ontology of international politics. For a good treatment of these theoretical and ontological issues see A. Wendt, *Social Theory of International Politics* (Cambridge, Cambridge University Press, 1999); E. Nadelmann, 'Global Prohibition Regimes: The Evolution of Norms in International Society', *International Organization*, 44 (1990) 479–526; M. Finnemore, 'Norms, Culture and World Politics: Insights from Sociology's Institutionalism', *International Organization*, 50 (1996), 325–48; P. Katzenstein, *The Culture of National Security: Norms and Identity in World Politics* (New York, Columbia University Press, 1996).

53 P. Taylor, *International Organization in the Modern World: The European and the Global Process* (London, Pinter, 1993), p. 3.

54 J. T. Checkel, 'International Institutions and Socialization', *ARENA Working Papers*, WP 99/5, 1999.

55 Jervis, 'Security Regimes', in Krasner (ed.), *International Regimes*, p. 173.

56 D. N. Chryssochoou, M. Tsinisizelis, S. Stavridis and K. Ifantis, *Theory and reform in the European Union* (Manchester and New York, Manchester University Press, 1999), p. 25.

57 A. Jünemann, 'Europe's Interrelations with North Africa in the New Framework of Euro-Mediterranean Partnership – A Provisional Assessment of the Barcelona Concept', *Conference Proceedings: The European Union in a Changing World* (Luxembourg, 1998), p. 365.

58 G. Edwards and Eric Philippart, '*Mare Nostrum* – the European Union and the Mediterranean in the 1990s and Beyond', Paper presented at the Fifth Biennial ESCA–USA Conference, Seattle 29 May–1 June 1997, p. 18.

59 See J. P. Derisbourg, 'The Euro-Mediterranean Partnership After Barcelona', Paper presented at the MEDAC Conference 'Prospects After Barcelona', Malta, March 1996.

60 Jünemann, 'Europe's Interrelations with North Africa', p. 383.

61 *Ibid.*, p. 373.

62 N. Fahmy, 'After Madrid and Barcelona: Prospects for Mediterranean Security', Paper presented at the MEDAC Conference 'Prospects After Barcelona', Malta, March 1996.

63 R. King and M. Donati, 'The "Divided" Mediterranean: Re-defining European Relationships', in R. Hudson and A. M. Williams (eds), *Divided Europe: Society and Territory* (London, Sage, 1999), p. 156.

64 Malcolm Rifkind, 'British Initiative in Investment Barriers', British Foreign Secretary Briefing at the Barcelona Conference, 28 November 1995, British Foreign Office.

65 E. Kienle, 'Destabilisation through Partnership? Euro-Mediterranean Relations after the Barcelona Declaration', *Mediterranean Politics*, 3: 2 (1998) 4.

66 The distinction between *Gemeinschaft* (community) and *Gesellschaft* (society) draws from Tönnies' sociological writings in the late nineteenth century. In a *Gemeinschaft*-type association, as opposed to the more instrumental notion of *Gesellschaft*, one may perceive the embryo of a genuine community that constitutes the identity of the individuals forming it. *Gemeinschaft* is also regarded as a stable form of association that best suits the prospering of mutually responsive relations: its members have developed a 'sense of community' – also known as 'community spirit' or 'community of attachment' – strong enough to overcome any potentially divisive issues. Thus, a *Gemeinschaft* is qualitatively distinct from and presumably higher than the numerical sum of the personal well-being of its individual members. In it, people associate themselves together because they think of their relationships as valuable in the dual sense of being important both as an end in and of itself. Thus, it is perceived as an internal living and organic 'collective entity', whose 'norms of order' are based on 'concord', as opposed to a *Gesellschaft* that rests on a contractual arrangement or 'convention'. Resting on relationships of mutual affirmation, the members of a *Gemeinschaft* develop strong feelings of 'togetherness', 'we-ness' or even 'oneness', which works towards the eventual framing of a collective consciousness. Thus, they are bound together by symbiotic relationships, think of their collective existence as dominating their individuality and perceive their close association as a means of improving their domestic conditions of living. An entity which is formed through this positive type of relationship points to 'a lasting and genuine form of living together', as opposed to its counterpart form of 'human *Gesellschaft*' which is considered as a mere co-existence of people otherwise independent of each other. In short, whereas the 'common sphere' of a *Gesellschaft* rests on the concept of contract, its 'secret' lying in 'a rational coming together of ends that remain individual', that of a *Gemeinschaft* rests on the concept of 'one people', its 'secret' being an internally oriented relationship among its members. Finally, it is important to note that no actual society or institution conforms completely to Tönnies' theoretical selections, for they are conceptual entities representing two ideal types of social organisation.

67 S. M. Nsouli, A. Bisat, and O. Kanaan, 'The European Union's New Mediterranean Strategy', *Finance and Development*, 33: 3 (1996), 14–17.

68 For a more detailed analysis of the economic benefits and costs of the EMP, see *ibid.*

69 Commission of the European Communities, Communication from the Commission to the Council and the European Parliament, 'Progress Report on the Euro-Mediterranean Partnership and Preparations for the Second Conference of Foreign Affairs Ministers', COM(97) 68 final, Brussels, 19 February 1997.

70 See A. Marquina, 'Security and Political Stability in the Mediterranean', *Revista CIDOB d'Afers Internacionals*, 37 (1997).

71 G. Luciani, 'Where to Start with Multilaterism – An Agenda for Cooperation Between Europe, the Middle East and North Africa', *Working Papers*, Research Group on European Affairs, University of Munich, August 1996.
72 R. Aliboni, 'The Euro-Mediterranean Partnership: An Interpretation from Italy', Paper presented at the MEDAC Conference 'Prospects After Barcelona', March 1996.
73 See Kienle, 'Destabilisation Though Partnership?'
74 G. Joffé, 'The Euro-Mediterranean Partnership Today', Informal EuroMeSCo–Senior Officials' Seminar, 'Euro-Mediterranean Security Dialogue', Bonn, Ministry of Foreign Affairs, 20 March 1999; *EuroMeSCo News*, 5: April 1999.
75 R. Gillespie, 'The Euro-Mediterranean Partnership', *Mediterranean Politics*, 2: 1 (1997), 4–5.
76 See also D. K. Xenakis, 'From Policy to Regime: Trends in Euro-Mediterranean Governance', *Cambridge Review of International Affairs*, 13: 1 (1999), 254–70.
77 E. Barbé, 'The Barcelona Conference: Launching Pad of a Process', *Mediterranean Politics*, 1: 1 (1996), 32.
78 Keohane, 'Neoliberal Institutionalism', in Keohane (ed.), *International Institutions*, p. 4.
79 Hasenclever *et al.*, *Theories of International Regimes*, p. 7.
80 J. P. Olsen, 'European Challenges to the Nation State', *ARENA Reprints*, 97/11, 1997, p. 182.
81 *Ibid.*, p. 175.
82 Jervis, 'Security Regimes', in Krasner (ed.), *International Regimes.*
83 Krasner, 'Structural Causes and Regime Consequences', in Krasner (ed.), *International Regimes*, p. 5.
84 *Ibid.*, p. 6.
85 *Ibid.*, p. 9.
86 *Ibid.*, p. 10.
87 See A. Bin, 'Mediterranean Diplomacy: Evolution and Prospects', *Jean Monnet Working Papers in Comparative and International Politics*, 5, University of Catania, January 1997.
88 Concluding Statement of the UK Presidency by the Foreign Secretary Mr Robin Cook, Ad-Hoc Euro-Mediterranean Ministerial Meeting, Palermo, 3–4 June 1998.

6

The emerging Euro-Mediterranean system

Drawing insights

'Current political transformations and reforms in Europe as well as in other parts of the world', writes Olsen, 'are redefining the terms of political life',[1] reactivating basic questions of governance across a wide range of policy domains. Fundamental changes in the structure and operation of institutionalised shared rule among distinct culturally defined and socially organised polities pose new challenges to the interminable search for a viable political order based on stable authority patterns of governance not only within but, increasingly, between states and peoples. These ascending challenges necessitate the integration of domestic and international politics and, by extension, the conditions for developing a more profound understanding of the relationship between continuity and change, unity and fragmentation, sovereignty and interdependence, autonomy and control. Defining elements of separateness thus proceeds hand in hand with the need to identify degrees of common understanding among a plethora of public, semi-public and private actors operating under conditions of globalisation.

Against this background, defining the Mediterranean is no easy task. One plausible way of doing so is by locating it in the midst of the 'global village', while another is to do so in terms of history, socio-economic realities, prevailing value spheres, compatibility of belief systems, cultural interaction and so on. Whatever the definitional approach, however, the Mediterranean remains a heterogeneous synthesis of various religious and ethic groups, as well as a region characterised by unequal economic development, a plurality of political regimes, divergent perceptions of security (threats), and uneven demographic growth. As stated in Chapter 2, 'the Mediterranean' refers to a regional space where geography, history and politics intermesh with culture and religion with enormous complexity, resulting in a composite system of partial regimes, each reflecting a particular sense of being and belonging. Such a definition is specific enough to map the peculiarities of the region and broad enough to allow for the accommodation of complementary variables.

Contemporary analysts pay due attention to the ways in which mental maps, ideologies, belief systems and worldviews impinge on the actors' perceptions and behaviour, while influencing political interaction. For instance, Arabic communities perceive the EMP as a mechanism to counterbalance American economic hegemony in the Middle East.[2] Moreover, the creation of a common framework for regional co-operation touches upon sensitive issues of Arab identity, to which concepts like 'Middle Easternism' or 'North-Africanism' are not accepted as viable alternatives. In this context, it is worth noting that the EMP seems to be more acceptable to Arab states since 'Mediterraneanism' is seen as less threatening. Kramer writes:

> In a broad Mediterranean framework, Israel is not an economic giant but one more partner, effectively balanced by Europe. The 'Mediterranean option' also marginalizes the United States and offers a flicker of hope that some kind of great power rivalry might be reintroduced into the region, and enhance Arab manoeuvrability *vis-à-vis* Israel. Nevertheless, Mediterraneanism is also not readily accepted as an alternative to Arab–Islamic identity.[3]

In terms of such broad concepts as 'the West' or 'the Orient', the Mediterranean remains a divided construct, with its embedded complexity occupying a prominent position between order and disorder.[4] This makes the development of co-operative politics in the region an open-ended endeavour. However useful, as opposed to merely convenient, the division of the Mediterranean into 'Europe' and 'others' generates mental constructs that fail to capture the dynamic (or even dialectic) between Europe and the Mediterranean. Such analogies underestimate the conditions required for a meaningful regional partnership that can not only prevent the outbreak of autochthonous conflicts, but can activate processes of international regime formation. Despite the fact that current Euro-Arab relations are still nurtured by prejudices preserved in Islamic–Christian relations,[5] the new challenges confronting the region demand a coherent response from all the actors involved in its transformative order. Interestingly, the active engagement of multiple actors in the politics of order building may exacerbate the possibilities for reaching substantive agreement on many sensitive issues, such as immigration, the economic aspects of security, the external protection of citizens, respect for human rights and even the resolution of protracted conflicts. At the same time, the very process of advocating such common goods may lead to regional reconciliation. As Zartman and Bergman convincingly maintain, successful negotiations change established perceptions of conflict from a 'zero-sum' to a 'win–win' situation.[6] Confidence building and a shared commitment to mutually rewarding outcomes can feed this process, constituting an essential adjunct to successful bargaining in 'deciding upon allocation of commonly desired utilities'.[7] In this endeavour, the institutionalisation of the EMP, defined as 'the emergence of enduring practices and rules, structures of meaning and resources',[8] is deemed necessary given the prevailing levels of Mediterranean complexity. But equally imperative is a new civilisational dialogue that will do away with the subjectivist approach that wants the West acting as a universal human rights protector, on the basis of fixed notions of democratic governance informed by a predominantly liberal understanding of political order.

Limited as it may be, the potential for systematising regional conflict prevention and conflict management in the Mediterranean awaits utilisation. This issue was also raised at the Second Ministerial Conference in Malta, without however achieving any significant progress in institutional terms. Working on the concept of 'co-operative security' implies making maximum use of non-military mechanisms and less use of military or defence structures. Applied to the region, co-operative security is essentially about conflict prevention, as it is about improving transparency and the predictability of factors that characterise security considerations in the region. Historically, European nations have used conflict prevention as a means to an end: that of strengthening their sense of security. Throughout the Cold War era, large-scale security regimes like the CSCE eased East–West confrontation and helped to prevent superpower conflict. What is more, post-1989 Helsinki experience, which witnessed the transformation of the CSCE into the OSCE, illustrates that, even today, security regimes remain effective policy tools. As Spencer notes, 'where OSCE is the confidence-building institution *par excellence*, elements of its approaches and vocabulary have crept into the policies of other organisations. This is most evident in the EU's Euro-Mediterranean Partnership.'[9] Here, the Helsinki Process may offer a suitable model for the institutionalisation of the EMP, as the CSCE has evolved from a process-driven system to an international organisation.

The adoption of C/OSCE-like mechanisms and monitoring structures by the EMP would be a welcome development, for such instruments carry out specific tasks that help to transform the constitutive principles of the EMP into a practical political achievement.[10] A difficulty associated with this line of development is that the EMP has not yet operationalised or even regularised political co-operation to any significant degree, despite the adoption of the Action Plan that was set out at the beginning of the Barcelona Process. Aliboni writes: 'While the Action Plan would be a list of measures and policies that the Partners would pick up and negotiate over time according to priorities and modes they would remain free to gradually agree upon, the Charter would be an institutional framework with a normative ambition and a stronger mechanism of political dialogue.'[11] Speaking of tangible endeavours, Calleya suggests that the partners must introduce a basic type of confidence-building measure that will enable them to manage and contain the new security challenges in the region.[12] The levels of complexity stemming from the particular nature of protracted conflicts and threat (mis)perceptions constrain the implementation of the agreed PBMs. Thus, the creation of conflict-prevention mechanisms should provide PBMs with at least a minimal capacity to intervene in real or potential conflict situations.

Central to this study has been the claim that effective order-building can not be realised under the present institutional configuration of the EMP. Although the flexibility of the latter is a positive element in managing regional interdependence, its weak institutional structure makes it more difficult for partners to sacrifice the pursuit of short-term interests on the altar of international co-operation. But what model of institution building should the Barcelona Process proceed with so as to foster regional security and reorganise the Mediterranean order? A plausible answer is that, without investing further in concrete PBMs on issues of substance, such as developing a Charter for Peace and Stability in the region, then the prospects for a meaningful partnership will be particularly grim.[13] To that end, the partner states would have to foster an atmosphere in which norms of good governance act as a system-steering agency in the construction of a larger pluralist order. The prospective Charter may also come to resemble an exercise in pre-emptive diplomacy and, above all, a form of institutionalised governance based on legitimate patterns of shared rule. Let us for a moment recall that the 1990 Paris Charter, by establishing a timetable of regular political consultations, and by giving the CSCE a modest degree of institutional underpinning, has substantially contributed to its successful structural transformation into an international organisation with operational capabilities of its own. Moreover, a Euro-Mediterranean Charter can provide the much-needed levels of transparency, stability and trust that any meaningful regional partnership requires, along with the establishment of the necessary machinery for effective conflict management.

Turning to the economic domain, it is neither realistic nor even desirable to expect that the development efforts of southern Mediterranean partners will converge on a single model of 'good economic behaviour'. International experience shows that the economies that have performed well have done so by employing their own set of policies. Macroeconomic stability and high investment rates have been common, but beyond that many details have varied. Correspondingly, the rules governing the economic framework of the EMP must be flexible enough to allow southern Mediterranean countries to develop their own 'styles' of market liberalisation, in the same way that countries like Germany, Japan and the US did in the past. According to Rodrik's recent analysis, there is evidence to suggest that developing countries can thrive in the new global economy only if they combine economic openness with a clear domestic investment strategy and effective civil and political institutions.[14]

In this light, one can draw important insights form the experience offered today by the transformative polities of central and eastern Europe. In particular, the evolution of systemic transition and macroeconomic performance have benefited from a new cultural environment, the emergence of which in the Euro-Mediterranean space will be difficult. Building the rules and institutions of a working market economy calls for tenacious and continual political action.

Although the process can go ahead only by trial and error, it is imperative to keep to a fundamental direction: designing efficient systems of internationalised co-operation requires a maximum, not a minimum, of what might be called 'capacity for governance'. At the level of the emerging Euro-Mediterranean system, such a capacity is presently lacking not only because of various institutional weaknesses *per se*, but because of the absence of substantive political will and, by extension, of credible commitments to make effective use of the existing institutional infrastructure in the process of managing the regional arrangements.

Over the past decade, the political economies of the Mediterranean region have become more open to global pressures, offering greater autonomy to their respective private sectors. Today, countries like Egypt, Morocco, Tunisia and Jordan are regarded as cases of successful, albeit partial, economic reform and restructuring, for they have managed, in large measure, to avoid shock therapy, preferring instead a gradual and heterodox economic approach that emphasises the centrality of states in processes of economic governance. In this context, the process of 'marketisation' is accompanied by the preservation of public policies intended to mitigate the inevitable social costs that economic reform involves. Yet, as Couloumbis and Veremis note,

> the central question, in theory as well as in practice, is whether the Mediterranean region, despite its structural asymmetries ... will manage fit into a functionalist paradigm which permitted Western Europe ... to move forward toward economic and political integration employing the geoeconomic premises of Jean Monnet and abandoning the military power considerations of Clausevitzian geopolitics.[15]

On this view, the basket-based arrangements of the EMP, combining both low and high politics areas, may prove instrumental in fostering a new co-operative ethos among the partner states. The argument here is that interest convergence around economic arrangements acts as a means of contributing to a relaxation of tensions in areas where controversy is more likely to arise, areas like democratisation, human rights' issues, etc. The composite nature of the EMP offers a wide range of opportunities for the functionalist expectations of the actors involved to become part of a consensually pre-determined set of policies that are crucial to overall systemic stability. In other words, the MEFTA can be seen as a system of rules governing the interaction of actors around functionally specific tasks. By elevating the creation of rules of transaction to a systemic property of the EMP, a certain economic bias may prevail, whose liberalising effects may offer a platform from which substantive rewards can be gained for all. This of course points to a preference for a functionalist strategy, which is nevertheless embedded within the practice of market-oriented regimes.

Linked to the functionalist process is a notion of co-operation whereby individuals develop a greater awareness of their mutual needs and are prepared to make better use of the nascent common institutions. Drawing from a Mitranian logic to international co-operation,[16] collective action in functionally linked areas emanates as a real option for human governance. The basis of the functionalist hypothesis is that as individuals gradually come to identify with the problem-solving capacity of the new functional agencies, habits of co-operative interaction will emerge that would indicate, alongside the functionalist reorganisation of (regional) society, 'a sense of the whole'. At the same time, processes of social learning, attitudinal change and even (security) community growth by functional association may be set in train, dissociating the art of governance from any rigid adherence to a 'set' political ideology, as opposed to 'a "way" of thinking'. The end-result of this elaborate action process may be a kind of pragmatic politics which, although it does not dispense with the idea of power, focuses more on the role of task-oriented international agencies, as well as on non-coercive means of rational problem solving and the peaceful settlement of conflicts.

In general terms, there seems to be a cumulative effect in the functionalist thesis: once problems are recognised as common, and as solutions to these problems arise from collective rational thinking, there is a tendency to expand such co-operative behaviour to other relevant spheres of action. Another point here is that 'functional regionalism' is about the application of carefully examined, but not necessarily 'apolitical' strategies for transcending territorial boundaries in tackling common problems. In this respect, regional institution building becomes conditional on the (functionally determined) needs of the general system, rather than the preferred lines of action taken by states according to narrowly conceived territorial interests. These reflections lead to the wider assumption that international functional synergies should be acknowledged as crucial factors in Euro-Mediterranean order building.

International relations emphasises the role of international regimes as institutional devices for co-operative problem solving in areas characterised by the horizontal co-ordination of states. Arguably, torrents of ink have been used in writing about the effectiveness of international institutions, their transforming qualities, as well as their adaptive capacities in relation to the new world order requirements. Our investigation into the prospects for accommodating dialogue in the fragmented Euro-Mediterranean system has demonstrated that the preservation of regional stability is also closely linked to institutions. Likewise, in the security domain, and particularly in collective conflict management, the relevance of institutionalised co-operation becomes apparent.[17] But to understand liberalism as the cause of the wider security agenda one needs to focus on economic liberalism and, by extension, on the global market economy that so heavily impacts upon the evolving Barcelona Process. Buzan and Waever provide the theory:

> Along with democratisation, market economics played a big role in liberalism's apparent success in solving the problem of war for a substantial part of the international system. But now that liberalism, and especially economic liberalism, has become both the hegemonic ideology and the dominant mode of organisation, a new framework for (in)security unfolds that is quite unlike the Cold War one. With

> liberalism defining many of the most important political and economic spaces on the planet, it simultaneously spreads the classical version of the liberal peace, and opens up a new set of insecurities. The new agenda of insecurity arises in large part from the operation of the global market economy itself. It is not an aim of liberalism (quite the contrary), but an often unintended and unanticipated effect of liberal policy in practice. It is partly about economic insecurity directly, and partly about the spillover of effects from the operation of global markets into the military, political, societal and environmental sectors.[18]

The problem is thus how to organise regional security out of the systemic complexity of the Mediterranean. As noted earlier in the study, the latter represents a regional space where several civilisations and religions have mutually influenced and enriched each other, as well as a crossroads for multiple cultural, human and economic exchanges. But to break down Mediterranean complexity one has first to recognise diversity as an essentialistic principle in the 'heterarchical' Mediterranean order: the system is itself constituted in the clash of different systems. Its peoples have not yet laid down the foundations of a communal journey. The idiosyncratic nature of the constituent actors makes the possibility of a functionalist strategy a more plausible means of co-operation than one based on overrated assumptions about the socialisation of the state actors involved. A heterarchical order minimises homogeneity/universality as the principal referent for sub-systemic co-operation. This form of enhanced particularity through the reflexive appropriation of difference becomes normative for the system itself. This resonates with a broader aspiration for partnership, one that transcends any mono-dimensional configuration of power, stressing instead the complex character of an allegedly common destiny. This is exactly where a heterarchical regime is better equipped to manage the existing levels of Mediterranean complexity. The plausibility of this claim to the importance of reflexivity as opposed to co-ordinated hierarchy rests on a systemic perspective, whereby 'sub-systems do not [necessarily] join together into higher level systems … nor can they be conceived of as instances of a totality'.[19]

Turning again to the question of international regime creation, neither neorealism nor interpretations of the 'power of power politics' offers an objective basis for the emergence of a regional order that is, in turn, based on a predetermined strategy for the promotion of Western liberalism in exchange for regional co-operation. True, a hierarchy of norms may prove necessary for the sustenance of different collective arrangements in the Mediterranean, but such a construct should also reflect the praxis of mutualism and respect for 'the other'. On a positive interpretation of regional heterarchy, the aim is twofold: for 'others' to be brought into the management processes of the EMP; and for regional diversity to transform itself from a self-referential property of distinct segments (emphasising the separateness of the actors) into an identifiable pluralist order. As to the question whether international regimes matter in complex, fragile and fragmented orders, a plausible answer is that regimes do not play such a crucial role in issues where states can realise their own interests directly through unilateral applications of leverage. Rather, regimes are formed to overcome collective goods dilemmas by means of co-ordinating the actors' behaviour. Although actors may keep pursuing their own interests, they also create common institutional frameworks to structure and co-ordinate collective action. This is where regimes offer an indispensable service, by making international co-operation possible even within such diverse orders as the Euro-Mediterranean heterarchy, providing a framework for further agreement, encouraging transactions and reducing cheating among states.

Concluding notes

Mediterranean politics has gained a higher profile since the signing of the Barcelona Declaration. As stated in the Introduction to this study, it has come alive, sparking new interest in issues of Euro-Mediterranean governance in terms of studying the envisaged transformation of the region from a dispersed system of bilateral ties to the eventual framing of institutionalised patterns of rule based on shared understandings and mutually rewarding interactions between units with diverse social traditions and cultural perspectives. A new phase of intensified interaction between the European and southern Mediterranean economies has emerged, including trade, financial investment and the initiation of new forms of industrial relations. The MEFTA objective will provide for the free circulation of manufactured products, a progressive liberalisation of trade in agricultural products, liberalisation of the right of establishment for companies, trans-border services and the free movement of capital. The problem that still persists, however, is that the region's economic accomplishments do not match its potential for utilising political governance to facilitate the identification of a commonality of interests, aspirations and, crucially, a shared political vision of the shape of things to come. Regional complexity, different conceptions of order and the 'good polity', and a multitude of distinct economic strategies are the principal reasons underlying this shortfall. At a more practical level, stimulating economic growth based on mutually compatible schemes for collective (social) action requires a higher level of interdependence among the partners as well as between them and external actors, so that economic activity is re-oriented in the interest of higher and more equitably distributed gains. The pursuit over time of a more open trade and investment regime both within the region and with the outside world points in the direction of developing rules of the game based on transparency, predictability, non-discrimination and progressive liberalisation in an ever-globalising market economy.

As the latter will predictably continue to expand, the Mediterranean will become even more important as a regional economic space as well as a channel for the movement of vital resources. The emergence of globalised and regionalised markets makes the systemisation and structuring of Euro-Mediterranean relations increasingly possible, yet not inevitable. While bright opportunities exist post-1995, they could well slip by without adequate levels of institutionalisation and, given that the EU has been more concerned with the perceived threats of migration and Islamic activism than with the opportunities offered by shared interests, it is hardly surprising that its Mediterranean policy has been criticised for being limited, betraying a lack of credible long-term commitment.[20] Yet, should the Mediterranean continue to serve as a barrier rather than a bridge between a prosperous and heavily institutionalised Europe and a poor and fragmented Mediterranean south, it is likely that the resulting regional order will be characterised by elements of instability. Progress in developing co-operative relations is by no means irreversible. Failure to empathise with the other's perspectives and security needs could lead to an increase in hostility and mistrust. It is in this sense that regional diversity should be seen more as an asset than as an obstacle.

Moreover, contrary to the expectations of their advocates, policies of internal and external economic liberalisation are not likely to increase the economic performance of the southern Mediterranean partners.[21] Reactions to socio-economic inequities and suspicions about the motives of both Mediterranean rims could conceivably result in a resurgence of forces of disorder. Thus, of particular importance in the years to come will be the institutional format chosen to transcend the peculiarities underlying the transformation of this complex regional order. But institutionalisation of existing rules alone will not be sufficient to manage the Euro-Mediterranean security agenda. New rules and norms on how to handle change and instability should emerge given that behaviour, and not just proclamations, will determine the outcome of confidence and security building in the region. Methods of conflict management like mediation and arbitration can also become available, and new techniques like third-party consultation and problem solving be established. In a nutshell, 'a new era requires new ideas'.

As argued earlier, nationalistic and religious cleavages are a major feature of the Mediterranean's social structure. Such fragmentation is responsible for the slowing down of democratic consolidation and viable socio-economic reform. Beneath such tensions lie differences in the historical trajectories for constructing and sustaining differentiated identities in the region. These trajectories reflect different models of socio-political integration underpinned by different philosophies, ascribing different meanings to such general and even essentially contested concepts as democracy and modernity. Whatever the legitimising ethos of the prevailing worldviews, there are good grounds for thinking that preventive diplomacy, trust-building measures, transparent politico-economic structures, acknowledgement of cultural pluralism and symbiotic association, along with the prevalence of an open dialogue are useful tools for revitalising a cross-fertilisation between heterogeneous units in order that a meaningful, binding and balanced regional partnership can emerge and consolidate its strength.

The search for a new legitimacy in Euro-Mediterranean relations depends on the partners' capacity to resist the forces of polarisation and segmentation, as well as on the credibility of their commitment to rediscovering a sense of process (and purpose too) based on humanism, pluriformity and social justice. The flexibility of the fledging EMP, the way in which it is valued by the partners themselves, and the means through which its constitutive norms can facilitate agreement on the basis of mutualism, reciprocity and, where possible, reconciliation, will all affect its potential for acquiring substantive operational capabilities of its own and adjusting itself to a new and creative politics of institutional accommodation. What is most needed is a set of system-transforming mechanisms to alleviate regional complexity, absorb order-building vibrations and stabilise the emerging Euro-Mediterranean system. And given that 'forgetfulness about important things can be dangerous',[22] the making of a vibrant and enduring Euro-Mediterranean space should counsel an end to that neglect.

Notes

1 J. P. Olsen, 'The Changing Political Organization of Europe: An Institutional Perspective on the Role of Comprehensive Reform Efforts', *ARENA Working Papers*, 97/5, 1997, p. 1.

2 As El-Sayed Selim put it: 'They would like to see a more active European role in the Middle East as Europe is perceived to be less biased towards Israel than the United States is.' See M. El-Sayed Selim, 'Arab Perceptions of the European Union's Euro-Mediterranean Projects', in S. J. Blank (ed.), *Mediterranean Security into the Coming Millennium* (Strategic Studies Institute, US Army War College, 1999), p. 148.

3 M. Kramer, 'The Middle East, Old and New', *Daedalus*, 126: 2 (1997) 102.

4 See D. K. Xenakis, 'Order and Change in the Euro-Mediterranean System', *Mediterranean Quarterly*, 11: 4 (2000), 75–90.

5 See H. Köchler, 'Muslim–Christian Ties in Europe: Past, Present and Future', paper presented at the Second International Seminar 'Civilizational Dialogue: Japan, Islam and the West', Kuala Lumpur, 2–3 September 1996.

6 See W. Zartman and M. R. Bergman, *The Practical Negotiator* (New Haven, CT, Yale University Press, 1982).

7 G. H. Snyder and P. Diesing, *Conflict Among Nations: Bargaining, Decision Making, and System Structure in International Crises* (Pinceton, NJ, Princeton University Press, 1977), p. 1.

8 J. P. Olsen, European Challenges to the Nation State', *ARENA Reprints*, 97/11, 1997, p. 160.

9 C. Spencer, 'Building Confidence in the Mediterranean', *Mediterranean Politics*, 2: 1 (1997) 39.

10 See D. K. Xenakis, 'The Barcelona Process: Some Lessons from Helsinki', *Jean Monnet Working Papers in Comparative and International Politics*, 17, University of Catania, 1998. For a more detailed account see D. K. Xenakis, 'Transforming Regional Orders: The Helsinki and Barcelona Processes Compared', unpublished PhD dissertation, School of Historical, Political and Sociological Studies, University of Exeter, 2000.

11 R. Aliboni, 'European Union Security Perceptions and Policies Towards the Mediterranean', in Blank (ed.), *Mediterranean Security*, p. 137.

12 S. C. Calleya, 'Providing New Dynamism to the Euro-Med Process', *Euro-Mediterranean Magazine* 3, EuroMed Internet Forum, 1998.

13 Concluding Statement of the UK Presidency by the Foreign Secretary Mr Robert Cook, Ad-Hoc Euro-Mediterranean Ministerial Meeting, Palermo, 3–4 June 1998.

14 According to Rodrik, emerging market nations must participate in the world economy on their own terms and not on those 'dictated' by global markets and multilateral institutions. The pursuit of 'international competitiveness' has too often crowded out traditional development concerns related to industrialisation and poverty in many emerging economies. See D. Rodrik, 'Making Openness Work', *Policy Essay*, 24, Overseas Development Council, January 1999.

15 T. Couloumbis and T. Veremis, 'Introduction: The Mediterranean in Perspective', in S. Stavridis *et al.* (eds), *The Foreign Policies of the European Union's Mediterranean States and Applicant Countries in the 1990s* (London, Macmillan, 1999), p. 10.

16 See D. Mitrany, *A Working Peace System* (London, Royal Institute of International Affairs, 1943). See also D. Mitrany, *The Functional Theory of Politics* (London, Martin Robertson, 1975).

17 See J. S. Duffield, 'Explaining the Long Peace in Europe: the Contributions of Regional Security Regimes', *Review of International Studies*, 20: 4 (1994), 369–88.

18 B. Buzan and O. Waever, 'Liberalism and Security', *CSD Bulletin*, 5, Centre for the Study of Democracy, University of Westminster, 1998, p. 96.

19 Z. Bankowski and E. Christodoulidis, 'The European Union as an Essentially Contested Project', *European Law Journal*, 4: 4 (1998) 350.

20 I. Romeo, 'The European Union and North Africa: Keeping the Mediterranean "Safe" for Europe', *Mediterranean Politics*, 3: 2 (1998) 21–38.

21 Both Kienle and El-Sayed Selim note that as long as the EU insists on its unidirectional approach, the Arabs will be ambivalent partners in the Barcelona Process. See E. Kienle, 'Destabilization Through Partnership? Euro-Mediterranean Relations After the Barcelona Declaration', *Mediterranean Politics*, 3: 2 (1998), 1–20; and El-Sayed Selim, 'Arab Perceptions', in Blank (ed.), *Mediterranean Security*, pp. 143–58.

22 This phrase is borrowed from T. A. Spragens, Jr, *Civic Liberalism: Reflections on Our Democratic Ideals* (Lanham, Rowman & Littlefield, 1999), p. 208.

Select Bibliography

Books

Adams, N., *Worlds Apart: The North–South Divide and the International System* (London, Zed Books, 1993).

Adler, E. and Barnett, M. (eds), *Security Communities* (Cambridge, Cambridge University Press, 1998).

Allan, P. and Goldmann, K. (eds), *The End of the Cold War: Evaluating Theories of International Relations* (The Hague, Martinus Nijhoff, 1995).

Alexander, D. and Alexander, P., *The Lion Handbook to the Bible* (London, Lion, 1983).

Aliboni, R. (ed.), *Southern European Security in the 1990s* (London, Pinter, 1992).

Aliboni, R., Joffé, G. and Niblock T. (eds), *Security Challenges in the Mediterranean Region* (London, Frank Cass, 1996).

Allen, D. and Pijpers A. (eds), *European Foreign Policy-Making and the Arab–Israeli Conflict* (The Hague, Martinus Nijhoff, 1984).

Al-Mani, S. A., *The Euro-Arab Dialogue: A Study in Associative Diplomacy* (London, Pinter, 1983).

Archibugi, S. and Held, D. (eds), *Cosmopolitan Democracy: An Agenda for a New World Order* (Cambridge, Polity Press, 1995).

Ashworth, L. M. and Long, D. (eds), *New Perspectives on International Functionalism* (London, Macmillan, 1999).

Ayubi, N. (ed.), *Distant Neighbors: The Political Economy of Relations between Europe and the Middle East/North Africa* (Reading, Ithaka Press, 1995).

Baldwin, D. (ed.), *Neorealism and Neoliberalism: The Contemporary Debate* (New York, Columbia University Press, 1993).

Barston, R. P., *Modern Diplomacy* (London, Longman, 1988).

Bekemans, L. and Tsoukalis, L. (eds), *Europe and Global Economic Interdependence* (Brussels, European Inter-University Press, 1993).

Black, C. E., *The Dynamics of Modernization: A Study in Comparative History* (New York, Harper & Row, 1966).

Blackwill, R. D. and Stürmer, M. (eds) *Allies Divided: Transatlantic Policies for the Greater Middle East* (Cambridge, MA, MIT Press, 1997).

Blank, S. J (ed.), *Mediterranean Security into the Coming Millennium* (Strategic Studies Institute, US Army War College, 1999).

Booth, K. (ed.), *New Thinking about Strategy and International Security* (London, HarperCollins, 1991).

Booth, K. and Smith, S. (ed.), *International Relations Theory Today* (Cambridge, Polity Press, 1997).

Braudel, F., *The Mediterranean and the Mediterranean World in the Age of Philip II*, 2 vols, 5th edn (London, Fontana Press, 1987).

Brown, L. C., *International Politics in the Middle East: Old Rules, Dangerous Games* (Princeton, NJ, Princeton University Press, 1984).

Buchan, D., *Europe: The Strange Superpower* (Dartmouth, Aldershot, 1993).

Bull, H., *The Anarchical Society: A Study of Order in World Politics* (New York, Columbia University Press, 1977).

Buzan, B., *People, States and Fear: The National Security Problem in International Relations* (Brighton, Wheatsheaf Books, 1983).

Buzan, B., Waever, O. and de Wilde J., *Security: A New Framework for Analysis* (London, Lynne Rienner, 1998).

Calleya, S. C., *Navigating Regional Dynamics in the Post-Cold War World: Patterns of Relations in the Mediterranean Area* (Dartmouth, Aldershot, 1997).

Cantori, L. and Spiegel S., *The International Politics of the Regions: A Comparative Approach* (Englewood Cliffs, NJ, Prentice-Hall, 1970).

Carr, F. (ed.), *Europe: The Cold Divide* (London, Macmillan, 1998).

Carr, F. and Ifantis, K., *NATO in the New European Order* (London, Macmillan, 1996).

Chryssochoou, D. N., *Democracy in the European Union* (London and New York, I. B. Tauris, 1998).

Chryssochoou, D. N., *Theorizing European Integration* (London, Sage, 2001).

Chryssochoou, D. N., Tsinisizelis, M., Stavridis, S. and Ifantis, K., *Theory and reform in the European Union* (Manchester and New York, Manchester University Press, 1999).

Coffey, P., *The Future of Europe* (Aldershot, Elgar, 1995).

Cohen, R., *International Politics: The Rules of the Game* (London, Longman, 1981).

Collinson, S., *Shore to Shore: The Politics of Migration in Euro-Maghreb Relations* (London, Royal Institute of International Affairs, 1997).

Couloumbis, T. and Dokos, T. (eds) *Arms Control and Security in the Middle East and the CIS Republics* (Athens, Hellenic Foundation for European and Foreign Policy, 1995).

Cox, R. O. (ed.), *The New Realism: Perspectives on Multilateralism and World Order* (Tokyo, United Nations University Press, 1997).

Cox, R. O., *Approaches to World Order* (Cambridge, Cambridge University Press, 1996).

Dawisha, A. and Zartman, I. W. (eds), *Beyond Coercion: The Durability of the Arab State* (London, Croom Helm, 1988).

Deutsch, K. W. *et al.*, *Political Community and the North Atlantic Area* (Princeton, NJ, Princeton University Press, 1957).

Dewitt, D. B., Haglund, D. and Kirton, J. (eds), *Building a New Global Order: Emerging Trends in International Security* (Oxford, Oxford University Press, 1993).

Diamond, J., Linz, J. and Lipset, S. M. (eds), *Democracy in Developing Countries: Asia* (Boulder, CO, Lynne Rienner, 1989).

Diamond, L. and Plattner M. F. (eds), *The Global Resurgence of Democracy* (Baltimore, MD, Johns Hopkins University Press, 1993).

Dokos, T. P. and Pierros, F. T., *The Mediterranean Towards the 21st Century: Greece's Position* (in Greek) (Athens, Papazisis, 1996).

Dowall, D. D., *Europe and the Arabs: Discord or Symbiosis?* (London, Pinter, 1992).

Duchene, F. *et al.*, *The European Community and the Mediterranean Basin* (Luxembourg, Commission of the European Communities, 1984).

Duffy, M., Farrell T. and Sloan, G. (eds), *European Defence in 2020* (Exeter, University of Exeter, 1998).

Edwards, G. and Regelsberger, E. (eds), *Europe's Global Links: The European Community and Inter-Regional Cooperation* (London, Pinter, 1990).

Ehteshami, A. and Noneman, G., *War and Peace in the Gulf: Domestic Politics and Regional Relations into the 1990s* (Reading, Ithaca Press, 1991).

Espozito, J. L. (ed.), *The Islamic Threat: Myth or Reality* (Oxford, Oxford University Press, 1992).

Espozito, J. L., *Islam and Politics*, 4th edn (Syracuse, NY, Syracuse University Press, 1998).

European Commission, *The European Union in a Changing World* (Luxembourg, European Commission, 1998).

Falk, R. A. and Mendlovitz, S. H. (eds), *Regional Politics and World Order* (San Francisco, W. H. Freeman, 1973).

Falkenrath, R. A., *Shaping Europe's Military Order: The Origins and Consequences of the CFE Treaty* (Cambridge, MA, MIT Press, 1995).

Feldman, S. and Levite A. (eds), *Arms Control in the New Middle East Security Environment* (Jerusalem, Tel Aviv University, 1994).

Forsyth, J., *Unions of States: The Theory and Practice of Confederation* (Leicester, Leicester University Press, 1981).

Fukuyama, F., *The End of History and the Last Man* (New York, Free Press, 1992).

Fuller, G. E. and Lesser I. O., *A Sense of Siege: The Geopolitics of Islam and the West* (Boulder, CO, Westview Press, 1995).

Gasteyger, C., *An Ambiguous Power: The European Union in a Changing World* (Gutersloh, Bertelsmann Foundation, 1996).

Gillespie, R. (ed.), *Mediterranean Politics*, vol. II (London, Pinter, 1996).

Gillespie, R. *Spain and the Mediterranean: Developing a European Policy Towards the South* (London, Macmillan, 1999).

Ginsberg, R. H., *Foreign Policy Actions of the European Community: The Politics of Scale* (London, Adamandine Press, 1989).

Gompert, D. C. and Larrabee, S. F. (eds), *America and Europe: A Partnership for a New Era* (Cambridge, Cambridge University Press, 1997).

Golden, J. *et al.* (eds), *NATO at Forty: Change, Continuity and Prospects* (London, Westview, 1989).

Gould, P. and White, R., *Mental Maps* (Harmondsworth, Penguin, 1974).

Grabbe, H. and Hughes, K., *Eastward Enlargement of the European Union* (London, Royal Institute of International Affairs, 1997).

Greider, W., *One World, Ready or Not: The Manic Logic of Global Capitalism* (New York, Shimon & Schuster, 1997).

Grenon, M. and Batisse, M. (eds), *Futures for the Mediterranean Basin: The Blue Plan*, United Nations Environmental Programme (Oxford, Oxford University Press, 1989).

Grilli, E., *The EC and Developing Countries* (New York, Cambridge University Press, 1993).

Groom, A. J. R. and Taylor P. (eds), *Frameworks for International Cooperation* (London, Pinter, 1990).

Haas, E. B., *When Knowledge Is Power: Three Models of Change in International Organizations* (Berkeley, University of California Press, 1990).

Haas, P. E., *Saving the Mediterranean: The Politics of International Environmental Cooperation* (New York, Columbia University Press, 1992).

Haftendorn, H. and Tuschoff ,C. (eds), *America and Europe in an Era of Change* (Boulder, CO, Westview Press, 1993).

Haglund, D. and Ehrhart, H. G. (eds), *The 'New Peacekeeping' and European Security: German and Canadian Interests and Issues* (Baden-Baden, Nomos, 1995).

Hamlyn, D. W., *Metaphysics* (Cambridge, Cambridge University Press, 1995).

Hampsher-Monk, I. and Stanyer, J. (eds), *Contemporary Political Studies* (Exeter, Short Run Press, 1996).

Hasenclever, A., Mayer, P. and Rittberger, V., *Theories of International Regimes* (Cambridge, Cambridge University Press, 1997).

Heindenson, K., *Europe and World Trade* (London, Cassell, 1995).

Held, D. (ed.), *Political Theory Today* (Cambridge, Polity Press, 1991).

Held, D., McGrew, A., Goldblatt, D. and Perraton, J., *Global Transformations* (Cambridge, Polity Press, 1999).

Hill, C. (ed.), *The Actors in Europe's Foreign Policy* (London, Routledge, 1996).

Hiro, D., *Dictionary of the Middle East* (London, Macmillan, 1996).

Hoffman, S., *World Disorders: Troubled Peace in the Post-Cold War Era* (Oxford, Rowman & Littlefield, 1998).

Holm, H. H. and Sorensen, G. (eds), *Whose World Order?* (Boulder, CO, Westview Press, 1995).

Holmes, J. W. (ed.), *Maelstrom: The United States, Southern Europe, and the Challenges in the Mediterranean* (Cambridge, MA, World Peace Foundation, 1995).

Hudson, R. and Williams, A. M. (eds), *Divided Europe: Society and Territory* (London, Sage, 1999).

Huntington, S. P., *The Clash of Civilizations and the Remaking of World Order* (London, Touchstone Books, 1996).

Ignatieff, M., *Blood and Belonging: Journeys into the New Nationalism* (Toronto, Viking, 1993).

Jenkins, B. and Willets, P., *Subnational Conflict in the Mediterranean Region* (London, RAND, 1983).

Jervis, R., *Perception and Misperception in International Politics* (Princeton, NJ, Princeton University Press, 1976).

Jervis, R., *System Effects: Complexity in Political and Social Life* (Princeton, NJ, Princeton University Press, 1997).

Joffé, G. (ed.), *North Africa: Nation, State and Region* (London, Routledge, 1993).

Kaplan, L., Clawson, R. W. and Luraghi, R. (eds), *NATO and the Mediterranean* (Wilmington, Scholarly Resources, 1985).

Katzenstein, P. J., *The Culture of National Security: Norms and Identity in World Politics* (New York, Columbia University Press, 1996).

Keagley, C. W. and Reymond, G., *A Multipolar Peace? Great-Power Politics in the Twenty-First Century* (New York, St. Martin's Press, 1994).

Kegley, C., Jr (ed.), *The Long Postwar Peace* (New York, 1991).

Kennedy, P., *Preparing for the Twenty-First Century* (New York, Random House Press, 1993).

Keohane, R. O., *After Hegemony Cooperation and Discord in the World Political Economy* (Princeton, NJ, Princeton University Press, 1984).

Keohane, R. O. (ed.), *Neorealism and its Critics* (New York, Columbia University Press, 1986).

Keohane, R. O. (ed.), *International Institutions and State Power: Essays in International*

Relations Theory (Boulder, CO, Westview Press, 1989).
Keohane, R. O. and Nye, J. S. *Power and Interdependence: World Politics in Transition* (Boston, MA, Little, Brown, 1977).
Keohane, R. O., Nye, J. S. and Hoffman, S. (eds), *After the Cold War: International Institutions and State Strategies in Europe, 1989–1991* (Harvard, Harvard University Press, 1993).
King, G., Keohane, R. O. and Verba, S., *Designing Social Inquiry: Scientific Inference in Qualitative Research* (Princeton, NJ, Princeton University Press, 1994).
King, R., Proudfoot, L. and Smith, B. (eds), *The Mediterranean: Environment and Society* (London, Arnold, 1997).
Kipp, J. (ed.), *Central European Security Concerns: Bridge, Buffer or Barrier?* (London, Frank Cass, 1993).
Kissinger, H., *Diplomacy* (New York, Touchstone Books, 1994).
Klieman, A. and Levite, A. (eds), *Deterrence in the Middle East: Where Theory and Practice Converge* (Boulder, CO, Westview Press, 1993).
Korany, B. and Dessuki, A. E. H. (eds), *The Foreign Policies of the Arab States: The Challenge of Change* (Boulder, CO, Westview Press, 1991).
Koufoudakis, V., Tsardanides, C. and Sotirelis, K., *The Policy of the Superpowers for the Eastern Mediterranean and the Persian Gulf* (in Greek) (Athens, Institute for Mediterranean Studies, 1989).
Krasner, S. D. (ed.), *International Regimes* (Ithaca, NY, Cornell University Press, 1983).
Krause, K. and Williams, M., *Critical Security Studies: Concepts and Cases* (London, University College Press, 1997).
Kurth, J. and Petras, J. (eds), *Mediterranean Paradoxes: Politics and Social Structure in Southern Europe* (Providence, Berg, 1993).
Laffin, J., *The World in Conflict*, War Annual 7 (London, Brassey's, 1996).
Lane, J.-E. and Ersson, S., *The New Institutional Politics: Performance and Outcomes* (London, Routledge, 2000).
Lapidus, G. W. and Tsalik, S. (eds), *Preventing Deadly Conflict: Strategies and Institutions* (New York, Carnegie Corporation of New York, 1994).
Latouche, E. J., *The Westernization of the World* (Cambridge, Polity Press, 1996).
Lauren, P. G. (ed.), *Diplomacy: New Approaches in History, Theory and Policy* (New York, Free Press, 1979).
Lebow, R. N. and Risse-Kappen, T. (eds), *International Relations Theory and the End of the Cold War* (New York, Columbia University Press, 1995).
Leebaert, D. (ed.), *European Security Prospects for the 1980s* (Lexington, MA, Heath, 1979).
Lesser, I. O., *Mediterranean Security: New Perspectives and Implications for US Policy* (Santa Monica, CA, RAND, 1992).
Lesser, I. O., *Future Vision 2010: Mediterranean Europe and Turkey* (Santa Monica, CA, RAND, 1997).
Lesser, I. O. and Tellis, A. J., *Strategic Exposure: Proliferation Around the Mediterranean* (Santa Monica, CA, RAND, 1996).
Lieber, R. J., *Theory and World Politics* (London, Allen & Unwin, 1973).
Lippman, T. W., *Understanding Islam* (New York, Penguin Group, 1990).
Lister, M., *The European Community and the Developing World* (Aldershot, Avebury, 1988).
Lister, M., *The European Union and the South: Relations with Developing Countries* (London, Routledge, 1997).

Little, R. and Smith, M. (eds), *Perspectives on World Politics*, 2nd edn (London, Routledge, 1996).

Loughlin, J. (ed.), *Southern European Studies Guide* (London, Bauker-Saur, 1993).

Luciani, G. (ed.), *The Mediterranean Region: Economic Interdependence and the Future of Society* (London, Croom Helm, 1984).

Luciani, G. and Salame, G. (eds), *The Politics of Arab Integration* (London, Croom Helm, 1988).

Ludlow, P. (ed.), *Europe and the Mediterranean* (London, Brassey's, 1994).

Lynn-Jones, S. M. (ed.) *The Cold War and After: Prospects for Peace. An International Security Reader* (Cambridge, MA, MIT Press, 1991).

Manwaring, M. (ed.), *Gray Area Phenomena: Confronting the New World Disorder* (Boulder, CO, Westview Press, 1993).

Mandelbaum, M. (ed.), *The New Russian Foreign Policy* (Washington, DC, Brookings Institute, 1998).

Maoz, Z., *Regional Security in the Middle East: Past, Present and Future* (London, Frank Cass, 1997).

Markusen, J. Y. and Yudken, A., *Dismantling the Cold War Economy* (New York, Basic Books, 1992).

Marquina, A. and Brauch H. G. (eds), *Confidence Building and Partnership in the Western Mediterranean: Tasks for Preventive Diplomacy and Conflict Avoidance* (London, UNISCI, 1994).

Marsh, D. and Stoker, G. (eds), *Theory and Method in Political Science* (Basingstoke, Macmillan, 1995).

Matthews, K., *The Gulf Conflict and International Relations* (London, Routledge, 1993).

Mayer, A. E., *Islam and Human Rights: Tradition and Politics* (Boulder, CO, Westview Press, 1995).

Miall, H. (ed.), *Redefining Europe: New Patterns of Conflict and Cooperation* (London, Pinter, 1994).

Mitrany, D., *A Working Peace System* (London, Royal Institute of International Affairs, 1943).

Mitrany, D., *The Functional Theory of Politics* (London, Martin Robertson, 1975).

Moffett, G., *Global Population Growth: 21st Century Challenges* (New York, Foreign Policy Association, 1994).

Mueller, J., *Quiet Cataclysm: Reflections on the Recent Transformation of World Politics* (New York, HarperCollins, 1995).

Niblock, T. and Murphy, E. (eds), *Economic and Political Liberalization in the Middle East* (London, British Academic Press, 1993).

Nierop, T., *Systems and Regions in Global Politics: An Empirical Study of Diplomacy, International Organisation and Trade 1950–1991* (Chichester, John Wiley, 1994).

Nonneman, G. (ed.), *The Middle East and Europe: An Integrated Communities Approach* (London, Federal Trust, 1992).

Nonneman, G. (ed.), *The Middle East and Europe: The Search for Stability and Integration* (London, Federal Trust, 1993).

Nye, J. and Smith, R. (eds), *After the Storm: Lessons from the Gulf War* (Lanham, MD, Madison Books, 1992).

O'Brien, M. (ed.), *Security Issues in the Mediterranean Basin* (Washington, DC. Institute for National Strategic Studies, 1992).

O'Connell, D. P., *International Law*, 2nd edn (London, Stevens, 1970).

O'Donell, G., Schmitter P. C. and Whitehead, L. (eds), *Transitions from Authoritarian Rule* (Baltimore, MD, Johns Hopkins University Press, 1986).

Orwell, G., *In Front of Your Nose 1945–1950*, 3rd edn vol. IV, (London, Penguin, 1992).

Osiander, A., *The States System of Europe, 1640–1990: Peacemaking and the Conditions of International Stability* (Oxford, Clarendon Press, 1994).

Park, W. and Wyn Rees, G. (eds), *Rethinking Security in Post-Cold War Europe* (London, Longman, 1998).

Parry, G. and Morran, M. (eds), *Democracy and Democratization* (London, Routledge, 1994).

Paul, T. V. and Hall, J. A. (eds), *International Order and the Future of World Politics* (Cambridge, Cambridge University Press, 1999).

Piening, C., *Global Europe: The European Union in World Affairs* (London, Lynne Rienner Publishers, 1997).

Peters B. G., *Institutional Theory in Political Science: The 'New Institutionalism'* (London, Pinter, 1999).

Peters, I. (ed.), *New Security Challenges: The Adaptation of International Institutions* (New York, St. Martin's Press, 1996).

Peters, I., *Pathways to Peace: The Multilateral Arab–Israeli Peace Talks* (London, Pinter, 1996).

Porte, A. D., *Europe Between the Superpowers* (London, Yale University Press, 1979).

Pounds, N., *Europe and the Mediterranean* (New York, McGraw-Hill, 1953).

Promfred, R., *The Mediterranean Policy of the European Community: A Study of Discrimination in Trade* (London, Macmillan, 1986).

Qureshi, A., *The World Trade Organization: Implementing International Trade Norms* (Manchester, Manchester University Press, 1996).

Redmont, J., *The Next Mediterranean Enlargement of the EC: Turkey, Cyprus, Malta?* (Dartmouth, Aldershot, 1993).

Research Group on European Affairs, *Challenges in the Mediterranean: The European Response* (Gutersloh, Bertelsmann Foundation, 1991).

Rittberger, V. (ed.), *International Regimes in East–West Politics* (London, Pinter, 1990).

Rittberger, V. (ed.), *Regime Theory and International Relations* (Oxford, Clarendon Press, 1993).

Roberson, B. A. (ed.), *The Middle East and Europe: The Power Deficit* (London, Routledge, 1998).

Rosamond, B., *Theories of European Integration* (Basingstoke, Macmillan, 2000).

Rosenau, J. N., *Turbulence in World Politics: A Theory of Change and Continuity* (Princeton, NJ, Princeton University Press, 1990).

Rosenau, J. N., *Along the Domestic–Foreign Frontier: Exploring Governance in a Turbulent World* (Cambridge, Cambridge University Press, 1997).

Rosenau, J. N. and Czempiel, E. (eds), *Governance Without Government: Order and Change in World Politics* (Cambridge, Cambridge University Press, 1992).

Rosenthal, G. G., *The Mediterranean Basin: Its Political Economy and Changing International Relations* (London, Butterworth, 1982).

Ruggie, J. G., *Constructing the World Polity: Essays on International Institutionalization* (New York, Routledge, 1998).

Rummel, R. (ed.), *The Evolution of an International Actor: Western Europe's New Assertiveness* (Boulder, CO, Westview Press, 1990).

Russett, B. M., *International Regions and International System: A Study in Political Ecology* (Chicago, RAND, 1967).

Said, E., *Orientalism* (New York, Vintage, 1979).

Said, E., *Covering Islam: How the Media and the Experts Determine How We See the Rest of the World* (London, Routledge and Keegan Paul, 1981).

Salamé, G. (ed.), *The Foundations of the Arab State* (London, Croom Helm, 1988).

Sanderson, S. K. (ed.), *Civilisations and World Systems* (Walnut Creek, Altamira, 1995).

Schlaim, A. and Yannopoulos, G. N. (eds), *The EEC and the Mediterranean Countries* (Cambridge, Cambridge University Press, 1976).

Shafik, N., *Economic Challenges Facing Middle Eastern and North African Countries: Alternative Futures* (Basingstoke, Macmillan, 1998).

Scholte, J. A., *International Relations of Social Change* (Buckingham, Open University Press, 1993).

Siegfried, A., *The Mediterranean* (London, Jonathan Cape, 1984).

Singer, M. and Wildavsky, A., *The Real World Order: Zones of Peace–Zones of Turmoil* (Chatham, NJ, Chatham House, 1993).

SIPRI Yearbook 1991, *World Armament and Disarmament* (Oxford, Oxford University Press, 1992).

SIPRI Yearbook 1997, *Armaments, Disarmament and International Security* (Oxford, Oxford University Press, 1997).

Smith, M., *The United States and the European Community in a Transformed World* (London, Pinter, 1993).

Snyder, G. H. and Diesing, P., *Conflict Among Nations: Bargaining, Decision Making, and System Structure in International Crises* (Princeton, NJ, Princeton University Press, 1977).

Spencer, S. (ed.), *Immigration as an Economic Asset: The German Experience* (Staffordshire, Trentham Books, 1994).

Sperling, J. and Kirchner, E. (eds), *Recasting the European Order* (Manchester and New York, Manchester University Press, 1997).

Spragens, T. A., Jr, *Civic Liberalism: Reflections on Our Democratic Ideals* (Lanham, MD, Rowman & Littlefield, 1999).

Stavridis, S. *et al.* (eds), *New Challenges to the European Union: Policies and Policy-Making at the End of the Century* (Aldershot, Dartmouth, 1997).

Stavridis, S., Couloumbis, T., Veremis, T. and Waites, N. (eds), *The Foreign Policies of the European Union's Mediterranean States and Applicant Countries in the 1990s* (London, Macmillan, 1999).

Stein, D. L. (ed.), *Lectures in the Sciences of Complexity* (Redwood City, CA, Addison-Wesley, 1989).

Steunenberg, B. and Vught, F. V. (eds), *Political Institutions and Public Policy* (Dordrecht, Kluwer, 1997).

Strange, S., *The Retreat of the State: The Diffusion of Power in the World Economy* (Cambridge, Cambridge University Press, 1996).

Strange, S., *Casino Capitalism* (Manchester and New York, Manchester University Press, 1997).

Stubbs, R. and Underhill, G. R. D. (eds), *Political Economy and the Changing Global Order* (London, Macmillan, 1994).

Tanner, F. (ed.), *Arms Control, Confidence-Building and Security Cooperation in the Mediterranean, North Africa and the Middle East* (Malta, MEDAC, 1994).

Taylor, P., *International Co-operation Today: The European and the Global Patterns* (London, Elek, 1971).

Taylor, P., *International Organization in the Modern World: The European and the Global Process* (London, Pinter, 1993).

Taylor, P. J. (ed.), *Political Geography of the Twentieth Century* (London, Belhaven Press, 1993).

Taylor, R., *Implications for the Southern Mediterranean Countries of the Second Enlargement of the European Community* (Brussels, Commission of the European Communities, 1980).

Tovias, A., *Foreign Economic Relations of the European Community: The Impact of Spain and Portugal* (Boulder, CO, Lynne Rienner,1990).

Tsardanides, C., *The Renewed Mediterranean Policy of the European Community and Greece* (in Greek) (Athens, Papazisis, 1992).

Tsoukalis, L., *The European Community and its Mediterranean Enlargement* (London, George Allen & Unwin, 1981).

Unger, R. M., *Knowledge and Politics* (New York, Free Press, 1975).

Vasquez, J. A., *The Power of Power Politics: From Classical Realism to Neotraditionalism* (Cambridge, Cambridge University Press, 1998).

Vatikiotis, P. G., *Islam and the State* (in Greek) (Athens, Hellenic Institute of European and Foreign Policy, 1991).

Waever, O. *et al.*, *Identity, Migration and the New Security Agenda in Europe* (New York, St. Martin's Press, 1993).

Waites, N., *European Community Mediterranean Policy and Agricultural Problems of the Maghreb: A View from Northern Europe* (Reading, University of Reading, 1988).

Wallace, W. (ed.), *The Dynamics of European Integration* (London, Pinter, 1990).

Wallace, W., *The Transformation of Western Europe* (London, Pinter, 1990).

Webb, M., *The Political Economy of Policy Co-ordination: International Adjustment Since 1945* (Ithaca, NY, Cornell University Press, 1995).

Weidenfeld, W. (ed.), *Europe and the Middle East* (Gutersloh, Bertelsman Foundation, 1995).

Weidenfeld, W., *Challenges in the Mediterranean: The European Response* (Gutersloh, Bertelsman Foundation, 1991).

Weidenfeld, W. and Janning, J. (eds), *Global Responsibilities: Europe in Tomorrow's World* (Gutersloh, Bertelsmann Foundation, 1991).

Weidenfeld, W. and Janning, J. (eds), *Europe in Global Change* (Gutersloh, Bertelsmann Foundation, 1993).

Weisberger, B., *Cold War, Cold Peace: The United States and Russia Since 1945* (New York, American Heritage Press, 1985).

Wendt, A. *Social Theory of International Politics* (Cambridge, Cambridge University Press, 1999).

Wessels, W., *Europe and the North–South Dialogue* (Paris, Atlantic Institute, 1978).

White, B., Little, R. and Smith, M. (eds), *Issues in World Politics* (London, Macmillan, 1997).

Williams, A. M., *Southern Europe Transformed* (London, Harper & Row, 1984).

Williams, P., Goldstein D. and Shafritz J. (ed.), *Classic Readings of International Relations*, 2nd edn (Fort Worth, TX, Harcourt Brace, 1999).

Wilson, W., *The State: Elements of Historical and Practical Politics* (London, Isbister, London, 1899).

Wolfe, R., *Farm Wars: The Political Economy of Agriculture and the International Trade Regime* (London, Macmillan, 1998).
Woods, N. (ed.), *Explaining International Relations Since 1945* (Oxford, Oxford University Press, 1996).
Woodward, S. L., *Balkan Tragedy* (Washington, DC, Brookings Institutie, 1995).
Wyn Rees, G. (ed.), *International Politics in Europe: The New Agenda* (London, Routledge, 1993).
Yachir, F. (ed.), *The Mediterranean: Between Dependency and Autonomy* (London, Zed Books, 1989).
Young, O. R., *Compliance and Public Authority* (Baltimore, MD, Johns Hopkins University Press, 1979).
Young, O. R., *International Cooperation: Building Regimes for Natural Resources and the Environment* (Ithaca, NY, Cornell University Press, 1989).
Young, O. R., *International Governance: Protecting the Environment in a Stateless Society* (Ithaca, NY, Cornell University Press, 1994).
Young, O. R. (ed.), *Global Governance: Drawing Insights from the Environmental Experience* (Cambridge, MA, MIT Press, 1997).
Zartman, W. I., *The Politics of Trade Negotiations Between Africa and the European Economic Community: The Weak Confront the Strong* (Princeton, NJ, Princeton University Press, 1971).

Articles

Adler, E., 'Imagined (Security) Communities: Cognitive Regions in International Relations', *Millennium*, 26: 2 (1997), 249–77.
Agnoletti, E. E., 'The Difficult Construction of a Coherent Policy', *Politica Internazionale*, 5: 1 (1986), 5–22.
Ajami, F., 'The End of Pan-Arabism', *Foreign Affairs*, winter (1978–79), 355–73.
Aliboni, R., 'The Mediterranean Scenario: Economy and Security in the Regions South of the EC', *International Spectator*, 25: 2 (1990), 138–54.
Aliboni, R. *et al.*, 'Co-operation and Stability in the Mediterranean: An Agenda for Partnership', *International Spectator*, 29: 3 (1994), 5–20.
Allen, D., 'The Euro-Arab Dialogue', *Journal of Common Market Studies*, 16 (1977–78).
Allen, D. and Smith, M., 'Western Europe's Presence in the Contemporary International Arena', *Review of International Studies*, 16: 1 (1990), 19–39.
Asmus, R., Larrabee, F. S. and Lesser, I. O., 'Mediterranean Security: New Challenges, New Tasks', *NATO Review*, 44: 3 (1996), 25–31.
Aust, A., 'Theory and Practice of Informal International Instruments', *International and Comparative Law Quarterly*, 35 (1986), 787–812.
Baldwin, D., 'Security Studies and the End of the Cold War', *World Politics*, 48: 1 (1996), 117–41.
Bankowski, Z. and Christodoulidis, E., 'The European Union as an Essentially Contested Project', *European Law Journal*, 4: 4 (1998), 341–54.
Barbé, E., 'The Barcelona Conference: Launching Pad of a Process', *Mediterranean Politics*, 1: 1 (1996), 25–42.
Barber, B., 'Jihad Versus McWorld', *The Atlantic Monthly*, March (1992), 53–63.

Benyaklef, M., 'Socio-Economic Disparities in the Mediterranean', *Mediterranean Politics*, 2: 1 (1997), 93–112.

Bersani, G., 'North–South Relations', *European Digest*, 47 (1982), 171–9.

Bin, A., 'Strengthening Cooperation in the Mediterranean: NATO's Contribution', *NATO Review*, 46: 4 (1998), 24–7.

Blunden, M., 'Insecurity in Europe's Southern Flank', *Survival*, 36: 2 (1994), 134–49.

Booth, M., 'Global Warring', *The Independent Magazine* (End Lines), 30 January 1999.

Boyer, Y., 'Europe's Future Strategic Orientation', *Washington Quarterly*, 16: 4 (1993), 141–53.

Brauch, H. G., 'Energy Interdependence in the Western Mediterranean', *Mediterranean Politics*, 1: 3 (1996), 295–319.

Budd, L., 'Regional Integration and Convergence and Problems of Fiscal and Monetary Systems: Some Lessons for Eastern Europe', *Regional Studies*, 31: 6 (1997), 559–70.

Burnell, P., 'Democratisation and Economic Change Worldwide – Can Societies Cope?', *Democratisation*, 1: 1 (1994) 1–7.

Bush, K. D. and Keyman, E. F., 'Identity-Based Conflict: Rethinking Security in a Post-Cold War World', *Global Governance*, 3: 3 (1997).

Buzan, B., 'New Partners of Global Security in the Twenty-First Century', *International Affairs*, 67: 3 (1991), 431–51.

Buzan, B. and Little, R., 'Reconceptualizing Anarchy: Structural Realism Meets World History', *European Journal of International Relations*, 2: 4 (1996), 403–38.

Caldwell, H. M., 'Western Competition for the Middle East Market', *Survival*, 28: 1 (1986) 32–53.

Caligaris, L., 'Security Challenges in Alliance: The Southern Periphery', *International Spectator*, 27: 4 (1992), 5–23.

Calleya, S. C., 'The Euro-Mediterranean Process After Malta: What Prospects?', *Mediterranean Politics*, 2: 2 (1997), 1–22.

Chayes, A. and Handler Chayes, A., 'On Compliance', *International Organization*, 47: 2 (1993), 175–205.

Checkel, J. T., 'Russian Foreign Policy: Back to the Future?', *RFE/RL Research Report*, 1: 41 (1992), 15–29.

Checkel, J. T., 'International Norms and Domestic Politics: Bridging the Rationalist–Constructivist Divide', *European Journal of International Relations*, 3: 4 (1998), 473–95.

Coffey, J. I., 'Security in the Middle East: Can the Allies Do Better?', *NATO Review*, 37: 5 (1989), 20–5.

Colas, A., 'The Limits of Mediterranean Partnership: Civil Society and the Barcelona Conference of 1995', *Mediterranean Quarterly*, 8: 4 (1997), 63–80.

Copeland, D. C., 'Economic Interdependence and War: A Theory of Trade Expectations', *International Security*, 20: 4 (1996), 5–41.

Couloumbis, T. and Veremis, T., 'In Search of New Barbarians: Samuel P. Huntington and the Clash of Civilizations', *Mediterranean Quarterly*, 5: 1 (1994), 36–44.

Crawford, B., 'The New Security Dilemma Under International Economic Dependence', *Millennium*, 23: 1 (1994), 25–56.

Dickson, A. K., 'The EC and its Associates – Changing Priorities', *Politics*, 5: 3 (1995), 147–52.

Dienstbier, J., 'The Future of European Security. Prague Conference Confirms Agreement on Basic Ideas', *NATO Review*, 39: 3 (1991), 22–7.

Downs, G. D., Rocke, D. M. and Barsoom, P. N., 'Is the good news about compliance good news about cooperation?', *International Organization*, 50: 3 (1996), 379–406.

Downs, G. D., Rocke, D. M. and Barsoom, P. N., 'Managing the Evolution of Multilateralism', *International Organization*, 52: 2 (1998), 397–419.

Duffield, J. S., 'Explaining the Long Peace in Europe: The Contributions of Regional Security Regimes', *Review of International Studies*, 20: 4 (1994), 369–88.

Duffield, J. S, 'NATO's Functions After the Cold War', *Political Science Quarterly*, 109: 5 (1994–95), 763–88.

Edis, R., 'Does the Barcelona Process Matter?', *Mediterranean Politics*, 3: 3 (1998), 93–105.

Edwards, G. and Philippart, E. 'The EU Mediterranean Policy: Virtue Unrewarded or ...?', *Cambridge Review of International Affairs*, 11: 1 (1997) 185–207.

Edwards, G. and Philippart, E., 'The Euro-Mediterranean Partnership: Fragmentation and Reconstruction', *European Foreign Affairs Review*, 2: 4 (1997), 465–89.

Faria, F., 'The Mediterranean: A New Priority in Portuguese Foreign Policy?', *Mediterranean Politics*, 1: 1 (1996), 212–30.

Farley, J., 'Mediterranean – Southern Threats to Northern Shores', *The World Today*, 50: 2 (1994), 33–6.

Farrar-Hockley, D., 'Future Instability in the Mediterranean', *European Security*, 3: 1 (1994), 58–81.

Fearon, J. D., 'Bargaining, Enforcement and International Cooperation', *International Organization*, 52: 2 (1998), 269–305.

Fenech, D., 'East–West to North–South in the Mediterranean', *Geojournal*, 31: 2 (1993), 129–40.

Fenech, D., 'The Relevance of European Security Structures to the Mediterranean (and Vice Versa)', *Mediterranean Politics*, 2: 1 (1997), 149–76.

Finnemore, M., 'Norms, Culture and World Politics: Insights from Sociology's Institutionalism', *International Organization*, 50, (1996), 325–48.

Fukuyama, F., Hobsbawm, E., Garton Ash, T., Cooper, R., Luttwak, E. and Hassner, P., 'The Global Order in the 21st Century: A Round Table', *Prospect*, August/September (1999), 50–8.

Gaddis, J. L., 'International Relations Theory and the End of the Cold War', *International Security*, 17: 3 (1992–93), 5–58.

Gale, F., '"*Cave! Hic Dragones*": A Neo-Gramscian Deconstruction and Reconstruction of International Regime Theory', *Review of International Political Economy*, 5: 2 (1998), 252–84.

Gallarotti, G. M., 'The Limits of International Organization: Systematic Failure in the Management of International Relations', *International Organization*, 45: 2 (1991), 183–220.

Gaspar, C., 'Europe and the Middle East: At the Crossroads', *NATO Review*, 42: 5 (1994), 26–30.

Gawdat, B., 'Democracy in the Arab World: An Elitist Approach', *International Relations*, 12: 2 (1994), 49–60.

Gellner, E., 'Up From Imperialism', *The New Republic*, 22 May (1989), 35–6.

Gellner, E., 'Nationalism and Politics in Eastern Europe', *New Left Review*, 189: September/October (1991), 127–34.

Ghebali, V. Y., 'Toward a Mediterranean Helsinki-Type Process', *Mediterranean Quar-*

terly, 4: 1 (1993), 92–101.

Gillespie, R., 'Spain and the Mediterranean: Southern Sensitivity, European Aspirations', *Mediterranean Politics*, 1: 2 (1996), 193–211.

Gillespie, R., 'The Euro-Mediterranean Partnership', *Mediterranean Politics*, 2: 1 (1997), 1–5.

Gillespie, R., 'Spanish Protagonismo and the Euro-Mediterranean Partnership', *Mediterranean Politics*, 2: 1 (1997), 33–48.

Gowan, P., 'Western Economic Diplomacy and the New Eastern Europe', *New Left Review*, 180: March/April (1990), 63–84.

Grieco, J. M., 'Anarchy and the Limits of Cooperation: a Realist's Critique of the Newest Liberal Institutionalism', *International Organization*, 42 (1988), 485–507.

Gunder Brauch, H., 'Energy Interdependence in the Western Mediterranean', *Mediterranean Politics*, 1: 3 (1997), 295–319.

Halliday, F., 'The Gulf War and its Aftermath: First Reflections', *International Affairs*, 67: 2 (1991), 223–34.

Henrikson, A. K., 'The Geographical "Mental Maps" of American Policy-Makers?, *International Political Science Review*, 1: 4 (1980), 495–530.

Hollis, R, 'Europe and the Middle East: Power by Stealth?', *International Affairs*, 73: 1 (1997), 15–29.

Holmes, J. W., 'Italy: In the Mediterranean, But *of* it?', *Mediterranean Politics*, 1: 2 (1996), 176–92.

Howorth, J., 'France and the Mediterranean in 1995: From Tactical Ambiguity to Inchoate Strategy?', *Mediterranean Politics*, 1: 2 (1996), 157–75.

Hughes, M., 'Western Pain and Western Promise: The Reaction of Western Governments to the Economic Plight of the "New Eastern Europe"', *International Relations*, 11: 6 (1993), 585–604.

Humphreys, S., 'Islam and Political Values in Saudi Arabia, Egypt and Syria', *Middle East Journal*, 33 (1979), 6–7.

Hunter, R. E, 'The United States' Role in the Middle East', *Current History*, February (1990), 49–54.

Huntington, S. P., 'The Clash of Civilizations?', *Foreign Affairs*, 72: 3 (1993), 22–49.

Huntington, S. P., 'If Not Civilizations, What? Paradigms of the Post-Cold War World', *Foreign Affairs*, 72: 5 (1993), 186–93.

Huntington, S. P., 'The West Unique, Not Universal', *Foreign Affairs*, 75: 6 (1996), 28–46.

Hurrell, A., 'Explaining the Resurgence of Regionalism in World Politics', *Review of International Studies*, 21: 2 (1995), 121–39.

Itta, E., 'The Mediterranean Between Europe and Africa: New Institutions for a New Economic and Monetary Order', *Journal of Regional Policy*, 2: 8 (1988), 269–79.

Jawad, H. A., 'Islam and the West: How Fundamental Is the Threat?', *RUSI Journal*, 140: 4 (1995), 34–8.

Jbili ,A. and Enders, K., 'The Association Agreement Between Tunisia and the European Union', *Finance and Development*, 33: 3 (1996), 18–23.

Joffé, G., 'Southern Attitudes Towards an Integrated Mediterranean Region', *Mediterranean Politics*, 2: 1 (1997), 12–32.

Joffé, G. *et al.*, 'The Mediterranean: Risks and Challenges', *International Spectator*, 28: 3 (1993).

Joffe, J., 'Collective Security and the Future of Europe', *Survival*, spring (1992), 36–50.

Kaldor, M., 'After the Cold War', *New Left Review*, 180: March/April (1990), 25–40.

Kaplan, R. D., 'The Coming Anarchy', *The Atlantic Monthly*, February (1994), 44–76.

Kaufman, S. J., 'The Fragmentation and Consolidation of International Systems', *International Organization*, 51: 2 (1997), 173–208.

Kennan, G., 'Peaceful Coexistence: A Western View', *Foreign Affairs*, 38: 2 (1960), 171–90.

Keohane, R. O., 'Reciprocity in International Relations', *International Organization*, 40: 1 (1986), 1–27.

Keohane, R. O. and Martin, L. L., 'The Promise of Institutionalist Theory', *International Security*, 20: 1 (1995), 39–51.

Kienle, E., 'Destabilization through Partnership? Euro-Mediterranean Relations After the Barcelona Declaration', *Mediterranean Politics*, 3: 2 (1998), 1–20.

Kindleberger, C. P., 'Dominance and Leadership in the International Economy', *International Studies Quarterly*, 25 (1981), 250–69.

Koekkoek, A., 'Europe 1992 and the Developing Countries: An Overview', *Journal of Common Market Studies*, 29: 2 (1990), 111–32.

Kratochwill, F. V., 'The Embarrassment of Changes: Neo-Realism as the Science of *Realpolitik*', *Review of International Studies*, 19 (1993), 63–80.

Krause, K., 'Insecurity and State Formation in the Global Military Order: The Middle Eastern Case', *European Journal of International Relations*, 2: 3 (1996), 319–54.

Krebs, R. R., 'Perverse Institutionalism: NATO and the Greco-Turkish Conflict', *International Organization*, 53: 2 (1999), 343–77.

Ladeur, K., 'Towards a Legal Theory of Supranationality – the Viability of the Network Concept', *European Law Journal*, 3 (1997), 33–54.

Laipson, E., 'Europe's Role in the Middle East: Enduring Ties, Emerging Opportunities', *Middle East Journal*, 44: 1 (1990), 7–17.

Laipson, E., 'Thinking About the Mediterranean', *Mediterranean Quarterly*, 1: 1 (1990), 50–65.

Laulan, Y., 'East–West Economic Relations', *NATO Review*, 21: 2 (1973), 15–16.

Lesser, I. O., 'Southern Europe and the Maghreb: US Interests and Policy Perspectives', *Mediterranean Politics*, 1: 2 (1996), 231–42.

Levy, M., Young O. R. and Zürn, M., 'The Study of International Regimes', *European Journal of International Relations*, 1: 3 (1995), 267–330.

Lewis, B., 'Islam and Liberal Democracy. A Historical Overview', *Journal of Democracy*, 7: 2 (1996), 52–63.

Licari, J., 'The Euro-Mediterranean Partnership: Economic and Financial Aspects', *Mediterranean Politics*, 3: 3 (1998), 1–20.

Lieven, A., 'A New Iron Curtain', *Atlantic Monthly*, 277: 1 (1996), 20–25.

Lipson, C., 'Why Are Some International Agreements Informal?', *International Organization*, 45 (1991), 495–538.

Lorca, A., 'The EU and the Mediterranean: Is an "Us" Versus "Them" Situation Inevitable?', *International Spectator*, July/September (1996), 51–69.

March, J. G and Olsen, J. P., 'Institutional Perspectives on Political Institutions', *Governance: An International Journal of Policy and Administration*, 9: 3 (1996), 247–64.

Marco, G. de, 'A Dynamic Europe', *Studia Diplomatica*, 47: 3 (1994), 23–8.

Marks, J., 'High Hopes and Low Motives: The New Euro-Mediterranean Partnership Initiative', *Mediterranean Politics*, 1: 1 (1996), 1–24.

Mearsheimer, J. J., 'Why We Will Soon Miss the Cold War', *The Atlantic Monthly*, 266: 2 (1990), 35–50.

Mearsheimer, J. J., 'The False Promise of International Institutions', *International Security*, 19: 3 (1994), 5–49.

Michelis, G. D., 'The Mediterranean After the Gulf War', *Mediterranean Quarterly*, 2: 2 (1991), 1–8.

Monar, J., 'Institutional Constraints of the European Union's Mediterranean Policy', *Mediterranean Politics*, 3: 2 (1998), 39–60.

Moreau, A. S, Jr, 'The Defense of NATO: Southern Region', *NATO Review*, 34: 4 (1986), 13–20.

Mitchell, R. B., 'Modeling the Forms of International Cooperation: Distribution Versus Information', *International Organization*, 48: 3 (1994), 387–423.

Mortimer, E., 'The Party of God', *Prospects*, 42: June (1999), 36–40.

Munslow, B. and Ekoko, F., 'Is Democracy Necessary for Sustainable Development?', *Democratisation*, 2: 1 (1995), 158–78;

Munuera, G. and Wrede, H., 'Prospects for Security and Cooperation in the Mediterranean After the PLO–Israel Agreement: A CSCM Revisited?', *Helsinki Monitor*, 2 (1994), 48–59

Nadelmann, E., 'Global Prohibition Regimes: The Evolution of Norms in International Society', *International Organization*, 44 (1990), 479–526.

Nsouli, M., Bisat, A, and Kanaan, O., 'The European Union's New Mediterranean Strategy', *Finance and Development*, 33: 3 (1996), 14–17.

Renaud, J. C., 'Security and Energy in the Post-Crisis Period', *NATO Review*, 39: 1 (1991).

Rieff, D., 'Imperialism or Barbarism?', *Prospect*, 43: July (1999), 36–40.

Roberts, A., 'A New Age in International Relations', *International Affairs*, 67: 3 (1991), 509–25.

Romeo, I., 'The European Union and North Africa: Keeping the Mediterranean "Safe" for Europe', *Mediterranean Politics*, 3: 2 (1998), 21–38.

Roper, J., 'Vulnerable Continent or Secure Community: Western Europe in the Twenty-First Century', *The World Today*, 52: 2 (1996), 35–6.

Rosenau, J. N., 'Before Cooperation: Hegemons, Regimes, and Habit-Driven Actors in World Politics', *International Organisation*, 40 (1986), 879–84.

Ruggie, J. G., 'International Responses to Technology: Concepts and Trends', *International Organization*, 29: 3 (1975), 557–84.

Sachedina, E., 'Religion and Global Affairs: Islamic Religion and Political Order', *SAIS Review*, 18: 2 (1998), 59–64.

Salmon, T., 'Testing Times for European Political Co-operation: The Gulf and Yugoslavia 1990–1992', *International Affairs*, 68: 2 (1992), 233–53.

Sammut, D., 'Libya and the Islamic Threat', *The World Today*, 50: 10 (1994), 198–200.

Santis, N. D., 'The Future of NATO's Mediterranean Initiative', *NATO Review*, 46: 1 (1998), 32–5.

Sayigh, Y., 'The Gulf Crisis: Why the Arab Regional Order Failed?', *International Affairs*, 67: 3 (1991), 487–507.

Serre, F., 'The Community's Mediterranean Policy After the Second Enlargement', *Journal of Common Market Studies*, 19: 4 (1981), 377–87.

Silvestri, S., 'Political Factors Affecting Co-operation between Italy, Greece and Turkey', *International Spectator*, 22: 1 (1987), 20–3.

Smith, M., 'The European Union and a Changing Europe: Establishing the Boundaries of Order', *Journal of Common Market Studies*, 34: 1 (1996), 5–28.

Spencer, C., 'Algeria in Crisis', *Survival*, 36: 2 (1994), 149–64.

Spencer, C., 'Building Confidence in the Mediterranean', *Mediterranean Politics*, 2: 1 (1997), 23–48.

Stein, J. G., 'Detection and Defection: Security "Regimes" and the Management of International Conflict', *International Journal*, 40 (1985), 599–627.

Taft, W. H., 'European Security: Lessons Learned From the Gulf war', *NATO Review*, 39: 3 (1991), 7–11.

Tanner, F., 'An Emerging Security Agenda for the Mediterranean', *Mediterranean Politics*, 1: 3 (1996), 279–95.

Tarzi ,S. M., 'The Role of Norms and Regimes in World Affairs: A Grotian Perspective', *International Relations*, 14: 3 (1998), 71–84.

Taylor, P., 'Interdependence and Autonomy in the European Communities: The Case of the European Monetary System', *Journal of Common Market Studies*, 18: 4 (1980), 370–87.

Tsardanides, C., 'The Southern EU Member States' Policy Towards the Mediterranean: Regional or Global Co-operation', *Journal of Area Studies*, 9: 3 (1996), 53–69.

Tsoukalis, L., 'The EEC and the Mediterranean: Is "Global" Policy a Misnomer?', *International Affairs*, 53: 3 (1977), 422–38.

Tsoukalis, L., 'The EU in Search of a Mediterranean Policy', *European Expression: A Quarterly Edition on European Issues* (in Greek), 28 (1998), 35–7.

Tucker, R. W., '1989 and All That', *Foreign Affairs*, 69: 4 (1990), 96–7.

Vandewalle, D., 'The Middle East Peace Process and Regional Economic Integration', *Survival*, 36: 4 (1994), 21–34.

Vasconcelos, A. de, 'Southern Europe, United States and NATO', *NATO Review*, 37: 5 (1989), 26–30.

Vasconcelos, A. de, 'The New Europe and the Western Mediterranean', *NATO Review*, 39: 5 (1991), 27–31.

Vieroucci, L., 'The Role of the WEU in the Maintenance of International Peace and Security', *International Peacekeeping*, 2: 3 (1995), 309–29.

Wallace, H., 'The Europe that Came in From the Cold', *International Affairs*, 67: 4 (1991), 647–63.

Wallerstein, I., 'The World System After the Cold War', *Journal of Peace Research*, 30: 1 (1993).

Waltz, K. N., 'The Emerging Structure of International Politics', *International Security*, 18: 2 (1993), 44–79.

Watkins, E., 'The Unfolding US Policy in the Middle East', *International Affairs*, 73: 1 (1997), 1–14.

Welch, D. A., 'The "Clash of Civilizations" Thesis as an Argument and as a Phenomenon', *Security Studies*, 6: 4 (1997), 197–216.

Wiarda, H. J., 'Southern Europe's Transformation', *Current History*, February (1990), 390–3.

Winrow, G. M., 'A Threat From the South? NATO and the Mediterranean', *Mediterranean Politics*, 1: 1 (1996), 43–59.

Wrede, H., 'Applicability of the CSCE Experience to the Middle Eastern Conflict Area', *Jerusalem Journal of International Relations*, 14: 2 (1992), 114–21.

Wright, R., 'Islam's New Political Face', *Current*, January (1991), 25–9.

Xenakis, D. K., 'Euro-Mediterranean Formations and the Emerging European System: The Role of Cyprus', *The Cyprus Review*, 11: 1 (1999), 59–82.

Xenakis, D. K., 'From Policy to Regime: Trends in Euro-Mediterranean Governance', *Cambridge Review of International Affairs*, 13: 1 (1999), 254–70.

Xenakis, D. K., 'Order and Change in the Euro-Mediterranean System', *Mediterranean Quarterly*, 11: 4 (2000), 75–90.

Young, O. R., 'International Regimes: Problems of Concept Formation', *World Politics*, 32 (1980), 331–56.

Young, O. R., 'International Regimes: Toward a New Theory of Institutions', *World Politics*, 39 (1986), 104–22.

Research papers

Aguirre, M., 'NATO Needs a New Approach to the Mediterranean', *Summit Briefing Paper*, 97/4, Berlin Information Centre for Transatlantic Security, July 1997.

Aliboni, R., 'European Security Across the Mediterranean', *Chaillot Papers*, 2, WEU Institute for Security Studies, Paris, 1991.

Aliboni, R., 'The Euro-Mediterranean Partnership: An Interpretation From Italy', Paper presented at the MEDAC Conference 'Prospects After Barcelona', Malta, March 1996.

Attinà, F., 'International and Internal Security in the European, the Transatlantic, and the Mediterranean Region', Paper presented at the MEDAC Conference 'Prospects After Barcelona', Malta, March 1996.

Attinà, F., 'Regional Cooperation in Global Perspective. The Case of the 'Mediterranean' Regions', *Jean Monnet Working Papers in Comparative and International Politics*, 4, University of Catania, December 1996.

Bin, A., 'Mediterranean Diplomacy: Evolution and Prospects', *Jean Monnet Working Papers in Comparative and International Politics*, 5, University of Catania, 1997.

Brzezinski, Z., 'The Consequences of the End of the Cold War for International Security', *Adelphi Papers*, 265, International Institute for Strategic Studies, London, 1991–92.

Bulmer, S., 'New Institutionalism, the Single Market and EU Governance', *ARENA Working Papers*, 97/25, 1997.

Bussutil, S., 'Security and Co-operation: Economic Security in the Mediterranean', Paper presented at the MEDAC Conference 'Prospects After Barcelona', Malta, March 1996.

Buzan, B. and Waever, O., 'Liberalism and Security', *CSD Bulletin*, 5, Centre for the Study of Democracy, University of Westminster, 1998.

Calleya, S. C., 'Providing New Dynamism to the Euro-Med Process', *Euro-Mediterranean Magazine*, 3, EuroMed Internet Forum, 1998.

Checkel, J. T., 'International Institutions and Socialization', *ARENA Working Papers*, 99/5, 1998.

Checkel, J. T., 'Why Comply? Constructivism, Social Norms and the Study of International Institutions', *ARENA Reprints*, 99/24, 1999.

Chtatou, M., 'Central-Eastern Europe and Mediterranean Region: Similarities and Differences', Paper presented at the ELIAMEP Halki International Seminar, Greece, September 1996.

Church, C. H., 'European Integration Theory in the 1990s', *European Dossier Series*, 33, University of North London, 1996.

Claes, D. H., 'What Do Theories of International Regimes Contribute to the Explanation of Cooperation (and Failure of Cooperation) among Oil-Producing Countries?', *ARENA Working Papers*, 99/12, 1999.

Clément, S., 'Conflict Prevention in the Balkans: Case Studies of Kosovo and the FYR of Macedonia', *Chaillot Papers*, 30, WEU Institute for Security Studies, Paris, 1997.

Collinson, S., 'Migration and Security in the Mediterranean: A Complex Relationship', Paper presented at the Conference 'Non-Military Aspects of Security in Southern Europe: Migration, Employment and Labour Market', organised by the Institute of International Economic Relations and Regional Network on Southern European Societies, Santorini, 19–21 September 1997.

Cremasco, M., 'Two Uncertain Futures: Tunisia and Libya', in *Prospects for Security in the Mediterranean, Adelphi Papers*, 231, International Institute for Strategic Studies, London, 1988, pp. 41–60.

Curdy, G., 'Security and Peace in the Middle East: Experiments with Democracy in an Islamic World', *Maxwell Papers*, 4, Air War College, 1996.

Derisbourg, J. P., 'The Euro-Mediterranean Partnership After Barcelona', Paper presented at the MEDAC Conference 'Prospects After Barcelona', Malta, March 1996.

Desjardins, M. F., 'Rethinking Confidence-Building Measures. Obstacles to Agreement and the Risks of Overselling the Process', *Adelphi Papers*, 307, International Institute for Strategic Studies, London, 1996.

Dokos, T., 'Security Problems in the Mediterranean', *ELIAMEP Occasional Papers*, OP97/04, Hellenic Foundation for European and Foreign Policy, Athens, 1997.

Driss, R., 'The Cultural Aspects of Co-operation and Security in the Mediterranean', Paper presented at the MEDAC Conference 'Prospects After Barcelona', Malta, March 1996.

Duke, S., 'Security Regimes in the New Europe', *TKI Working Papers on European Integration and Regime Formation*, 7/97, Thorkil Kristensen Institute, South Jutland University Centre, 1997.

Echeverria, C. J., 'Euro-Mediterranean Political Relations: Confidence- and Security-Building Measures', *ELIAMEP Occasional Papers*, OP97/07, Hellenic Foundation for European and Foreign Policy, Athens 1997.

Edwards, G. and Philippart, E., '*Mare Nostrum* – the European Union and the Mediterranean in the 1990s and Beyond', Paper presented at the Fifth Biennial ESCA–USA Conference, Seattle 29 May–1 June 1997.

Ehteshami, A., 'Southern Europe, the Community and the Middle East', Paper presented at the Political Studies Association Annual Conference, April 1989.

Eyskens, M. *et al.*, 'How can Europe Prevent Conflicts', *Discussion Papers*, 14, The Philip Morris Institute for Public Policy and Research, 1997.

Fahmy, N., 'After Madrid and Barcelona: Prospects for Mediterranean Security', Paper presented at the MEDAC Conference 'Prospects After Barcelona', Malta, March 1996.

Faria, F. and Vasconcelos, A. de, 'Security in Northern Africa: Ambiguity and Reality', *Chaillot Papers*, 25, WEU Institute for Security Studies, Paris, 1996.

Fenech, D., 'Ways and Means of Security Around the Mediterranean Sea: A Euro-Mediterranean Partnership', Fondation Méditerranéenne des Etudes Stratégiques, Séminaire de la Tour Blanche, Toulon, 21–4 June 1995.

Fenech, D., 'A Euro-Mediterranean Partnership: Whose Security?', Paper presented at the MEDAC Conference 'Prospects After Barcelona', Malta, March 1996.

Fhamy, N., 'After Madrid: Prospects of Mediterranean Security', Paper presented at the MEDAC Conference 'Prospects After Barcelona', Malta, March 1996.

Follesdal, A., 'Justifying Human Rights: The Challenge of Cross-Cultural Toleration', *ARENA Reprints*, 96/4, 1996.

Gambles, I. (ed.), *A Lasting Peace in Central Europe?*, *Chaillot Papers*, 20, WEU Institute for Security Studies, Paris, 1995.

Gasteyger, C., 'European Security and the New Arc of Crisis', in *New Dimensions in International Security*, *Adelphi Papers*, 266, International Institute for Strategic Studies, London, 1992, 69–81.

Gnesotto, N. (ed.), *War and Peace: European Conflict Prevention*, *Chaillot Papers*, 11, WEU Institute for Security Studies, Paris, 1993.

Gnesotto, N., 'Lessons of Yugoslavia', *Chaillot Papers*, 14, WEU Institute for Security Studies, Paris, 1994.

Gordon, P. H., 'The Transatlantic Allies and the Changing Middle East', *Adelphi Papers*, 322, International Institute for Strategic Studies, London, 1998.

Greenwood, T., 'US and NATO Force Structure and Military Operations in the Mediterranean', *McNair Papers*, 14, Institute for National Strategic Studies, National Defence University, Washington, DC, 1993.

Grizold A., 'The Challenges of Central-Eastern Europe and the Mediterranean Regions for Creating a New European Security Order', Paper presented at the ELIAMEP Halki International Seminar, Greece, September 1996.

Hamdani, S., 'Barcelona Declaration: A Partnership looking for implementation and improvement', Paper presented at the MEDAC Conference 'Prospects After Barcelona', Malta, March 1996.

Hassner, P., 'Change and Security in Europe: In Search of a System', *Adelphi Papers*, 49, Part II, International Institute for Strategic Studies, London, 1968.

Heisbourg, F., 'Challenges to European Security and How to Meet Them', Speech to the European Movement's Conference on European Foreign and Security Policies, 7 June 1991.

Hoekman, B., 'The World Trade Organization, the European Union, and the Arab World: Trade Policy Priorities and Pitfalls', *Working Papers in International Economics*, Private Sector Development Division, World Bank, September 1995.

Ibrahim, S. E., 'The Demographic Factors in the Security of the Mediterranean: From the Battle of Tours to the Battle of Algiers', Fondation Méditerranéenne des Etudes Stratégiques, Séminaire de la Tour Blanche, Toulon, 21–4 June 1995.

Ireland, P. R., 'Europe's Rio Grande? The Mediterranean Basin, Islam and the EU's Southern Strategy', paper presented at the Fifth Biennial ECSA–USA Conference, Seattle, WA, May 1997.

Jacomet, A., 'Regional and State Security Challenges in the Mediterranean: The WEU's Response', *Discussion Paper*, University of Reading, 1995.

Jones, P., 'Towards a Regional Security Regime for the Middle East: Issues and Options', SIPRI, Stockholm, December 1998.

Joffé, G., 'European Security and the New Arc of Crisis', in *New Dimensions in International Security*, *Adelphi Papers*, 266, International Institute for Strategic Studies, London, 1992, 53–68.

Joffé G., 'Integration and Peripheral Dependence: The Dilemma Facing the South Mediterranean States', Paper presented at the MEDAC Conference 'Prospects After Barcelona', Malta, March 1996.

Joffé, G., 'The Euro-Mediterranean Partnership: Two Years After Barcelona', *Briefing*

Papers, 44, Middle East Programme, Royal Institute of International Affairs, London, May 1998.

Joffé, G., 'The Euro-Mediterranean Partnership Today', Informal EuroMeSCo–Senior Officials Seminar 'Euro-Mediterranean Security Dialogue', Bonn, Ministry of Foreign Affairs, 20 March 1999, *EuroMeSCo News*, 5: April 1999.

Kaminski, A., 'The Geostrategic Implications of Enlargement', Paper presented at the Second Meeting of the Working Group, 'The Eastern Enlargement of the European Union', Robert Schuman Centre, European University Institute, Brussels, 1997.

Katzenstein, P. J., 'Regionalism in Comparative Perspective', *ARENA Reprints*, 1, 1996.

Kessler, B. R., 'Bush's New World Order: The Meaning Behind the Words', *Research Paper*, Department of Air Command and Staff College, 1997.

Khader, B., 'Euro-Mediterranean Partnership (EMP): The Unaccomplished Tasks', *The IPTS Report*, 25 (special Euro-Mediterranean issue), European Science and Technology Observatories Network, June 1998.

Khader, B. and Legrand, V., 'Democratization in the Arab–Muslim World', *ELIAMEP Occasional Papers*, OP98/09, Hellenic Foundation for European and Foreign Policy, Athens, 1998.

King, M., 'Muslims in Europe: A New identity for Islam', *EUI Working Papers in Cultural Studies*, 93/1, European University Institute, Florence, 1993.

Klebes, H., 'The Quest for Democratic Security', *Peaceworks*, 26, United States Institute of Peace, 1998.

Köchler, H., 'Muslim–Christian Ties in Europe: Past, Present and Future', Second International Seminar on Civilizational Dialogue, 'Japan, Islam and the West', Kuala Lumpur, 2–3 September 1996.

Köchler, H., 'US–European Relations After the End of the East–West Conflict: Implications for Euro-Mediterranean Co-operation', *Occasional Papers Series*, 1, International Progress Organization, 1997.

Köchler, H., 'Philosophical Foundations of Civilizational Dialogue: The Hermeneutics of Cultural Self-Comprehension Versus the Paradigm of Civilizational Conflict', *Occasional Papers Series*, 3, International Progress Organization, 1998.

Kovalski, N., 'The Mediterranean Process: Dimensions of the 90s', *Occasional Papers*, 8, International Institute for Peace, Vienna, 1995.

Lenzi, G. 'European Security and the Mediterranean', Paper presented at the MEDAC Conference 'Prospects After Barcelona', Malta, March 1996.

Lister, M., 'Issues of Dependency: The Mediterranean Enlargement of the European Union', *Working Paper*, 1, Centre for Documentation and Research on the European Communities, University of Poznan, 1995.

Luciani, G., 'Where to Start with Multilaterism – an Agenda for Cooperation Between Europe, the Middle East and North Africa', *Working Papers*, Research Group on European Affairs, University of Munich, August 1996.

Mahncke, D., 'Parameters of European Security', *Chaillot Papers*, 10, WEU Institute for Security Studies, Paris, 1993.

March, J. G and Olsen, J. P., 'Institutional Perspectives on Governance', *ARENA Reprints*, 94/2, 1994.

March, J. G. and Olsen, J. P., 'The Institutional Dynamics of International Political Orders', *ARENA Reprints*, 98/5, 1998.

Marco, G. D., 'The Mediterranean Roots of Europe', Paper presented at the Seminar 'Europe After 1992: Which Europe?', organised by the European Christian Democrats

of Malta, 23–6 September, 1992.
Marco, G. D., 'North–South relations in the Mediterranean', MEDAC Colloquium, Malta, 30 November–3 December 1992.
McLin, J., 'The European Community and the Mediterranean: Co-Prosperity Sphere or North–South Confrontation Zone', *American Universities Field Staff Reports*, New York, 1973, 1–23.
Melasuo, T., 'The Mediterranean Revisited', *Research Report*, 57, TAPRI, 1994.
Minasi, N., 'The Euro-Mediterranean Free Trade Area and its Impact on the Economies Involved', *Jean Monnet Working Papers in Comparative and International Politics*, 16, University of Catania, 1998.
Mortimer, E., 'Dealing with the South', *European Security After the Cold War, Adelphi Papers*, 271, International Institute for Strategic Studies, London, 1992, 35–46.
Munuera, G., 'Preventing Armed Conflict in Europe: Lessons From Recent Experience', *Chaillot Papers*, 15/16, WEU Institute for Security Studies, Paris, 1994.
Niblock, T., 'Economic Liberalisation in the Arab World: The Social and Political Significance', *RUSEL Working Papers*, 1, University of Exeter, 1990.
Nonneman, G., 'Economic Liberalisation in the Developing World: The State of the Debate, and the Case of the Middle East', *RUSEL Working Papers*, 12, University of Exeter, 1993.
Olsen, J. P., 'European Challenges to the Nation State', *ARENA Reprints*, 97/11, 1997, p. 182.
Olsen, J. P., 'Organising European Institutions of Governance: A Prelude to an Institutional Account of Political Integration', *ARENA Working Papers*, 00/2, 2000.
Olsen, J. P. and Peters, B. G., 'Learning from Experience', *ARENA Reprints*, 96/5, 1996.
Pace, R., 'The European Union's Next Mediterranean Enlargement: Challenges and Uncertainties', *Jean Monnet Working Papers in Comparative and International Politics*, 6, University of Catania, 1997.
Picheca, G., 'The Follow-Up of the Security Aspects of the Barcelona Declaration with Regard to Other Initiatives in the Area', Paper presented at the MEDAC Conference 'Prospects After Barcelona', Malta, March 1996.
Politi, A., 'European Security: The New Transnational Risks', *Chaillot Papers*, 29, WEU Institute for Security Studies, Paris, 1997.
Rodrik, D., 'Making Openness Work', *Policy Essay*, 24, Overseas Development Council, January 1999.
Sachs, J. D. and Warner, A., 'Economic Reform and the Process of Global Integration', *Brookings Papers on Economic Activity*, 25th anniversary issue, 1995, 1–95.
Sato, H., 'International Political Economy in the Changing World', *TKI Working Papers on European Integration and Regime Formation*, 1/96, Thorkil Kristensen Institute, South Jutland University Centre, 1996.
Schake, K., 'Europe After NATO Expansion: The Unfinished Security Agenda', *Policy Papers*, 38, University of California Institute on Global Conflict and Cooperation, 1998.
Schneider, H. and Zomer H., 'European Union and the Mediterranean (MEDA)', APRODEV Information Document, August 1997.
Sebesta, L., 'The Middle East and European Security in the Fifties: A Historical Assesment', *EUI Working Papers in History*, 10, European University Institute, Florence, 1991.
Spencer, C., 'The Mediterranean Region', Paper presented at the 23rd Annual Conference of the British International Studies Association, 'European Security II:

Regional Cooperation', Session 8, University of Sussex, 14–16 December 1998.
Tanner, F., 'The Malta Meeting Revisited: The Middle East Is Catching Up with the Barcelona Process', Director's editorial on the Second Ministerial Meeting of the Barcelona Process, Malta 15–16 April 1997.
Tarrow, S., 'Building a Composite Polity: Popular Contention in the European Union', *Institute for European Studies Working Paper*, 98/3, Cornell University, 1998.
Tarschys and Rotfeld, A. D., *A Future Security Agenda for Europe*, Report of the Independent Working Group on 'A Future Security Agenda for Europe', International Peace Research Institute, Stockholm, 1996.
Toukan, A., 'A Plan for Euro-Med Conflict Prevention', *How Can Europe Prevent Conflicts?, Discussion Papers*, 14, Philip Morris Institute for Public Policy and Research, 1997.
Tovias, A., 'The Mediterranean Challenge III: EEC Enlargement – the Southern Neighbours', *Sussex European Papers*, 5, European Research Centre, University of Sussex, 1979.
Ulrich, S., 'The Mediterranean Challenge: Europe and North Africa', *Libertas Europdische Zeitschrift*, 1–2, Stuttgart, 1992.
Usher, R., 'A Bigger, Better Club Med: Europe and its Southern Neighbors Plot Stability', *Time Magazine*, 146, 11 December 1995.
Vanhaeverbeke, G., 'Survey of Europe's Mediterranean Policy. Where it Comes From – Where it Stands Today – Where it Is Likely to Go', Euro-Med Training and Information Programme for Diplomats, Mediterranean Academy of Diplomatic Studies, University of Malta, 15–17 March 1997.
Vasquez, J., 'Peace and the New World Order', *AntePodium*, 4, Victoria University of Wellington, 1995.
Waites, N., 'France and the Post-Colonial Mediterranean Region', *Occasional Papers*, 33, University of Reading, September 1994.
Waites, N., 'Dynamics of EU Mediterranean Policy', Paper presented at the ELIAMEP Halki International Seminar 'The European Union and the Mediterranean Region', Hellenic Foundation for European and Foreign Policy, Halki Island, Greece, September 1996.
Whitman, R., 'The European Union's Common Foreign and Security Policy. Achievements and Prospects', *CSD Perspectives, Research Papers*, 11, Centre for the Study of Democracy, University of Westminster, 1996.
Whitman, R., 'The EU and the Mediterranean: Looking Towards the Millennium', *CMS Occasional Papers*, 18, Centre for Mediterranean Studies, University of Bristol, February 1998.
Worner, M. *et al.*, *What Is European Security After the Cold War?, Discussion Papers*, 2, Philip Morris Institute for Public Policy and Research, 1993.
Xenakis, D. K. 'The Barcelona Process: Some Lessons from Helsinki', *Jean Monnet Working Papers in Comparative and International Politics*, 17, University of Catania, 1998.
Zanders, J. P., 'A New Security (Dis)Order for the Gulf', *POLE Papers*, 1, Centrum voor Polemologie, Vrije Universiteit Brussel, March 1995.

Official documents and publications

Chairman's Formal Conclusions, Third Euro-Mediterranean Conference of Foreign Ministers – Barcelona III, Stuttgart, Germany, 15–16 April 1999.

Commission of the European Communities, Communication to the Council, *The Future of Relations Between the Community and the Maghreb*, COM(92) 401 final, Brussels, 1992.

Commission of the European Communities, Communication to the Council, *Future Relations and Co-operation between the Community and the Middle East*, COM(93) 375 final, Brussels, 1993.

Commission of the European Communities, *EC Support to Middle East Peace Process*, COM(93) 458 final, Brussels, 1993.

Commission of the European Communities, Communication to the Council, *Strengthening the Mediterranean Policy of the European Union: Establishing A Euro-Mediterranean Partnership*, COM(94) 427 final, Brussels, 1994.

Commission of the European Communities, Proposal for a Council Regulation on *Aid for Population Policies and Programmes in the Developing Countries*, COM(95) 295 final, Brussels, 1995.

Commission of the European Communities, 'Implementation of Financial and Technical Cooperation with the Mediterranean Non-Member Countries and on Financial Cooperation with those as a Group',Report from the Commission to the Council and the European Parliament, COM(95) 384 final, Brussels, 1995.

Commission of the European Communities, Working Document on *Report on the Situation of Oil Supply, Refining and Markets in the European Community*, COM(96) 143 final, Brussels, 1996.

Commission of the European Communities, Communication to the Council and the European Parliament, 'Progress Report on the Euro-Mediterranean Partnership and Preparations for the Second Conference of Foreign Affairs' Ministers', COM(97) 68 final, Brussels, 1997.

Commission of the European Communities, Europe Information: Development, *The European Community, the Mediterranean and the Middle East*, X/20/90, Brussels, 1990.

Commission of the European Communities, *EU–ACP Co-operation* (special issue), Directorate General for Development, Brussels, April 1994.

Commission of the European Communities, *Barcelona Declaration adopted at the Euro-Mediterranean Conference* (final version), Barcelona, 28 November 1995.

Commission of the European Communities, *How Does the European Union Relate to the World?*, European Documentation, Luxembourg, 1996.

Commission of the European Communities, Program 95/C 180/07 for *Immigration From the Mediterranean Countries (Med-Migration)*, C180/10.

Commission of the European Communities, Regulation 1763/92 of the Council Concerning *Financial Co-operation for the Non-EU Mediterranean Countries*, L181.

Commission of the European Communities, Regulation Proposal 94/C 214/8 of the Council Concerning *Creation of Labour Posts and the Support of the Small Enterprises in the Maghreb Countries*, C214/26.

Commission of the European Communities, Regulation Proposal 95/C 232/05 of the Council Concerning *The Financial and Technical Support of the Economic and Social*

Structures' Reform in the Mediterranean Non-EU Countries, C232/5.

Concluding Statement by Robin Cook, UK Presidency, Ad-Hoc Euro-Mediterranean Ministerial Meeting, Palermo, 3–4 June 1998.

Cuco P., *The Eastern Mediterranean*, Report submitted on behalf of the Defence Committee, Assembly of Western European Union, Document 1465, 24 May 1995.

Europe Documents, No. 1930, 27, Brussels, April 1995.

Europe Documents, No. 1961, Brussels, November 1995.

European Commission, *The Europe–South Dialogue*, Brussels 1988.

European Commission, *EU–ACP Co-operation* (special issue), Directorate General for Development, Brussels, April 1994.

European Community, *European Community and the Mediterranean*, Luxembourg 1991.

European Council at Corfu, 24–5 June 1994, Presidency Conclusions, SN 150/94.

European Council at Cannes, 26–27 June 1994, Presidency Conclusion, SN 211/95.

European Council at Essen, 9–10 December 1994, Presidency Conclusions, SN 300/94.

EuroMeSco, Working Group on 'Confidence-Building, Arms Control and Conflict Prevention', EuroMeSco Network, April 1997.

Eurostat, 'Euro-Mediterranean Statistics', *General Short-Term Statistics*, 2, Luxembourg, 1998.

Experts' Meeting on the Euro-Mediterranean Economic Area, Brussels, 27–8 April 1998.

Informal EuroMeSco–Senior Officials' Seminar, 'Euro-Mediterranean Security Dialogue', Bonn, Ministry of Foreign Affairs, 20 March 1999; *EuroMeSco News*, 5: April 1999.

Inter-Parliamentary Union, 'Employment Is Key to Stability in the Mediterranean, CSCM Meeting Concludes', press release of the Inter-Parliamentary Union, 2, Monte Carlo/Geneva, 4 July 1997.

Italian Foreign Ministry, *The Mediterranean and the Middle East After the War in the Gulf: The CSCM*, Rome, March 1991.

Moya, P., *Frameworks for Cooperation in the Mediterranean*, North Atlantic Assembly, Civilian Affairs Committee, Sub-Committee on the Mediterranean Basin, AM 259, 7 October 1995.

Netherlands Helsinki Committee, 'A Focus on the Future: Using an Enhanced Conference on Security and Co-operation in Europe', Utrecht, 15 August 1994.

Official Journal of the European Communities, Opinion on *The European Community and Economic Co-operation in the Middle East*, No. C73, Brussels 15 March 1993.

Rifkind, M., 'British Initiative in Investment Barriers', British Foreign Secretary Briefing at the Barcelona Conference, 28 November 1995, British Foreign Office, 1995.

World Bank, *Dept Tables 1994*, Washington, DC, 1995.

Other sources

Agence Europe, 'Western Mediterranean: Second Ministerial Session', *Europe Daily Bulletin*, No. 10–1990.

Euromed Internet Forum, 'The Euro-Mediterranean Economic Area', *Euromed Special Features*, 2: November 1998.

Euromed Internet Forum, 'The Euro-Mediterranean Cultural Partnership', *Euromed Special Features*, 3 December 1998.

Euromed Internet Forum, 'Euro-Mediterranean Conference On Regional Cooperation' *Euro-Med Special Features*, 5: 5 February 1999.

Euromed Internet Forum, 'The Middle East Peace Process and the Role of the European Union', *Euromed Special Features*, 7: 23 April 1999.

Euromed Internet Forum, 'EUROMESCO: The Network of Foreign Policy Institutes', *Information Note*, April 1999.

Eurostat Key Figures, 'European Union Trade with the Mediterranean Countries', DataShop Eurostat, in *Frontier-Free Europe*, 4, Luxembourg, 1996.

Philip Morris Institute, *Conference Proceedings: Mediterranean Partnerships*, Madrid, 5–6 October 1995.

World Trade Organization, *Regionalism and the World Trading System* (London, 1995).

Xenakis, D. K., 'Transforming Regional Orders: The Helsinki and Barcelona Processes Compared', unpublished PhD dissertation, School of Historical, Political and Sociological Studies, University of Exeter, 2000.

Index

Adler, E., 20
African states, 10
ageing population, 38
aid programmes, 58, 65, 68, 105
Aliboni, R., 28, 34, 39–41, 77, 81, 84, 107, 118
Amsterdam Treaty (1997), 39
Arab–Israeli dispute, 29–31, 42, 66–8, 75–9, 85–9
Arab League, 18
area of peace and stability, 77, 107
arms control, 77
Association Agreements, 58, 60–1, 69–71, 79–80, 85, 87
Athens Agreement (1962), 60
Ayubi, N., 32–3

Balladur Plan, 77
Balta, P., 29
Barber, B., 9
Barcelona Conference (1995), 69, 74–5, 77
Barcelona Declaration, 1, 3, 5, 19, 59, 76–9, 82–5, 105, 108, 123
Barcelona Process, 2, 17, 109, 121
  economic basket, 78–82, 86, 88
  evolution of, 85–90
  follow-up mechanism, 84
  institution building in, 119
  political basket, 75–8
  socio-cultural basket, 82–5, 89
Benyaklef, M., 37
Bergman, M. R., 117
bilateral agreements, 3, 58–63 *passim*, 79, 123
bi-multilateralism, 79
Bin, A., 36
Blunden, M., 32
Bournoville, Anne-Charlotte, 82
Boutros-Ghali, Boutros, 40
Brauch, H. Gunder, 37
Braudel, F., 28
Bush, George, 30
Buzan, B., 32, 121

Calleya, S. C., 86, 118
Chater, K., 31
Chechnya, 11
China, 10
Church, C. H., 98–9
civil society representatives, 82
Claes, D. H., 104
Colas, A., 82
Cold War, 1, 118
  ending of, 9–15 *passim*, 29
collective goods, 123
Collinson, S., 39–40
Combined Joint Task Force (CJTF), 16
Common Agricultural Policy, 63, 80
Common Foreign and Security Policy (CFSP), 44, 66, 77
Conference on Security and Co-operation in Europe (CSCE), 15, 19, 118–19
Conference on Security and Co-operation in the Mediterranean (CSCM), 19, 44, 64
confidence-building measures (CBMs), 78, 117–18
confidence and security-building measures (CSBMs), 77
conflict management, 4, 16, 118–19, 121, 124
conflict prevention, 77, 78, 118
conflict resolution, 16, 30, 121
conflicts endemic to the Mediterranean, 29, 124
'consciousness raising', 109
Constas, D., 44
Co-operation Agreements, 57, 61

Couloumbis, T., 26, 120
Cox, R. O., 12
Cox, R. W., 102
cultural cooperation, 82–3
culture, Mediterranean, 2–4
Curdy, D. G., 35
Cyprus, 29–30

Delors, Jacques, 66
democracy, 40, 63, 82–3, 118, 124
demography, 38–9
Derisbourg, J. P., 105
Dewit, D. B., 11
Diamond, J., 35
Duchene, F., 62

Echeverria, C. J., 78
Edwards, G., 61, 66, 77, 84, 105
Ersson, S., 103
Espozito, J. L., 33
Euro-Arab Dialogue, 18, 57, 63
Euro-Mediterranean Charter for Peace and Stability, 77, 85–9, 110, 118–19
Euro-Mediterranean Committee, 84
Euro-Mediterranean Conferences of Foreign Ministers, 85–7, 89, 118
Euro-Mediterranean Economic Area Experts Meeting (1998), 88
Euro-Mediterranean partnership (EMP), 20, 74–8, 82–90, 100, 105–11, 117–20, 125
EuroMeSCo report (1997), 81, 89, 92
European Commission, 77, 84
European Community/Union
  enlargement of, 16, 43–4, 61, 63, 66
  policy towards the Mediterranean, 3–4, 17–19, 31, 42–5, 57–60, 68–9, 124; *see also* Global Mediterranean Policy; Renovated Mediterranean Policy
European Council
  meeting at Berlin (1999), 89
  meeting at Cannes (1995), 67–9
  meeting at Copenhagen (1993), 67
  meeting at Corfu (1994), 67
  meeting at Essen (1994), 67
  meeting at Lisbon (1992), 66
  meeting at Rome (1990), 64
European Investment Bank (EIB), 65, 68
European Parliament (EP), 58, 64, 74, 87
European Security and Defence Identity (ESDI), 16, 31
European Union *see* European Community/Union

Fahmy, N., 83, 105
'Five plus Five' initiative, 19, 64
Fuller, G. E., 32

Gellner, E., 34
Gemeinschaft and *Gesellschaft* models of society, 101, 106, 114
Gillespie, R., 43, 107
Ginsberg, R. H., 59–60, 63
global governance, 13
Global Mediterranean Policy (GMP), 58–9, 61–3
globalisation, 11–12, 79, 81, 123
Gnesotto, N., 30
Gordon, P. H., 42
Gray, C., 13–14
Greek–Turkish dispute, 29–30, 64
Grilli, E., 60
Groom, A. J. R., 99
Gulf Co-operation Council, 65
Gulf Crisis (1990–91), 9–11, 17–18, 29–32, 42, 57

Hasan, King, 35
Hasenclever, A., 103
Hassner, P., 13, 15
hegemony, 102
Heisbourg, F., 15
Held, D., 12
Helsinki Process, 118
hermeneutics of civilisational dialogue, 4, 36
Hobbes, Thomas, 102
Hoekman, B., 19
Hoffmann, S., 98
Hollis, R., 42–3
Holmes, J. W., 41, 43
human rights, 9, 31, 33, 66–8, 73, 76, 82–3, 87, 90, 118
Huntington, S. P., 32, 34

Hussein, Saddam, 32

immigration, 39–40
income differentials, 65
institutions, significance of, 20, 102–3, 121–4
interdependence theory, 102
internal conflicts, 10
international institutions, 13, 20, 102
International Monetary Fund (IMF), 12
international orders and organisations, 100
international regimes, theory of, 102–4, 107–10
Iraq, 31
Ireland, P. R., 36
Islam, 26, 31–5, 83
'Islamic fundamentalism', 14–15, 31–5
Israel, 68, 117; *see also* Arab–Israeli dispute

Jervis, R., 30, 109
Joffé, G., 37–8, 63, 87, 107
Jünemann, A., 23, 75, 105

Kaminski, A., 43
Keohane, R. O., 10, 12, 15–16, 98, 100–2, 108
Khader, B., 81
Khalilzad, Z., 41
Kienle, E., 106
King, G., 10
Klebes, H., 16
Köchler, H., 42, 74
Kosovo, 42
Kramer, M., 117
Krasner, S. D., 101, 108–9, 112

laissez-faire, 106
Lane, J.-E., 103
Lapidus, I. M., 33–5
Lesser, I. O., 29, 32, 36, 42
Leviathan, the, 102
liberalisation, 106, 108, 119–24
of markets and trade, 12, 44, 59, 78, 81, 107, 123
political, 66; *see also* political reform
Libya, 31, 74
Licari, J., 85
Linz, J., 35
Lipset, S. M., 35
Lister, M., 28
Lomé Conventions, 60
Luciani, G., 37

Malta Conference (1997), 85–7, 118
marketisation, 120
Marks, J., 66
Marquina, A., 106
Marr, P., 41–2
Mayall, J., 14
Mayer, P., 103
MEDA programme, 81, 88
Mediterranean, definition of, 25, 27–8, 116–17
Mediterranean Forum, 19, 44
Mediterranean Free Trade Area (MEFTA), 78–81, 88–9, 105–7, 120, 123
Mediterranean Pact, 45, 78
'Mediterraneanism', 117
mental maps, 25, 117
Miall, H., 14
Middle East Peace Process *see* Arab-Israeli dispute
migration, 31, 39–40, 105–6
Minasi, N., 23
Mitrany, D., 120
Mjøset, L., 97
modernity, 34–5
Monar, J., 84
Monnet, Jean, 120
Mortimer, E., 31
multilateralism, 11–12, 15, 59, 79, 110
Munuera, G., 19

nationalism, 40
natural gas, 37–8
neoliberalism, 102, 108
neorealism, 11, 122
new European order, 14–15
new institutionalism, 102–3
new world order, 9, 11, 13, 30, 121
Nierop, T., 13
non-governmental organisations (NGOs), 82

non-intervention in domestic affairs, principle of, 10, 76
norms, 104, 108
North Atlantic Treaty Organisation (NATO), 15–16, 31, 42–3
Nye, J. S., 12, 15–16, 42, 101

oil supplies and prices, 36–8, 62
Olsen, J. P., 20, 103, 109, 116
Organisation for Security and Co-operation in Europe (OSCE), 15–16, 118
Orientalism, 32–3
Oslo Accords and Process, 86, 88–9

Palermo Ministerial Meeting (1998), 88
Palestinian Authority, 68, 85, 87
Paris Charter (1990), 119
Parliamentary Forum, 110–11
partnership, concept of, 84
partnership-building measures (PBMs), 78, 85, 110, 118–19
Permanent Joint Council (NATO–Russian), 16
Peters, B. G., 20, 103
Peters, J., 41
Philippart, Eric, 61, 66, 77, 84, 105
political reform, 66–7, 79
population, 38–9
Promfred, R., 61
protectionism, 62–3

rapprochement phase of Euro-Mediterranean policy, 60
realist theory, 11–12, 102, 104, 108
regime theory, 13, 110–11, 122–3; *see also* international regimes
renewable energy, 37
Renovated Mediterranean Policy (RMP), 58, 64–6
Rhodes Ministerial Conference (1998), 89
Rifkind, Malcolm, 105–6
Rittberger, V., 103
Roberson, B. A., 33
Rodrik, D., 119
Rosamond, B., 99, 103
Ruggie, J., 100
Russia, 15–16

Sachedina, A., 32
Said, E., 33
Schlaim, A., 61–2
secularism, 34
security
  architecture of, 15
  cooperative, 106–7, 118
  definition of, 11
  European, internal and external, 14–15
security community concept, 16, 24, 121
Smith, Adam, 106
Snyder, J. C., 43
social conditions, 37–8
socialising, 104
sovereignty of states, 12–13, 16
Spencer, C., 29–30, 118
Spencer, Herbert, 106
STABEX programme, 61, 70
state, the, role of, 12
Stavridis, S., 84
Stein, D. L., 10
Stoker, G., 99
Stuttgart Ministerial Conference (1999), 89
sub-regions of the Mediterranean, 27
Suez crisis, 41
SYSMIN programme, 61, 70

Tanner, F., 45, 77–8, 86
Taylor, P., 98, 104
theorisation
  of Euro-Mediterranean governance, 99–100
  of international governance, 100–5
  in the social sciences, 97–9
'tool box approach' to economic support, 80
Toukan, A., 36–7
Tovias, A., 43, 60
Treaty of Rome (1957), 60, 70
Treaty on European Union (1992), 39, 66
Tsardanides, C., 64
Tsoukalis, L., 80

Turkey, 68, 72; *see also* Greek–Turkish dispute

unemployment, 39
United Nations, 9, 15, 100
Charter, 76
Security Council Resolutions, 89
United States, 41–3, 86, 117
Universal Declaration of Human Rights, 76

Valencia Conference (1999), 90
Vasconcelos, A. de, 37
Verba, S., 10
Veremis, T., 26, 45, 120

Waever, O., 121
Waites, N., 61, 63, 84
Weidenfeld, W., 60, 65
Western European Union (WEU), 15
Wolf, M., 80
World Bank, 12, 38
World Trade Organisation (WTO), 12, 68, 80
Wrede, H., 19
Wye River Memorandum, 89

xenophobia, 40

Yannopoulos, G. N., 61–2
Young, O. R., 100–1
Yugoslav crisis, 10–11, 17, 19, 30, 66

Zartman, W., 117